CROWDFUNDING TH

Crowdfunding the revolution

The First Dáil Loan and the Battle for Irish Independence

Patrick O'Sullivan Greene

Eastwood

First published in 2020
Eastwood Books,
an imprint of the Wordwell Group.
Unit 9, 78 Furze Road, Sandyford Industrial Estate, Dublin 18
www.eastwoodbooks.com
www.wordwellbooks.com

Cover Image: The Sinn Féin Bank at 6 Harcourt Street after a raid,
November 1920. (National Library of Ireland)

ISBN: 978-1-9161375-8-5 (paperback)
ISBN: 978-1-913934-00-2 (mobi)
ISBN: 978-1-913934-01-9 (epub)

British Library Cataloguing-in-Publication Data.
A catalogue record for this book is available from the British Library.

Typeset in Ireland by Wordwell Ltd
Copy-editor: Emer Condit
Cover design and artwork: Wordwell Ltd
Printed by: Gráficas Castuera, Pamplona

Contents

Acknowledgements

The genesis of this book was an article published in the *Irish Times* on 4 April 2019, 'A century on: the Dáil loan that set the State on the road to financial sovereignty'. Ronan McGreevy, journalist and author, facilitated the publication of the article and has been a support throughout the project. Ronan introduced me to Wordwell, where Ronan Colgan, Nick Maxwell and Emer Condit provided the support and resources required to transform a manuscript into a published book. Eileen Kelleher gave much early encouragement and Elaina Galvin delivered invaluable research.

Historical records have become increasingly available on-line. Not only is it easier to source material but collections can also be interrogated in many new ways. This is made possible by professional archivists continuing to innovate in digital archival practice, so a special word of gratitude to the staff in the Bureau of Military History, the National Library of Ireland and the National Archives of Ireland, as well as to the staff of Kerry Library.

Thanks to the Nolan family, everyone from New Street, and friends at home and abroad. The book is dedicated to my siblings—Eileen, Maura and John—for their support at various stages in life, and to my brothers-in-law, Colm and Noel.

Note
Amounts in 'pounds, shillings and pence' (e.g. £815.4.9) have been rounded to the nearest pound number. Amounts translated into current value in dollars are shown in brackets rounded to the nearest thousand: £815 = $55,000. The Bank of England inflation calculator is used to bring sterling amounts up to present-day value, and the exchange rate at 31 December 2019 is used for conversion to dollar.

'Follow the money. Always follow the money.'
—*All the President's Men* (film, 1976)

'The enemy government quickly realised that the economic policy of the Dáil was as great a danger to them as its political policy, that in fact the elected Government of Ireland stood for social and economical deliverance, no less than for political deliverance. Without finance, however, the policy would be inoperative. The enemy must, therefore, at all costs prevent our getting the necessary funds. He attempted, certainly—and with a renewed determination and savagery.'
—Letter from Michael Collins to Éamon de Valera on 10 February 1920

'Can you say whether your Bank has an account in the name of a man called Michael Collins?'

'I would not like to say that from memory. I would have to go up and look it up. That is not a name in connection with certain societies you have mentioned.'

' "I cannot say from memory whether there is in my bank an account in the name of one Michael Collins" [answer repeated back].'

'That is quite right. It would be too dangerous for me to speak from memory.'
—Official transcript of the deposition of Henry Campbell, manager, Hibernian Bank, College Green, conducted by Alan Bell, resident magistrate, 8 March 1920

Prologue

Start-up government

'When we started as a Dáil in January, 1919,' Michael Collins reminded his fellow TDs after the truce had been signed, 'we started … on a loan of £1,000.' It was 26 August 1921 and the Minister for Finance was addressing the future funding requirements to carry on the government of the nation. It was two and a half years since Dáil Éireann had met for the first time, set up as a counter-state parliament in open defiance of the established and hostile British administration in Ireland. 'Then we had to start and take up all the Departments of a National Government. We had to … bring Ireland out of the corner and to make her known—in fact, to advertise her existence.'

Opened in a public session, with 70 Irish and international journalists present, the 'National Parliament' of the self-declared Irish Republic met for the first time on 21 January 1919.[1] A Declaration of Independence was read, and a message to the free nations of the world in English and French—'Aux Nations du Monde! Salut fraternal!'

Both London and Dublin Castle, the seat of British rule in Ireland, ignored the new assembly, dismissing it variously as a ludicrous farce, a stage play and a piece of political window-dressing. Nevertheless, the heads of the Dublin Metropolitan Police and the Royal Irish Constabulary did watch the elected representatives arrive at the Mansion House from a window in a building across the street. A military officer looked on from a neighbouring balcony. Police in plain clothes mingled with the large crowd that had gathered outside. No police intervention, however, was made or expected.

The first meeting of the Dáil was largely symbolic, lasting just two hours. Many of the Sinn Féin leaders were in prison, having been arrested on foot of the 'German Plot'. Accused of 'treasonable communication with the German enemy', they had been interned without trial and deported to England in early 1918.[2] Éamon de Valera, the leader of Sinn Féin, escaped in February 1919. The remaining Sinn Féin leaders were released in March, after one of the prisoners, Pierce McCann TD, died from influenza, which was ravaging the English prison system. Those released included Countess Markievicz, the first woman elected to the House of Commons.

In the first months of 1919, while waiting for the release of the prisoners and with almost no funding, Dáil Éireann had to 'fake it until it could make it'. The cabinet appointed in January could not make executive decisions in the absence of so many leaders, in particular Éamon de Valera and Arthur Griffith, the founder of Sinn Féin. No policy or government programmes were announced. The cabinet focused its efforts on trying to gain representation for Ireland at the peace conference in Paris. The Dáil met for the second time on 2 April and a new cabinet was appointed. Éamon de Valera was elected President of Dáil Éireann and Arthur Griffith was elected Minister for Home Affairs, replacing Michael Collins, who became Minister for Finance.

Even after the appointment of the new cabinet nothing substantial emerged in terms of policy and programmes. The Dáil government did not look like a credible alternative to the Dublin Castle administration. Police intelligence wondered why Dáil Éireann, 'which was to have usurped the government of Ireland, has made no attempt to do so'.[3] In June, a witty nationalist opponent of Sinn Féin commented that 'Dáil Éireann had been tried for six months and a very dull Éireann it had been'.[4] They were, however, mistaken.

'We are slave-driving here,' Diarmuid O'Hegarty wrote to George Gavan Duffy, the Dáil envoy in Paris. 'Committees on all conceivable form of project, flotation of loans, etc.'[5] The counter-state government was determined to replace British control of the courts system, policing, local government, foreign affairs and the provision of social needs. It was also developing its constructive programme in the areas of agriculture, fisheries, forestry, natural resources and industry and trade, as well as land reform policies.

At 27, Diarmuid O'Hegarty was the clerk of the Dáil and secretary to the cabinet. He was determined that the Dáil government would operate to the highest international standards, whatever the circumstances. Those who met him noticed that he spoke little and had a dishevelled appearance ('an untidy collar, an angled tie'), but also noted that he was a brilliant organiser with a first-class brain.[6] Ernie O'Malley said that his 'mind worked quickly, shrewdly and surely ... he used clear, clever imagery, often biting. I admired his type of quick intellect often disguised by a surface casualness.'[7]

O'Hegarty was close to Michael Collins and Harry Boland. This triumvirate exercised significant control over the civilian and military activity of the revolutionary government. O'Hegarty, a veteran of 1916, was also Director of Communications of the Irish Volunteers. He was a good friend of the Archer siblings, Liam and Claire. Liam was an intelligence officer and Claire worked with the Dáil government. O'Hegarty married Claire after the war and Michael Collins was best man at the wedding. Eilis Ryan was also part of this group of young revolutionaries, whose paths crossed frequently in government and intelligence activities.

Scrambling for money, the Dáil launched a national fund-raising campaign called the Self-Determination Fund.[8] The plan was to capture money being returned by the anti-conscription movement, which had raised substantial funds to fight the introduction of conscription to Ireland. Money for the self-determination fund started to arrive in early March. The Dáil received a small but important proportion of the anti-conscription money that was handed back, along with donations from individuals.

Democracy is expensive, however, and the costs of the national government were growing. By June 1919 the secretariat of the Dáil had seven employees, and each of the new government departments was recruiting staff. Office space had to be rented or acquired and ministerial salaries paid, and TDs—although not salaried—were entitled to travel and hotel expenses. Funding was needed for overseas diplomatic representation, the planned court system and the constructive programme. And the Ministry of Defence needed the sinews of war.

The Dáil had ambitious economic plans, in particular to open direct trading routes between Ireland and the rest of the world and to re-establish an Irish merchant marine. Trade opportunities were examined in America, Europe, Argentina and Chile, and even in Uruguay, Peru and Paraguay. The Irish and Overseas Shipping and Trading Company was formed with the dual purpose of developing international trade and arranging arms shipments.

'It is obvious that the work of our Government cannot be carried on without funds,' Éamon de Valera told the Dáil in April, but raising finance presented numerous challenges for the counter-state government. Institutional investors—banks and large financial institutions—were the traditional buyers of government bonds, but they invested only in sovereign governments. These could not be targeted for investment by Dáil Éireann. That left private individuals. The plan was to crowdfund the revolution.

Crowdfunding the revolution

On 4 April the Dáil approved a plan to raise a £250,000 bond in 'such amounts as to meet the needs of the small subscriber'. In June the size of the bond was increased to £500,000, of which £250,000 was to be raised in Ireland and £250,000 in America.[9]

The minimum investment was set at £1. Michael Collins said that his preference was to get '250,000 subscriptions of £1 per week [rather] than 25,000 of £10 each'.[10] He wanted individuals who could not afford to pay £1 to club together. Twenty individuals contributing one shilling each could purchase one bond every week. Participation in the Loan would enable individuals to become 'positively identified with the cause of Irish freedom'.[11]

On 19 June, at a private meeting in Fleming's Hotel, the Dáil approved the issue of the Loan prospectus and the appointment of three trustees. Two months later, after much preparatory work, the Loan was publicly announced at the annual meeting of the governing body of Sinn Féin. National newspapers reported extensively on a statement issued by Michael Collins outlining the purpose of the Loan, which included funding the consular service, the development of the fishing industry and a commission to investigate the resources available to develop Irish industry.[12]

'Ho Chi Minh Trail'

On 18 July, while Michael Collins was finalising plans for the Dáil Loan, two fighter biplanes flew over the centre of Dublin,[13] but they were not loaded with bullets or bombs. Instead, on that busy Friday evening the sky was filled with promotional leaflets for the Victory Loan, part of an impressive marketing campaign by the British government for the latest War Bond issue.[14] Victory Loan advertisements were placed in all the national papers. There was no small print, no financial watchdog and no consumer protection laws.

> 'Say to your Banker—"Put ALL my deposits into the Victory Loan. Lend me more money on the terms you've announced and put that in too. I want to be in up to the hilt".' [15]

Banks across the United Kingdom came together in an umbrella group to advertise advances at 0.5% below the standard rate to buy bonds. The Irish banks were part of the loyal umbrella group, including those with a nationalist disposition, the Hibernian, Munster & Leinster and National banks. The unionist Bank of Ireland had to issue an embarrassing clarification after its name was left out of the group advertisement in error.[16] The intensity of the promotional campaign increased as the closing date for subscriptions approached: 'The Golden Sands are running out!' screamed one newspaper advertisement.

Michael Collins must have watched the Victory Loan campaign with envy—not of the marketing budget and innovative advertising (he had his own ambitious plans to reach the people) but of the wide distribution network. Subscriptions could be made through the nationwide network of banks, post offices and stockbrokers. Collins, who had some investment banking exposure in London, understood that distribution was crucial to successful fund-raising. He had no bank or post office branch network to distribute the promotional material and application forms for the Dáil Loan; subscribers could not simply walk into the local bank and transfer £1 from their deposit account into the Loan, and the local post office or bank branch would not transfer the locally subscribed proceeds to a central Loan account in Dublin.

In the absence of an established distribution network, he built his own—a financial 'Ho Chi Minh Trail' between Dublin and the four corners of the country to target the people directly. Couriers had to distribute the prospectus, promotional material and receipts for the Loan, and carry subscriptions (cheques, notes, coin, gold) back to Dublin. The quantity of material and money to be moved was substantial. At the end of August, Collins told the Dáil that he was about to issue 5,000 copies of the prospectus to every constituency in Ireland and promotional leaflets for local distribution.

Collins planned a broad marketing campaign in support of the Loan, including full-page advertisements in national newspapers and a seven-minute promotional film featuring a who's who of Irish revolutionary figures at the time, including the mother and sister of Patrick Pearse, the widows of Tom Clarke and Eamon Ceannt, and Arthur Griffith, Eoin MacNeill and Erskine Childers.[17] Harry Boland in America wrote to Collins: 'That film of yourself and Hegarty selling Bonds brought tears to my eyes. Gee Boy! You are some movie actor. Nobody could resist buying a bond and we having such a handsome minister of finance.'[18]

New bank

Setting up a new national bank was the idea of Robert Barton, who had been appointed Director of Agriculture at the second meeting of the Dáil on 2 April.[19] Three weeks earlier he had escaped from Mountjoy prison, where he was awaiting trial for what he later called a 'rather foolish threat' against Lord French, the lord lieutenant of Ireland, and Frank Brooke, a director of the Bank of Ireland and a close associate of French.[20]

Barton had made a public promise that if arrested he would escape, 'So it had to be done'.[21] The escape was meticulously planned by Barton on the inside and organised on the outside by Michael Collins, who was in a nearby street waiting to congratulate Barton after his escape. Barton had left a note in his cell for the prison governor, saying that he felt compelled to leave owing to the discomfort of his surroundings.

A particularly warm friendship developed between Barton and Collins, despite very different starts in life. Barton was an Anglo-Irish Protestant farmer from Wicklow and a former British Army officer. Both of his younger brothers had been killed in France during the war. Collins respected the journey that Barton had taken to come over to the republican side.[22]

Robert Barton was appointed Director of Agriculture and Michael Collins was appointed Minister for Finance on the same day. They were the only heads of government departments on the run. Interruption to their work schedule was routine. The Dáil minutes for 17 June read: 'The Minister for Finance and the Director of Agriculture being temporarily prevented from attendance by enemy action, their reports were read by the Acting-President'.[23]

They met almost every evening at Collins's office at Cullenswood House in Ranelagh.[24] If Barton did not show up, Collins would send for him. At those evening meetings Collins told Barton everything that was going on. They shared a common opinion on most issues. As *Director* of Agriculture, Barton did not have the formal right to attend cabinet meetings, but he attended most anyway at Collins's urging. Collins wanted someone who shared his views at the meetings.[25]

They also shared a mutual friend in Batt O'Connor, a successful builder from Kerry. Barton first met Batt in the aftermath of the 1916 Rising, when Barton was a 2nd lieutenant in the British Army in charge of prisoners' effects. 'He brought my wife to the room where I was a prisoner,' Batt recalled, 'so that he could hand my money to her in my presence for which I signed a receipt. Then he saw her back to the gate. His manner was full of kindness and courtesy.'[26] Mrs O'Connor never forgot him. Three years later, it was arranged that Barton would stay with the O'Connors after his escape. When he arrived at the house, he and Mrs O'Connor immediately recognised each other. Batt remarked that Mrs O'Connor 'could never do enough for him while he was with us'.[27]

Barton, who described Collins as 'an indefatigable worker and a most efficient administrator', shared the same qualities.[28] Once appointed Director of Agriculture, he had to be immediately self-sufficient and productive. 'In all the Departments of Government,' Barton recalled, 'the machinery to make them effective had to be devised and operated by the Minister responsible.'[29] He had to find his feet quickly. The Dáil government required a solution to a problem that had the potential to derail not just Dáil Éireann but also the entire republican movement: the 'Land Question' was back on the political agenda.

Considerable progress had been made in the redistribution of land from mainly Anglo-Irish landlords to tenant farmers.[30] An innovative land purchase scheme had been introduced in 1909, compensating landlords with government-backed Land Stock paying a 3% interest rate. The scheme had come to a halt, however, because of the war—or, more precisely, because of the issue of British war bonds at much higher interest rates, which caused the value of the Land Stock to collapse on the financial markets. By the end of 1916, the value of '£100 Land Stock' had fallen to just £55 on the bond markets.[31] Landlords no longer wanted to sell land to tenants under the scheme, which was all but paralysed. [32]

The solution proposed by Dáil Éireann was to set up a new national bank to fund land purchases. On 18 June the Dáil approved the establishment of a 'Loan Fund', a code for the new bank.[33] Ambitions for the bank extended beyond land purchase: it would become a 'financial centre for Ireland'.

As the summer progressed, land agitation increased and fears arose of a new 'Ranch War', like that which had erupted in 1906 and had lasted for three years. Many farms purchased under the Land Acts were uneconomical in size. Struggling farmers eyed the untenanted land used by landlords for cattle grazing. The rallying cry became 'Land for the people, cattle for the road'. Farm labourers who wanted their own land took up the cry. Threats of violence and Wild West-type cattle drives increased. Sinn Féin feared that it would be forced into supporting a violent agrarian campaign. It needed the political agenda to remain focused on resistance to British rule. Robert Barton was concerned. He was receiving 'drastic proposals' from leaders of the land agitation campaign looking for his support.[34] Establishing the new bank had become a priority for the Dáil government.

Co-founders

On a summer's evening in June 1917, Michael O'Reilly could not hide his delight that the idea to which he had devoted so much thought was at last on its way to becoming a reality.[35] He had been determined for a long time to start an Irish-owned insurance business; it had become an obsession. While interned in Frongoch after the 1916 Rising, he spent much of his time discussing the idea with other prisoners, including Michael Collins and Jim Ryan. The idea was not new; it was just that no one had done it.

Arthur Griffith had frequently urged in his writings that something needed to be done to stop the flow of insurance premiums out of the country. English-owned companies had a near-monopoly on the insurance business in Ireland. On his release from internment, O'Reilly approached Collins, who heartily encouraged him to translate the idea into action and promised to render every possible assistance.[36]

O'Reilly needed to get a more 'intimate knowledge' of the insurance business. The secretary of the Royal Liver Society in Dublin put him in touch with his district agent in Enniscorthy, whose interest O'Reilly promptly purchased. Before moving his family to Wexford to live in a flat over a shop, he again discussed the idea with Collins, who showed a growing interest in the project and renewed his promise of assistance when required. While learning the intricacies of the insurance business, O'Reilly renewed his acquaintance with Jim Ryan, who was a doctor in Wexford town and who constantly urged him to launch the new business.

After six months O'Reilly was ready to take the big step. Meanwhile, Collins had interested four of his friends in the idea: Michael Staines, Frank Thornton, Liam Tobin and Dick Coleman. All four had fought in 1916 and had been interned. Michael Staines, in his early 30s, was a senior officer in the Volunteers and a senior employee in Henshaw's wholesale ironmongery and hardware business. Liam Tobin, the youngest of the group at 23, worked in the same business.[37] Only Dick Coleman had experience in insurance, having worked as a Prudential agent for three years.[38]

In June 1917 Michael O'Reilly arranged a meeting in Enniscorthy with his potential new co-founders. Only Dick Coleman could not travel for the meeting. They met in O'Reilly's flat over the shop and Jim Ryan joined the group shortly after the others arrived. It was on that evening that O'Reilly knew that his idea was on its way to becoming a reality. The five young men spent hours discussing the project, the possibilities, the difficulties and of course, given the times, the dangers.[39] They agreed to help find the necessary finance. Dick Coleman—and probably Tobin and Thornton—invested £100 that he had received from the National Aid Fund on his release from internment.[40]

Six months later, after a great deal of preparation and organisation, the first official meeting of the 'New Ireland Assurance' business was held on 5 January 1918. Éamon de Valera attended the meeting, a sign of the importance that the Sinn Féin leadership attached to the launch of the new business. Michael O'Reilly was appointed managing director and Michael Staines was appointed treasurer and secretary. Dr Jim Ryan and George Nesbitt, treasurer of Sinn Féin, were elected trustees. Dick Coleman could not attend the meeting, as he had been imprisoned in July for parading in military uniform.

Frank Thornton, Liam Tobin and Dick Coleman became divisional inspectors for the business, operating respectively in the border counties, Cork and Dublin. Five months later, Coleman was imprisoned for the third time as part of the 'German Plot'. He died in prison on 7 December 1918, a victim of the 'flu pandemic, his body weakened by harsh conditions, a severe winter and the absence of proper medical care. He was just 29 years of age.

Meanwhile, Thornton and Tobin combined their roles in New Ireland with their work as organisers of the Irish Volunteers, which were being reorganised nationwide. Frequent travel and meetings with insurance agents provided an ideal cover for their Volunteer activities. And only Volunteers were recruited into positions of trust in New Ireland.

During 1919 Tobin and Thornton were transferred to GHQ Intelligence. Both took an indefinite leave of absence without pay from New Ireland, though they remained on the management committee. Tobin was the first recruit into the new unit, as deputy director reporting to Michael Collins. Thornton followed later in the year. The New Ireland head office and its network of insurance agents were a valuable resource for the new intelligence department. And Michael Collins made it an important part of the 'Ho Chi Minh trail', using insurance agents to collect funds and the head office in Dublin as a drop-off point for couriers coming up from the country to deposit the subscriptions.

A (useful) slow failure

The Sinn Féin Bank had been launched in 1908 with great hopes. It was going to support industrial growth, promote credit in towns and do for Ireland 'what the banks of England, France, Germany … do for the trade and finance of their respective countries'.[41]

The bank acquired 6 Harcourt Street in 1910. Reporting on the official opening of the building, the *Freeman's Journal* wrote that 'one of the finest mansions in this historic street has been taken over and entirely refitted and decorated.'[42] The offices of the bank were on the ground floor. Arthur Griffith and the Sinn Féin organisation, from which the bank was legally independent, leased offices on the upper floors.

The Act of Union in 1800 and the merger of the Irish and British exchequers in 1817 had made Ireland politically, administratively and fiscally part of the United Kingdom of Great Britain and Ireland. From January 1817 the exchequer of the United Kingdom received the tax revenues of Ireland and paid for its capital and administrative costs.[43] Although Ireland had a vibrant banking sector, the domestic banks invested the savings of the Irish people in short-term investments in financial institutions in London and in British government bonds.[44]

Arthur Griffith railed against this export of Irish money.[45] The key to industrial growth was access to capital. 'Business cannot succeed without capital,' Michael Collins later commented. 'Millions of Irish money are lying idle in banks.' One nationalist commentator believed that the English private sector saw Ireland purely as 'a field for exploitation' and regarded every effort to start independent industries in Ireland 'as an impertinent menace to themselves, to be resisted by any possible method'.[46]

When Arthur Griffith founded Sinn Féin in 1905, a large part of his motivation was to promote a nationalist economic programme. He wrote that Irish banks were 'deliberately withholding any substantial loans to Irish traders, entrepreneurs and private individuals'. He decided to set up the Sinn Féin Bank, but it was doomed to failure from the beginning.

The three-member founding council was an eclectic and unstable mix of poet, trade unionist and centre-right political figure: George Russell, P.T. Daly and Arthur Griffith. George Russell, the poet who wrote under the pseudonym 'Æ', had experience organising co-operative banks, however; one biographer described him as 'a radical intellectual involved with anarchism, labor and Sinn Féin'.[47] P.T. Daly, a trade unionist, politician and member of the Irish Republican Brotherhood, and chairman of the Public Health Committee of Dublin Corporation, had 'the shadow of financial impropriety hanging over him' in both his republican and trade union activities.[48] Daly and Griffith would later fall out over the role of trade unions in society.

Members of the management committee also quarrelled.[49] Indeed, a rift was inevitable. On one side was William Shackleton, one of three brothers who owned a well-known flour-milling firm, Shackleton and Sons.[50] On the other was Richard O'Carroll, trade union leader and member of Dublin Corporation. Their relationship broke down completely during the Dublin Lockout of 1913, the most significant labour dispute in Irish history.

William Shackleton was something of a political maverick. From a unionist background, he was on the Sinn Féin executive from 1907 to 1909, sharing Griffith's economic nationalist views. At the onset of the labour dispute in 1913, he told his employees to choose between their jobs and 'Larkin's union'. They chose the latter and by evening the mill was closed. Shackleton Mills was the first company to lock out its workers. The Shackleton brothers received advice from William Martin Murphy, the leader of the employers.[51] After the Lockout ended, the mill reopened and flour production at the Shackleton Mill continued until 1998.

Richard O'Carroll was from the working-class Liberties area of Dublin.[52] During the Lockout he had been severely beaten by baton-wielding RIC officers and needed hospital treatment. He continued to fight for workers' rights after the Lockout ended. He was also a founding member of the Volunteers and was promoted to lieutenant during the fighting in 1916. On the day after his promotion, he was shot by the infamous Captain Bowen-Colthurst. He died of septicaemia ten days later, leaving behind his wife Annie and seven children. The youngest, Seán, was born two weeks after his father's death and died at the age of just eight months.

Arthur Griffith showed little interest in the bank's operations. According to James Kavanagh, an accountant in the Sinn Féin office, Griffith could write a fine article on finance but appeared to care nothing about money.[53] He described Griffith's unique filing system:

> 'He would open his letters and just throw them on his table, dealing with anything that could be dealt with at once and then leaving all on the table until "tomorrow". When "tomorrow" came he would push back everything on the table to make room for the current day's correspondence, and so on day after day ...'

An attempt was made to tidy Griffith's office. Cheques, cash and postal orders were found lying in a heap on the floor behind his table. Though many of the cheques and postal orders were out of date, 'a large amount of money was recovered'.[54]

Alderman Tom Kelly, treasurer of the bank, was a leading member of Sinn Féin and a highly regarded member of Dublin Corporation.[55] 'Tom Kelly was another man who had queer ideas regarding money,' recalled Kavanagh. He remembered a meeting of the Sinn Féin executive chaired by the alderman. A delegation appeared before the committee looking for financial assistance. As the secretary was explaining that there was no money available to help them, Alderman Kelly intervened: 'Yes, there's plenty of money here, I saw it over in that corner. You can have as much as you want.' That the money was allocated for another purpose was of no interest to Kelly. 'It was money and these boys wanted money, so that was that.'

A weak supervisory board, poor management and a lack of capital sealed the bank's fate. By the time of the opening of the Dáil in January 1919, it operated as a small savings bank for working-class customers.[56] David Kelly, the manager and sole employee, was the brother of Alderman Kelly.

But it was its slow failure that gave the bank its importance to Michael Collins. As a legally recognised bank, established under the Industrial and Provident Societies Act, 1893, it could issue its own cheques, and two of the more nationalist of the commercial banks accepted those cheques.[57] Dáil Éireann opened deposit and current accounts in the Sinn Féin Bank, which facilitated the payment of salaries and the day-to-day expenditure of the counter-state administration.

The Sinn Féin offices over the bank were frequently raided in early 1919, although the authorities, respecting the Sinn Féin Bank's legal independence, did not enter the bank's offices. There was no guarantee, however, that this legal nicety would continue to be respected. The question facing Michael Collins was for how long Dublin Castle would respect the legal independence of a bank whose antagonistic and provocative name was written in large gold letters across the front of 6 Harcourt Street.[58] He needed to find an alternative means of safeguarding the proceeds of the Dáil Loan.

Education in assassination

John McBride was a brief but important father-figure for Michael McDonnell. They met for the first time during the fighting in 1916. A strong bond developed between McDonnell, whose father had died when he was eight years old, and McBride, who was estranged from his twelve-year-old son, Seán, who lived in Paris with Maud Gonne.

> 'During the course of Easter Week, I became closely acquainted with Major John MacBride and had many conversations with him, the last of which remains vividly in my memory. As we were preparing to leave Jacobs to surrender in Bride Street I said to him: "Commandant, you had better get out of here". He replied by saying: "Mac, every G. man in Dublin knows me". And I said: "I had been upstairs looking out the window and there was not a G. man in sight and there is no chance of your escaping if you remain here, and my advice is to get out". He slightly bowed his head as if in deep emotion and replied: "Oh Mac! I wouldn't leave the boys". And he didn't. That is the last I saw of him.'[59]

Major John McBride was executed by the British five days later.

McDonnell had been promoted to the rank of 2nd lieutenant in the field and was interned in Frongoch, where he met Michael Collins. On his release, he was instrumental in redrafting the revolutionary strategy and was appointed captain quartermaster in the 2nd Battalion of the Dublin Brigade. Like many others, he had no intention of repeating the mistakes of 1916, and that was one of the reasons why he had a clear conscience when it came to shooting detectives. 'From an early stage,' he recalled, 'I advocated the execution of those who were responsible for the identity of the men executed in 1916 and who were at the same time watching us.'[60] In early May, three months after the opening of the Dáil, he broached his proposal to shoot detectives to Dick McKee, brigadier of the Dublin Brigade and *ex officio* member of GHQ, but McKee felt that the people were not yet ready for this type of action.

McDonnell could be intense and ill-tempered. After his father died, his mother had remarried. His own marriage, from which he had a young daughter, was in trouble, but he was always protective of his men and recognised when he was overly harsh in his criticism. A young Volunteer, after receiving an unwarranted dressing-down, saw McDonnell 'change immediately and [he] became very nice to me and said he was very sorry for all he had said'.[61] McDonnell was not slow to let his superior officers know his feelings. He was not happy when the same young Volunteer told him that a car borrowed for the use of Michael Collins and Dick McKee had broken down: 'You can go back and tell Mr Collins and McKee that they will never get a car from me again'.

By July, circumstances had changed to the point that Dick McKee asked McDonnell to select four men for a special job—the shooting of detectives. This type of work was not for everyone. Many of the Volunteers objected 'for one reason or another'.[62] The men who joined this new squad were undoubtedly brave and dangerous, but they were also inexperienced in the mechanics of assassination. And they botched their first job in July 1919: Detective Sergeant Patrick Smith, a father of seven children, survived the shooting, though he was in a critical condition in hospital.

The outcome could have been worse. Insufficient advance intelligence work and operating without scouts in covering positions left the assassination team exposed. Worse, they were using the wrong weapons. 'I thought that the minute we would fire at him he would fall,' recalled Jim Slattery, 'but after we hit him he ran.'[63] McDonnell gave Slattery a sharp dressing-down the following morning.[64] A mistake like that against a more experienced target could have been fatal, but it was an education in assassination. 'We never used .38 guns again, we used .45 guns after that lesson.'[65] McDonnell and his inexperienced part-time team of assassins survived their first months of operation through luck rather than the planning and attention to detail expected of a professional hit squad.

Ready to launch

In early August Michael Collins was anxious to get on with the public advertising campaign for the Loan. The launch had been delayed because enough copies of the prospectus had not yet been printed. Printing 250,000 copies of the document under the watchful eye of Dublin Castle was an 'extremely difficult undertaking'.[66] Days earlier, on 30 July, he had authorised the shooting of Detective Smith.

On 12 August the sixteen-member Finance Committee finalised the process for the issue of the Loan and the collection of subscriptions.[67] Each member of the Dáil had to establish a central committee made up of the most prominent Sinn Féin supporters in his constituency.[68] This central committee would form 'collecting and advertising committees' in every parish, or half-parish where necessary, throughout the constituency. Special arrangements were made for TDs in prison or who were in America or Paris, or where the Sinn Féin candidate had been withdrawn or defeated in the election.

Collins was concerned that the TDs would not implement the local organisational structures fast enough. In his written report presented to the Dáil on 19 August, he urged that 'the work must go ahead quickly. It will be essential to get on with a rush.'[69] On the following day he informed the Dáil that the prospectuses would be delivered to the constituencies in one week.

Meanwhile, the successful launch of the Loan in Ireland took on more urgency. News coming from America was not good. Although the Dáil passed a motion on 20 August to increase the amount of the American Loan from £250,000 to £5 million ($25 million), floating the Loan was facing unexpected obstacles. State regulators, implementing anti-fraud regulations known as 'Blue Sky' laws, were vigilant regarding non-US investments. The American Loan presented a specific problem for them. Dáil Éireann was not the sovereign government of Ireland and the Irish Republic was not legally recognised. The issue of an investment security described as a government bond, which implied lower risk for investors, was misleading. A technical solution was found, eventually, by calling the securities 'bond-certificates' and revising the repayment terms. Certificates could be exchanged for a gold bond paying a 5% interest rate issued by Dáil Éireann one month after the Republic received international recognition.

A fractious relationship had also developed between Éamon de Valera and Daniel Cohalan, a New York judge and the leading figure in the Friends of Irish Freedom (FOIF). The powerful Irish-American lobby group had launched its own fund-raising campaign—the Victory Fund—in early 1919. The money was to be used in America in a propaganda campaign to win support for recognition of the Irish Republic, and to oppose the Wilson administration and the League of Nations. When the funding campaign was just five months old, de Valera arrived in New York to launch the Dáil Loan. It was deemed not advisable to launch the Loan simultaneously with the Victory Fund. The FOIF agreed to terminate the Victory Fund in August 1919, after raising over $1 million, and the American or 'External Loan' was launched in January 1920.

Although the FOIF sent $100,000 (£25,000) to Ireland, this was not sufficient to meet the growing needs of the counter-state administration, in particular to fund the constructive programmes and the Department of Defence.[70] The credibility of the Dáil government as a viable alternative to the Dublin Castle administration was at stake. Without money, the Dáil Éireann experiment could end in failure—maybe even with the Sinn Féin elected representatives crawling back to Westminster, as many in London had predicted.[71] The future of Dáil Éireann and the republican movement depended on the loans.[72] With funds from America delayed, it was imperative that the domestic Loan should succeed.

Finally, on 6 September, Collins instructed the MacDonogh advertising agency to send copies of the Loan advertisement to the national newspapers to get quotes for publication on Friday 12 September, and to get quotes for publication in the provincial weeklies the following weekend.[73]

Collins was concerned that the British would block publication of the advertisements. He told the TDs that the 'type of advertising will of course largely depend on the action of the British Censorship towards our notices'.[74] If the advertisements were censored, the local organising committees would have an even more important role in promoting the Loan.

Dáil Éireann had been in existence for over seven months in open defiance of British rule in Ireland. Plans for the Loan and the constructive programme were reported extensively by the press. And although Dublin was quiet, 'outrages' had increased in the country, especially in Clare and Tipperary, where Sinn Féin had been prohibited. Yet there had still been no reaction from London or Dublin Castle to this unique challenge to the authority of the British Empire. Collins, however, expected a 'considerable' response to the launch of the Loan.[75] He underestimated the nature, depth and violence of that response.

1. Suppression

Prohibition

Fine-featured and handsome, he was his defiant self on the stage of the Town Hall in Macroom. 'They had received a direct challenge during the week, and the best way to answer it was to make this loan a big success.'[1] Terence MacSwiney TD, playwright and author, was addressing members of Sinn Féin from various parts of his Mid-Cork constituency. They were gathered to put in place the organising structure for the Loan campaign. 'The recent proclamation might make their work a little more difficult, but it would afford a stimulus to the proceedings which is always of advantage.' Before getting into the organisational details, he told those in attendance that the best way to get people to subscribe to the Loan was to give examples of the work being done by Dáil Éireann. He made a passionate appeal to them to subscribe liberally to the Loan for the sake of the cause and the country.

Seven days earlier, on Wednesday 10 September, Dáil Éireann had been prohibited under an order signed by Lord French and General Shaw, the military commander in Ireland. The announcement was promulgated in the *Dublin Gazette*, the official newspaper of the Irish executive, two days later on 12 September.

The timing of the prohibition so close to the press launch of the Loan was not coincidental. When the manager of Independent Newspapers received the Loan advertisement copy from the MacDonogh advertising agency on 6 September, he immediately contacted Dublin Castle. The office of the censor had been closed at the end of August and he wanted guidance on the legality of publication. Dublin Castle waited five days, until 11 September, the day before the prohibition was publicly announced, before replying. Independent Newspapers were informed that publication of the prospectus was 'illegal, and that if published your company must take the consequences'.[2]

An abrupt response from Dublin Castle was not unexpected. On the previous Sunday morning, in an attack by Volunteers in plain clothes in Fermoy, a British soldier had been killed, the first in Ireland since 1916. The killing of Private Jones as he was walking to church with other soldiers was widely condemned. The following day, Detective Patrick Smith died from the wounds he had received five weeks previously. King George V was provoked into writing a letter demanding 'to know what the government was going to do to protect the lives of suffering people in Ireland and what measures were to be brought into parliament for the government of the country'.[3]

Nevertheless, the shooting of Private Jones and the death of Detective Smith were not sufficient, either individually or combined, to motivate the proscription of Dáil Éireann by Dublin Castle. The response to the shooting of Private Jones was to prohibit Sinn Féin in Cork city and county.[4] Dublin Castle stopped short of banning Sinn Féin outright. This response was consistent with the Irish executive's previous responses to 'outrages'—the localised prohibition of Sinn Féin in the district where the attack took place: Tipperary on 4 July, then Clare on 13 August, and now Cork. On each occasion the Sinn Féin Clubs, the Irish Volunteers, Cumann na mBan and the Gaelic League were prohibited along with Sinn Féin. The death of Detective Smith, although tragic for his family and subject to wide media coverage, was only a minor catalyst. And although the king's letter was an important intervention, the order to prohibit Dáil Éireann had been signed the day before the letter was written.

Macpherson, the chief secretary, wrote to Bonar Law explaining the timing of the decision to prohibit Dáil Éireann. They could not intervene when the Irish elected representatives chose 'to sit together in *consultation*', but when they conspired by '*executive acts* … to overthrow the duly constituted authority' then they could act.[5] Macpherson may have been referring to the passing by Dáil Éireann on 20 August of the oath of allegiance to be taken by the Volunteers, soon to be more commonly known as the Irish Republican Army,[6] but this was no more treasonous than the Declaration of Independence read at the first meeting of the Dáil.

A newspaper article from April was prophetic as regards the reasoning behind the decision to prohibit the Dáil. Writing in *The Observer*, Captain Stephen Gwynn, a moderate Protestant nationalist who lost his Westminster seat in the 1918 Sinn Féin landslide, commented that 'two old hands in Irish politics told him they believed that the money would be found for the loan. If true, Sinn Féin would need to be taken very seriously indeed. Money talks'.[7]

Arthur Griffith said that 'it was interesting to find that it was only when the [constructive] programme was being put into operation that the enemy suppressed the Dáil'.[8] Terence MacSwiney agreed: 'These things were being taken in hand with every prospect of success, and that was the reason for the proclamation'.[9] Éamon de Valera, in a statement telegraphed from Rhode Island, shared the same view.[10] Patrick J. Little, editor of the *New Ireland* journal, was even more forthright in his opinion that 'the whole force of English violence comes into play when her trade jealousy is aroused'. Relating the prohibition of Dáil Éireann to the constructive programme, he added: 'The British Government now aims at making it physically impossible to float any loan which will establish industries and prevent emigration'.[11]

Media reaction to the prohibition of Dáil Éireann ran along expected lines. Nationalist media blamed Lloyd George for absenting himself from the Irish situation, leaving Lord French as the 'absolute ruler in Ireland' and Edward Carson pulling the strings of the Irish executive in Dublin.[12]

Lloyd George, however, had more pressing geopolitical issues on his desk.[13] The Paris peace conference had opened on 18 January, three days before the first meeting of Dáil Éireann. In the first half of the year, Lloyd George was rarely even in London, spending most of his time in Paris. Domestically, he also had to contend with mutinous demobilised soldiers, a strike by the metropolitan police and a perceived Bolshevik threat to national security.

The pro-Union *Irish Times* linked the decision to prohibit the Dáil to the failure of Sinn Féin and the elected assembly to condemn criminal acts, stating that the government 'must proceed fearlessly with its heavy task of punishing crime and of vindicating law against anarchy'.[14]

London papers generally expressed approval of the prohibition, though the Liberal press appealed to the government to find a settlement.[15] The conservative *London Express* said that Sinn Féin 'promises only a crank policy, and is supported by impracticable idealists or frank anarchists ... it has been put down with a firm hand ...'.[16]

DORA and the Crimes Act

Suppressing Dáil Éireann but not prohibiting Sinn Féin outright was a politically smart move by Dublin Castle, an administration that would make few smart decisions over the coming months. Sir Warren Fisher, one of the most senior civil servants in London, later described the Dublin regime as 'almost woodenly stupid and quite devoid of imagination'.[17]

London opposed the suppression of Sinn Féin. The political reality was that Sinn Féin had won 73 of the 105 seats in the 1918 elections. Bonar Law, leader of the Conservative party and a Union advocate, feared the repercussions of 'suppressing an organisation which represented a great part of the South of Ireland'.[18] London also had an eye on American public opinion. Éamon de Valera's sojourn in America to seek recognition for the Irish Republic and to promote the Dáil Loan had placed Ireland on the political agenda. Prohibiting the largest political party in Ireland would not be received positively in the former colony.

In any case, Dublin Castle did not need to prohibit Sinn Féin to curtail the advances made by the republican movement or to suppress the Dáil Loan. The Irish executive had special powers available to it under legislation passed in the 1880s. The Crimes Act, the more common name for the Criminal Law and Procedure (Ireland) Act, passed by the House of Commons in 1887, applied only in Ireland. And where the Crimes Act was deficient in dealing with the republican movement, Lord French and Macpherson could fall back on the Defence of the Realm Act (DORA) and its punitive regulations, which were still operable despite the end of the war.

Dublin Castle had considered using DORA regulations to suppress Dáil Éireann by declaring its members 'illegal personages' until it was judged unwise to apply wartime regulations to elected representatives.[19] To prohibit and supress Dáil Éireann under the Crimes Act, the body had to be declared a 'dangerous' association, but even the *Irish Times* admitted that on the surface Dáil Éireann was 'not a very dangerous association'.[20]

Some subtle legal interpretation was required. Sinn Féin had been declared 'dangerous' on 3 July 1918, giving the Irish executive the authority to prohibit the organisation, if it so chose, in individual districts or in all the districts in Ireland. To date, that authority had been used to prohibit

Sinn Féin in specific districts in response to localised 'outrages'. By establishing a link between Dáil Éireann and Sinn Féin, the former could also be declared a 'dangerous' association.

Lord French, under the advice of the solicitor-general for Ireland, Daniel Martin Wilson, a staunch unionist, declared that Dáil Éireann was 'formed and first employed for all purposes' of Sinn Féin.[21] (Sinn Féin, of course, would argue that the Dáil was an assembly for all the elected representatives in Ireland, not just Sinn Féin members.) With the link established, Lord French exercised the authority of the Privy Council to prohibit Dáil Éireann in all districts in Ireland.

Prohibiting Dáil Éireann under the Crimes Act held another advantage. Dublin Castle could suppress the promotion of the Dáil Loan and the solicitation of subscriptions. Section 2 of the Act gave Dublin Castle the power to prevent 'unlawful assembly', which, with a wide interpretation, could be used to prohibit Loan organising meetings and promotional events. Section 7 of the Act permitted the prosecution without a jury trial of persons soliciting subscriptions for a prohibited body.

Star Chamber

And Dublin Castle also used the Crimes Act in a surprising and controversial manner. On the same day that the order to prohibit Dáil Éireann was signed, the Irish executive enforced the 'Coercion Sections' of the Crimes Act in Dublin, Cork, Limerick, Tipperary and Clare. This enabled the establishment of 'Star Chamber' inquiries.[22]

Under Section I of the Crimes Act, an inquiry could be established by a resident magistrate with wide judicial and investigative powers. A single magistrate could examine under oath any persons whom he believed capable of giving material evidence concerning an offence. Inquiries were held behind closed doors and no legal representation was permitted. Witnesses were not excused from answering questions on the grounds that the answer might be self-incriminating and could be committed to prison for refusing to answer questions.

The move was even more controversial because it was enforced in Dublin, which as yet had seen little military activity. Sinn Féin had not even been banned there. The last time that Star Chamber powers were authorised in the city it had caused a general outcry. In 1888, speaking in Westminster, the then lord mayor of Dublin, also an MP, decried 'the humiliation and the insult of wantonly setting up a Star Chamber in their midst'.[23] Enforcing the legislation in Dublin was a pre-emptive move by the Castle. It indicated that the Irish executive was receiving advice from someone with prior experience in the suppression of illegal bodies and their funding.

Be calm and patient

Writing to de Valera in America following the prohibition of the Dáil, Michael Collins expected the worst: 'Of course, we don't know yet how the situation will work out under this, but presumably the position will be identical to that created by the German Plot proclamation last year'.[24] In other words, he expected the mass arrest and internment of TDs and Sinn Féin leaders. Preparing for that eventuality, Arthur Griffith and Collins put arrangements in place to ensure continuance of the Dáil government. The plans were sent to de Valera and the other TDs in America, including Harry Boland, and to the envoys in Paris.

A circular was issued from Dáil Éireann for the guidance of the Volunteers.[25] It opened ominously: 'The critical moment has now arrived in the history of the movement ... and we are sure that the next few days will no doubt bring our forces in closer touch than we have been for some time'. Volunteers were urged to be calm and patient, and to 'obey the orders that may come from our successors whom we've appointed in case of necessity'.

Raid on 6 Harcourt Street

At 10.30 in the morning of 12 September, Eithne Lawless was at a meeting on the second floor of 6 Harcourt Street, the headquarters of Sinn Féin, in the office of Diarmuid O'Hegarty, for whom she worked as a secretary.[26] Michael Collins was there, along with four other members of the Dáil Finance and Secretariat staff—Fintan Murphy, Jenny Mason, Kate O'Toole and Bob Conlon. The meeting was about to commence.

Someone had left the door of the office open. 'I was getting up to shut it when I saw a policeman standing on guard, outside. I shut the door and told Mick it looked like a raid.' Two military lorries had pulled up in front of the building.[27] While soldiers took up positions outside, the police and detectives were already entering the building. Taken by surprise, there was not a lot of time to react. 'I stuck Mick's revolver down my stocking and anything else incriminating we girls took charge of.' No escape was possible. Collins said: 'We are caught like rats in a trap'.

When the raiding party arrived upstairs and entered the room, Collins was pleased to see that it was Inspector McFeely. Ned Broy, one of his agents inside G Division, had already prepared him in the event of meeting McFeely.[28] Eithne Lawless thought that McFeely looked a little bit frightened. 'He went round searching the different desks and seemed desperately anxious to finish his task and get out.' Collins was sitting casually on the edge of his desk with one leg swinging. He decided to have a go at Inspector McFeely. 'What sort of a legacy will you leave to your family, looking for blood money,' he taunted. 'Could you not find some honest work to do?'[29] McFeely, known to be a Home Rule supporter, ignored the comments and left the room.

The atmosphere on the ground floor was more intimidating and threatening. When McFeely returned downstairs to join Detective Hoey, second in command on the raid, he approached James Kavanagh, an accountant with Sinn Féin, who described what happened in his own words:[30] ' "Are you Mr O'Keeffe?". "No" said I. "Where is Mr O'Keeffe?" said he. "I don't know" said I, "haven't seen him for a long time".' Paddy O'Keeffe was sitting at the same table as Kavanagh. A short while later, Detective Hoey was seen whispering to McFeely while looking in the direction of Patrick O'Keeffe. 'McFeely approached the table again: "Mr O'Keeffe, I have to arrest you". "Be so and so you won't," said Paddy. A long argument ensued between them then, but eventually Paddy gave in and was arrested.'

Detective Hoey then picked up a tray of papers from a desk. Brian Fagan warned him, 'Hoey, the last man to handle that tray of papers was Sergeant Smyth'. Fagan, badly wounded in 1916, had steel supports for his legs and used crutches. 'Hoey dropped the tray of papers like a hot potato.'

Word of the raid had spread. Arthur Griffith and Alderman Kelly, treasurer of the Sinn Féin Bank, arrived shortly after the raid commenced and, after some discussions with the police, were permitted to enter the building. Other TDs, including William Cosgrave and Michael Staines, treasurer of New Ireland Assurance, were refused entry when they arrived.[31] A fiery Jenny Wyse-Power, one of the most senior Sinn Féin leaders and ubiquitous during the revolutionary period, was also turned away, 'despite her persistent efforts to gain admittance'.

A large crowd had gathered in the street to watch the raid. Motor traffic and tram movements were blocked. Shortly after midday, to the delight of the onlookers, a huge republican flag was hung from a top-floor window, followed immediately by the American Stars and Stripes. A painter on a ladder casually and defiantly carried on painting the door of No. 6. He became a target of the comedians in the crowd.

The noise and the excitement reached fever pitch when Paddy O'Keeffe and Ernest Blythe, the Dáil Director of Trade, came down the steps in police custody. There was a wild dash forward. A number of young men were seized by the police. When one offered resistance, the crowd surged round the military vehicles. A Sinn Féin official pleaded with the police to let the man go. The situation risked getting out of control. No one knew how the young and inexperienced British soldiers would react— the war veterans had received early post-war discharges. Eventually, the young man was released.[32]

The raid lasted over two hours.[33] Eithne Lawless felt intense relief when the police left the building. Michael Collins, however, refused to leave in spite of her protests. 'We all remained at our work until the normal time for our departure.' Eithne Lawless entered a convent as a novice in 1920. One wonders whether she ever told the other nuns about the morning she stuck Michael Collins's revolver down her stocking.

Collins had had a close escape that morning. He was fortunate that it was McFeely and not Hoey who had searched upstairs. Hoey was known to have identified Seán MacDermott, one of the executed 1916 leaders. Paddy O'Keeffe had been put on a military lorry by Hoey. As the lorry pulled away from 6 Harcourt Street, Paddy shouted back: 'Hoey, you'll die for this to-night'.[34]

The Sinn Féin offices had been raided about every two months in

1919, but none of the previous raids were as extensive as the one that morning.[35] It was the first time that arrests had been made, though Ernest Blythe and Paddy O'Keeffe were taken on old warrants issued under DORA regulations. Paddy O'Keeffe was general secretary of Sinn Féin and a respected organiser. He was a loss to the republican movement. The police had been looking for him in respect of a 'seditious speech' he had made in May. He was sentenced to one year and six months in prison.[36]

That day, raids and searches and seizures were reported all over Ireland. The homes of six Sinn Féin TDs were raided in Dublin 'amidst considerable excitement',[37] including those of Alderman Kelly and Michael Staines. Lord French and Chief Secretary Macpherson were sending a message that it was no longer business as usual for Sinn Féin. The proclamation of Dáil Éireann was published later that evening in the *Dublin Gazette*.

In Cork, police armed with carbines and revolvers carried out 'exhaustive' searches of the Sinn Féin Clubs, while soldiers with fixed bayonets stood guard outside. The headquarters of Sinn Féin in the city were searched for over an hour. There was no one in the office at the time. Later, Sinn Féin activists put up a 'Business as Usual' sign on the window.[38]

Reports of raids came in from across Ulster. In Belfast many shops and private residences were searched. In Derry 'Numerous raiding parties were busy'.[39] The house of Joe O'Doherty TD was searched. An accountant's office in Enniskillen and two solicitors' practices in Omagh were raided. From Donegal it was reported that parties of police and military 'were engaged in a systematic search of Sinn Féiners throughout the North-west'.[40] The raids continued across the country on Saturday and into Sunday. The home of Daithi Ceannt TD was searched in Cork.[41] Nothing material was seized in the raids, though 'in a few cases revolvers were discovered'.[42]

The shooting of Detective Hoey

On the evening of the raid on 6 Harcourt Street, Michael McDonnell arrived at the home of Jim Slattery and asked him whether he would mind going on a job.[43] The squad had been looking for Detective Hoey for a fortnight and after his role in the raid that day it had become urgent to get him. 'They very nearly got the man we want to guard', McDonnell told

Slattery. For the latter, it was the first time he 'got an inkling that Collins was the heart of things'.[44]

About 10pm that evening, McDonnell, Slattery and Tom Ennis watched Detective Hoey as he walked towards the police station on Great Brunswick (now Pearse) Street. Walking past the main entrance, he turned down a side street to buy a glass of milk. 'It is him alright,' McDonnell told the others.[45] They crossed the street, walked towards Hoey and shot him through the throat, the chin and the heart. He fell at the back door of the police station. McDonnell went to Collins to report to him directly that the operation was complete.

Detective Hoey had made the mistake of identifying Paddy O'Keeffe in the Sinn Féin offices that morning. Slattery called him the 'leading spirit in the raiders'.[46] The *Irish Independent*, reporting on the shooting, said that Hoey 'was a well-known figure in connection with political affairs in the capital for several years past and was frequently to be seen accompanying the Lord Lieutenant and Chief Secretary'.[47] Paddy O'Keeffe had warned Detective Hoey that he would be killed that night, and, if Brian Fagan's words were true, Hoey was the second detective to die shortly after handling a Sinn Féin filing tray.

The shooting of Detective Hoey was a successful operation, but it was carried out without intelligence support and without scouts in covering positions. Although it was an urgent job and McDonnell had little preparation time, and although he knew Hoey by sight, the shooting showed that the squad was still not operating as a professional assassination unit.

Suppression Week

On 12 September, the *Cork Examiner* was the only daily newspaper to publish the full-page advertisement for the Loan. Five days later, military and police raided the newspaper's offices on Patrick Street, suppressed the publication and removed vital components from the printing machinery.[48] The paper had a moderate nationalist editorial stance and favoured a Home Rule solution, though it had welcomed the opening of the first session of Dáil Éireann as an 'event of the first importance'.[49]

The attack on press freedom caused an outcry in Ireland and Britain. The Irish executive tried to 'spin' a story that it had given advance notice to the newspapers that publication of the Loan advertisement was an illegal act. Dublin Castle released the letters exchanged between it and Independent Newspapers. Although it had informed the *Irish Independent* and probably indirectly the *Freeman's Journal*, the two nationalist daily papers in Dublin, it had made no effort to inform the *Cork Examiner*, despite knowing about the advertisement since 6 September. The paper's management did not even know that Dáil Éireann had been prohibited when it published the advertisement. The prohibition announcement had only been promulgated in the *Dublin Gazette* that evening.

The suppression of the *Cork Examiner* had taken place on Wednesday 17 September. Provincial newspapers and weekly journals had not gone to press yet. Owners and editors were concerned that their papers would meet the same fate as the *Examiner*. Darrell Figgis, editor of *The Republic*, remembered how, when the advertisement came to him in his editorial office on Ormond Quay, 'I held it before me in admiration of the tinder my poor paper was to make'.[50]

There was still time, however, to change the wording of the advertisement. Collins sought legal advice, probably through Michael Noyk, a solicitor and good friend, and the advertisement was reworded. Reference was now made to the 'National Loan' rather than to the 'Dáil Éireann Loan', and the address for subscriptions was changed from 6 Harcourt Street to 76 Harcourt Street, which had been acquired by the 'Irish Club' but was in fact the new home of the Department of Finance and the secretariat.[51]

Despite the change in wording, owners and editors were still concerned. One editor consulted his RIC county inspector before publishing. He was told that if the advertisement appeared his paper would be 'snuffed'.[52] Michael Collins could not really have believed that Dublin Castle would respect the apparent legality of the 'National Loan'. Nevertheless, the change in wording appeared to have worked, as the first batch of weekly papers that came out with the advertisement were not interfered with by the authorities.

The crackdown commenced on Saturday morning. Darrell Figgis described how military and police entered his office, melted font, broke type and issued a formal notice of suppression of the paper. Across the country, printing was stopped, machinery dismantled and components confiscated.[53] Newspapers were taken from shops, and even from boys selling them on the street.[54] By Tuesday, 35 newspapers had been suppressed.[55]

The scale of the attack on the freedom of the press in Ireland attracted global attention. The liberal *Daily News* in London openly challenged government policy by publishing the full text of the advertisement in an edition primarily intended for circulation in Ireland.[56] The Dublin correspondent of the *Manchester Guardian* declared that 'Proclamation Week has been followed by Suppression Week in Ireland'.[57]

The Times found itself in an editorial predicament. On the one hand, the paper believed that free expression was the 'inalienable heritage of every British citizen', and it wrote of a 'vigilant jealousy' of any departure from the 'great principle'.[58] On the other hand, it had advocated a firm policy in Ireland. It initially viewed the suppression of the *Cork Examiner* 'with some measure of apprehension', but 'doubtless' the present condition of Ireland justified the action.[59] Within days the paper had changed its line and focused its criticism on Dublin Castle policy, stating that the press had 'an indefeasible right to report faithfully the happenings of all events whether welcome to the Executive or not'.[60] It published a letter from Major Bryan Cooper, the former press censor in Ireland, condemning the suppression policy.[61]

On 22 September the *Cork Examiner* was allowed to publish again, and most of the provincial papers were permitted to resume publication shortly afterwards. Proprietors and printers were required to sign personal declarations that they would not publish seditious literature or any items contravening common law, DORA or the Crimes Act.[62] Seven Sinn Féin journals in Dublin, however, were permanently suppressed.[63] These included *Nationality*, Arthur Griffith's paper; *New Ireland*, edited by Patrick J. Little; and Darrell Figgis's *Republic*.[64]

Not all unionists were pleased with Dublin Castle's policy of nationwide raids and media suppression. Thomas Sinclair telegraphed Lord French from Armagh: 'We have no Sinn Féiners in Lisburn in the sense of the word. Raids have taken place here, and if this sort of police interference with the rights of the citizens is to be continued, the Government will turn every Home Ruler in Ireland into a Sinn Féiner.'[65] J. Quinnell, a non-political unionist and a Freemason, printed three of the newspapers in Kerry that had been suppressed. Two of his sons had been in the flying corps during the war, one of whom worked in the family business.

Direct marketing

Many believed that the publicity surrounding the suppression of newspapers would be a boon to Loan subscriptions. The *Manchester Guardian* said that Lord French's policy of suppression 'ensured a first-class subscription' for the Loan.[66] Bryan Cooper, the former press censor, wrote in his letter to *The Times*: 'Sinn Féin has its secret printing presses and the prospectus of the Dáil Loan is doubtless by now being passed from hand to hand all over Ireland'. He added that 'The Government have given it the best advertisement it could possibly desire'.[67]

Darrell Figgis later echoed the same view, though with a hint of sarcasm towards Michael Collins for his decision to advertise the Loan in newspapers in the first place. 'All of us who owned journals were to be thrown cheerfully into the conflagration,' he wrote, 'the blaze of which would prove a much more successful advertisement than any mass of printed matter.'

Collins must have read these comments with a wry smile. If only it was so easy to promote a national public subscription loan for an underground government when it was illegal to gather in groups of more than three people and illegal to solicit subscriptions! 'Of course, it is an awful disadvantage to be excluded from the Press,' he wrote to de Valera.[68] Collins understood how greatly the success of the British Victory Loan was underpinned by its press campaign.

Denied access to national and local media, Collins enhanced the direct marketing campaign by sending a special letter to 50,000 prominent Sinn Féin supporters throughout the country,[69] increasing the print run of the prospectus to 400,000,[70] printing 3,000,000 promotional leaflets in Dublin and sending them by courier to loan committees in every constituency.[71] The loan committees would have to conduct a house-to-house canvas to distribute the material and to collect subscriptions, organise a poster campaign in every town and village, and reactivate the 'painting squads' used in the general election to stencil and paint slogans on walls and hoardings.

The increased level of Loan marketing and subscription activity required more resources. Collins transferred four provincial organisers and 43 sub-organisers from the payroll of Sinn Féin to Dáil Éireann to manage the Loan.[72] The promotion of the Loan would also have to take advantage of the festivals of music and culture—known as Aeridheacht—that were taking place around the country. TDs and prominent Sinn Féin members would have to speak at these events, even at the risk of arrest.

2. Oppression

Arrest of Alex McCabe

On 22 October, the Speaker informed the House of Commons that he had received a letter from the clerk of Sligo County Court,[1] informing him that Mr Alexander McCabe, MP for the South Division of the county of Sligo, had been convicted and imprisoned for two offences under the Criminal Law and Procedure (Ireland) Act, 1887. Alex McCabe, the absentee MP, became the first member of Dáil Éireann to be arrested and imprisoned for Loan-related activity.

McCabe had been charged with illegal assembly ('unlawfully, riotously and routously') and soliciting funds for the Dáil Loan. He was brought before a Crimes Court in front of two resident magistrates, Captain Fitzpatrick and Mr Glass.[2] It quickly became clear that McCabe, representing himself, had no intention of co-operating with the court, which as a member of the 'Irish Republican Parliament' he refused to recognise, and that he had every intention of making a mockery of it. Seeing another magistrate who happened to be in the room looking in his direction, McCabe addressed the court: 'Your Worships, I object to have a face like this looking at me'.[3] Speaking to the offended magistrate, Captain Fitzpatrick advised him to treat the comment 'with the contempt that it deserves'. During a short adjournment, McCabe's friends supplied him with 'tea and its accompaniments', which he continued to consume after the proceedings resumed.[4] Captain Fitzpatrick was not amused. He sentenced McCabe to three months' imprisonment with hard labour.

Members of Dáil Éireann were not going to be intimidated by the actions of Dublin Castle. Two days after the suppression of the Dáil, Peter Paul Galligan, TD for West Cavan, spoke at an Aeridheacht attended by over 1,000 people. He told the gathering that the members of Dáil Éireann 'treated that suppression with contempt'.[5] Appealing for subscriptions to the Loan, he reassured them that the Dáil, 'despite that proclamation, would continue'.

On the following Sunday, Seán Etchingham was loudly cheered when he was introduced as the principal speaker at an Aeridheacht in his Wicklow constituency. His opening remark was defiant: 'Sinn Féin laughed at England'.[6] On the same day, however, police and soldiers from the Oxford and Bucks Regiment took possession of the Town Hall in Midleton half an hour before a Loan meeting was due to commence. The soldiers had bayonets fixed.[7]

On 5 October James Dolan, TD for Leitrim, was arrested for unlawful assembly and soliciting Dáil Loan subscriptions at Drumshanbo.[8] Tried in a Crimes Court whose authority he refused to recognise, Dolan was sentenced to two months' imprisonment.

On 11 October over 70 policemen arrived at a meeting in Ballinasloe. The crowd was told to disperse. 'They did not seem to take things seriously', reported the *Irish Times*. After the crowd was again spoken to, a baton charge was ordered. 'Men, women and children were knocked down in the rush.'[9] The *Connacht Tribune* said that the police could have avoided the extreme measures, but it also criticised the organisers, who 'should have taken the necessary precautions to avoid broken heads'.[10] On the following day the police also drew batons, but did not use them, at a prohibited Aeridheacht in Finglas.[11]

Things go well in a general way

Despite the prohibition of Dáil Éireann, the nationwide raids, the arrest of TDs and a police baton charge on a crowd, Michael Collins was surprisingly sanguine. 'Taking them all round, the repressions have been of benefit to us,' he wrote to de Valera in early October. 'For the moment, they have had the effect of delaying things somewhat, but the circumstances they produce— requiring as they will a house-to-house canvass—will ultimately achieve better results.'[12] Collins was pleased with the work effort, which 'is now achieving definite and satisfactory results'.[13]

Diarmuid O'Hegarty was equally upbeat. 'The British are out after the Loan—neck or nothing,' he wrote to Seán T. O'Kelly, another Dáil envoy in Paris, on 9 October. 'But the loan goes merrily along. They appear to have got into a blue funk about it, but they cannot stop its progress. Their activities so far have been an asset.'[14]

Meanwhile, Volunteers in Mullingar decided to print their own Loan posters. Gaining access after midnight to the former printing works of the *Westmeath Nationalist*, and using an old-fashioned hand-worked printing machine, they toiled through the night to design and print thousands of posters. 'The old printing machine made an awful noise when being operated,' recalled Michael McCoy, captain of the Mullingar company, 'and it was extraordinary that we were not found at it by the police.'[15]

On the following Saturday night, McCoy and his men covered the town—including the gate of the police barracks—with posters, to be seen by Mass-goers in the morning. Finding a donkey wandering about the streets, they covered it with left-over posters. 'The following day,' recalled McCoy fondly, '… the RIC spent hours removing the posters, and when they thought they had completed the job to their satisfaction, down the street came the donkey covered all over with them.'

Collins updated de Valera again on 14 October. 'You will be interested to hear that the enemy's chief offensive here at the moment is directed against the Loan.' He told de Valera that 'McCabe is in jail, awaiting trial, for having spoken in commendation of the Loan, and Etchingham is "on the run" for the same offence.' He signed off the letter remarkably positively: 'Things go well in a general way'.[16]

Pressure mounts

Terence MacSwiney needed extra promotional leaflets to start the house-to-house canvass in his constituency. Matthew Doyle was his 'go-to' person for printing requirements. Arranging local printing of Loan material was appreciated by Collins. Head office had designed twenty sample promotional leaflets and Collins had offered to supply each of the Loan organisers, including MacSwiney, with 5,000 copies of each, 'but it would be better if you could have them printed locally'.

An entrepreneurial young man, Matthew Doyle had set up his own printing business in November 1918. He printed promotional material for MacSwiney during the general election. Following MacSwiney's victory, police seized the type and machinery and it was never returned.[17] Doyle, back to being an employee, was working in Killarney Printing Works. On 30 September he wrote to MacSwiney, offering 'all assistance I can in [the] working of the movement at all times'.[18]

MacSwiney was arrested five days later during a raid by police on a Loan organising meeting in Macroom. Although released shortly after, important documents had been seized, including MacSwiney's notebook (probably with Matthew Doyle's details), copies of the Loan prospectus and correspondence with Michael Collins regarding the Loan.[19] On the following evening, a large force of armed military and police raided the printing works in Killarney. An exhaustive search was made of the premises and the files were closely examined. Later that evening, Matthew Doyle's home was raided. He and his wife were subjected to personal searches (it was unusual for women to be searched at the time) and their house was thoroughly gone through.[20]

MacSwiney's documents proved especially valuable to the police. Until then, operating with little understanding of how the Loan was being organised, the police had found it difficult to identify and arrest the organisers. Having analysed the documents, an upbeat RIC District Inspector wrote that '… the papers captured give us an outline of the scheme as proposed to be carried out, so that we now know!'[21]

Police pressure on MacSwiney's organising team intensified. On 10 October the Sinn Féin secretary in his constituency was arrested for possession of Loan material and imprisoned for six weeks.[22] On 15 October a Loan worker was picked up while carrying a 'parcel of literature' and taken to the police barracks in Macroom. He was permitted to leave a short time later, probably not being senior enough to bother arresting.[23] In nearby Bandon a man was sentenced to three months' hard labour for a speech made in support of the Loan. Another man was given two months for possession of the Loan prospectus. A chemist in Berehaven was arrested for displaying Loan notices in his shop window.[24]

No post today

On the morning of 7 October, staff at 6 Harcourt Street were surprised that no post had been received. When none arrived the following day, they knew that it was not an oversight. A rumour went round that a postman had been stopped by police and letters confiscated. No post was received on the following two days.

The press picked up the story. Assistant Under-Secretary Sir John Taylor, interviewed about the alleged stoppage of the mail, bluntly replied, 'I have no information to give. I will give you no information at all on the matter. Thank you.'[25] The secretary of the General Post Office incredibly suggested to the *Freeman's Journal* that 'there might have been none to deliver'.[26] The police were 'reticent' on the subject.[27] No one was talking.

The *Evening Standard* had an explanation. 'The National Loan is apparently to be dealt with drastically by the Government', reported the Dublin correspondent. 'Letters and communication dealing with subscriptions to it coming from the country are being held up for examination by the authorities in the Post Office.'[28]

Interference with the postal service was a serious matter even for the Irish executive. Dublin Castle could not officially acknowledge that mail was being intercepted, so to soothe the concerns of ordinary people it spun a story through the *Evening Standard* that only Loan-related mail was being blocked: '*it is believed* that the action of the authorities is directed towards the suppression of the loan only', reported the paper, though no explanation was given as to how Dublin Castle could see through sealed envelopes!

The story gathered momentum when a letter and cheque sent by Bishop Fogarty to Sinn Féin were not received. The *Chicago Tribune* (Paris edition) reported on the 'mystery' of what happened to Dr Fogarty's subscription for the 'Sinn Féin Loan'.[29] The manager of *Young Ireland*, the only Sinn Féin weekly not suppressed, which was published at 6 Harcourt Street, wrote to the secretary of the GPO. The reply received was that he should refer to the authorities at Dublin Castle for information, but simultaneously with this reply a large batch of letters was received.[30]

The interception of the post had a limited effect or none on the collection of subscriptions. Michael Collins was one step ahead of Lord French. On 27 September, he had issued a circular to the Loan committees, advising them not to send correspondence directly to Dáil Éireann at 6 Harcourt Street. Instead, he advised that an inner envelope be sent to a 'trusted friend' in Dublin, who could drop it in to the office by hand.[31]

Sinn Féin took further steps by setting up an alternative postal system.[32]

Several shops in the Dublin area were designated as posting centres where letters could be left. A team of 'postmen', Volunteers and members of Fianna Éireann, the nationalist youth organisation, managed the delivery services.[33]

Checkpoints

Dublin Castle adopted a second tactic to prevent Loan subscriptions from reaching Dublin. On 13 October, drivers crossing O'Connell Bridge were surprised to be held up by uniformed policemen and directed to drive down Burgh Quay. Two policemen examined driving licences and questioned drivers on the registered number of the vehicle and the name of the owner. As police checkpoints for driving licences were not a common sight, a crowd gathered to watch the proceedings. Checkpoints were established in multiple locations across the city from early that morning.[34]

The official explanation for this 'exceptional action' by the police was that many licences had not been renewed.[35] The *Daily News* had a different explanation: 'It was thought that the stoppage had something to do with the transmission of letters to the Sinn Féin Headquarters from the country, but that is denied'.[36] Dublin Castle was at pains to let it be known that none of the held-up vehicles were searched, but Lord French and Macpherson were already planning a new measure to restrict the use of motor vehicles by republicans.

Under a DORA regulation, the owners of motor vehicles had to attend in person at a police station to obtain a new permit.[37] The RIC Inspector General justified the introduction of permits to stop 'the employment of motorcars in attacks on police barracks and other acts of violence'.[38] With only 10,000 cars on the road in 1919, Dublin Castle could exercise tight control on road transport in Ireland.[39] Owners of motorbikes had been required to have a permit since the beginning of the war.

The prevention of use of the national transport network by couriers carrying Loan material and subscriptions, including close monitoring of rail passengers, became a serious impediment to the work of Loan organisers. The Motor Mechanics Association and the Transport Union went on strike in protest against the introduction of the permits.[40] So concerned was Dáil Éireann at the restriction placed on motor transport that the Cabinet allocated £1,000 out of its limited funds to support the strike.[41]

Michael Collins was beginning to understand what it meant for the suppression of the Loan to be the enemy's chief objective. 'Official action denied us the use of motor cars, searches and hold-ups denied us the advantages of even horse-vehicles and bicycles,' wrote Collins. 'Our people, in distributing leaflets and prospectuses, had to use the by-ways, and not infrequently had to cross country to avoid the enemy forces.'[42]

And raids and searches continued across the country. The home of Dr Jim Ryan, TD and co-founder of New Ireland Assurance, was subject to an 'exhaustive search' on 13 October.[43]

The 'Midnight Parliament'

On 15 October the lord mayor of Dublin received a letter from Colonel Edgeworth-Johnstone, chief commissioner of the DMP:

> 'I am directed by the Government to inform you that his Excellency the Lord Lieutenant has issued an Order prohibiting and suppressing the Sinn Féin Organisation, Sinn Féin Clubs, Irish Volunteers, Cumann na mBan and the Gaelic League, and that any meeting of any of these organisations is illegal, and will be prevented, including the meeting of the Ard Fheis (National Convention) of Sinn Féin, which it is proposed to hold in the Mansion House on the 16th inst.'[44]

Sinn Féin had been prohibited in Dublin, adding to the existing proclamations in Clare, Cork and Tipperary. As the capital was the hub out of which civil and military republican activities were directed, the prohibition was nearly equivalent to a nationwide ban. The catalyst for the decision was the National Convention of Sinn Féin that was due to take place in the Mansion House the following morning. Larry O'Neill, the independent nationalist lord mayor of Dublin, had made his mayoral residence available to Sinn Féin. Delegates were expected to arrive from all over Ireland.

The police and military practically surrounded the Mansion House before 9am the next morning. The front and rear entrances were guarded by over 100 policemen,[45] and around 400 fully equipped soldiers were posted opposite in the garage of the Irish Automobile Club. While Dawson Street was 'occupied' by the authorities, an armoured car with two machine-guns was seen going up Grafton Street.[46] Edgeworth-Johnstone arrived early to supervise the arrangements.[47]

Arriving by morning train, unaware that Sinn Féin had been prohibited in Dublin and that the meeting had been declared illegal, many delegates went straight to the Mansion House. Blocked from entering the building, they walked up Dawson Street in the direction of 6 Harcourt Street. A detachment of twenty policemen took up a position on St Stephen's Green, about 50 metres from the Sinn Féin headquarters, to monitor the growing crowd gathering outside.

Arthur Griffith, addressing the Sinn Féin delegates from the steps of the building, had something surprising to tell them: the National Convention had already taken place. At midnight, in the Mansion House, over 500 delegates had gathered in secret. Sinn Féin had known in advance of the plan to disrupt the convention.[48] The Press Association confirmed that the meeting had lasted until three in the morning and that the 'full agenda was gone through'.[49] A master-class of organisational subterfuge had made fools of Dublin Castle, the police and the military.

The *Irish Independent* called it the 'Midnight Parliament', though technically it was a Sinn Féin meeting rather than one of Dáil Éireann.[50] But it was a headline too good not to use. Rubbing salt in the wounds of the authorities, the paper had published multiple photos of policemen and soldiers waiting in vain outside the Mansion House.[51] A strong response was expected from Dublin Castle.

Move to 76 Harcourt Street

'We immediately started to organise the loan issue,' Eithne Lawless recalled concerning the move to 76 Harcourt Street in late September. 'All the staff migrated to that office ... people who had been working in scattered offices throughout the city.'[52] A Loan 'war room' was created in a large back office on the ground floor. Dan O'Donovan, an employee of the Department of

Finance, was in charge there,[53] and there the distribution of the prospectus and promotional material was organised and the Loan registers were maintained.

It had become 'absolutely necessary' to get more accommodation for the increased staff numbers working on the Loan.[54] Batt O'Connor acquired 76 Harcourt Street, a four-storey, red brick Georgian building, for £1,130.[55] 'As I was in the building trade it was easy for me to buy houses without arousing suspicion.'[56] He had to be cautious, though: 'With the propertied classes, Sinn Féin naturally was not popular'.[57] To further disguise the use of the building by the Department of Finance and the Dáil secretariat, the name of the occupant given to the Post Office was 'The Irish Club'.[58]

Diarmuid O'Hegarty, head of the secretariat, occupied a front office on the ground floor and the only office with a phone. Daithi O'Donoghue, secretary to the Loan trustees, and Fintan Murphy, a bookkeeper in the Department of Finance, had an office on the first floor at the back.[59] In this office Batt O'Connor created a secret storage area in a built-in wardrobe, accessible by a secret spring.[60] Eithne Lawless, Jenny Mason and Kate O'Toole, officially hired as secretaries and typists, acted as executive assistants to Diarmuid O'Hegarty, Michael Collins and Daithi O'Donoghue respectively.

Mail intended for the office was sent to 'covering addresses'.[61] Eithne Lawless, Joe O'Reilly and others called daily to these addresses to collect the correspondence. Two of Eithne's regular collection points were from 'the Rabbit' Flanagan on Camden Street and Keogh's photographers on St Stephen's Green.

Michael Collins had an office on the top floor of the building. He came to the office most mornings and sometimes at night.[62] Batt O'Connor arranged a means of escape for Collins through a skylight by leaving a light ladder in readiness that he could pull up after him.[63] Collins could also bolt the skylight from the outside. The front drawing room on the ground floor was for his use as well. It was always kept locked.[64]

Seán McCluskey, hand-picked by Collins as the caretaker for the building, moved into the basement flat with his wife and young family. No ordinary caretaker, Seán was a member of the 3rd Battalion of the Dublin Brigade and in 'special service' to Michael Collins, who trusted him implicitly.[65]

Cat and mouse

On 24 October Michael Collins was still lamenting the inability to advertise the Loan in the newspapers and the negative effect that this was having on the Loan campaign. 'It will, of course, take a much longer time than if we had been able to proceed uninterruptedly with the public campaign,' he wrote to de Valera.[66]

Across the country, a dangerous game of cat and mouse was being played daily between Loan organisers and the police. 'I was posting up some notices in connection with the loan at Scartaglin one Sunday morning about Mass time,' recalled one Loan worker. 'The local RIC sergeant saw me and came to tear them down. I prevented him and he had to go away. I was alone at the time but during the altercation three or four elderly men who were going into the church stepped up on either side of me. I did not see them but the sergeant did and, no doubt, considered it wiser to walk away.' A few days later a sergeant and three constables raided the activist's home, though fortunately for him nothing was found.[67]

In Tralee, an officer commanding Fianna Éireann was on duty while a local Volunteer unit was stencilling slogans and putting up posters.[68] Around 3am the Volunteers informed him that they had finished for the night. He withdrew the Fianna but on his way home saw the outline of some Volunteers still sticking up posters. 'I approached with the intention of informing them of the withdrawal of the IRA,' recalled Michael O'Leary, 'when I found to my surprise four RIC tearing down the posters.' Earlier that evening he had been given a .32 revolver, which was in his hip pocket, wrapped in an empty membership roll book. After giving him some 'rough handling', the police searched him and pulled out the roll book from his hip pocket. Fortunately for O'Leary, the book had slipped easily off the heavier gun. He was let go after making an excuse for being out at that late hour.

Frank Thornton had appointed Jimmy Hoey as the New Ireland Assurance agent in Longford town. In advance of a big promotional drive for the Loan, Jimmy had been carefully studying night-time police patrols. On the night before the marketing push, between one and two in the morning, Jimmy took a team of six men, with three ladders and paint cans and posters, to the police barracks on the main street. They plastered the barracks from top to bottom with large posters—'Buy Dáil Éireann

Bonds'.[69] Any nearby ladders had been removed, so that when the police discovered the overnight work they could not take down the posters.

Dublin did not escape the marketing campaign. Posters put up throughout the city early one morning were torn down by the police during the course of the day, but the painting squads had been active as well.[70] 'Buy Republican Bonds' was stencilled on footpaths, postboxes, lampposts, walls and in difficult-to-access positions all over the city and the suburbs.[71]

The campaign message was getting out. The country was 'flooded with Loan literature', according to Joseph Byrne, inspector general of the RIC.[72] He informed his bosses in Dublin Castle that 'No pains have been spared to obtain subscriptions for this Loan and a substantial sum has probably been raised'. The only solace he could offer was that there was 'reason to believe that the response in many districts is disappointing to the promoters and that the quarter of a million asked for has not been subscribed'.

The increasing number of raids, searches and arrests was taking a toll on the Loan campaign. 'I said in my last letter to you that the enemy's chief offensive was directed against the Loan,' Michael Collins wrote again to de Valera. 'This continues to be true, but its vigour has been increased, and the arrests of people who have been active in Loan work have now reached quite a respectable figure.'[73] Collins tried to remain positive: '... I am convinced that we shall get the money ... of course I never expected that we should be allowed to proceed without interruption'. But the pressure applied by Dublin Castle was mounting.

On 19 October Eamon Donnelly, the provincial Loan organiser in Ulster, was arrested for unlawful assembly. He had addressed a Loan meeting outside the chapel gates in the village of Tynan, Co. Armagh. He told the court that twelve armed men had lined up in front of his house to arrest him: 'Why, Dick Turpin and Charles Peace [an infamous English murderer] had an easy passage to the scaffold compared to what I was going to get'.[74] Donnelly was a man of energy, a renowned organiser and, according to one colleague, 'capable of doing the work of at least half a dozen ordinary men'.[75] He was a loss to the Loan campaign.

Conor Maguire, a solicitor in Castlebar and the son of a local doctor, was arrested at his family home and marched through the town by policemen and soldiers with bayonets fixed. He was charged with soliciting contributions for the Loan and illegal assembly on 12 October at a meeting held outside Mayo Abbey Chapel, and with soliciting contributions at a meeting on 26 October, when he spoke in front of 200 people.[76] Refusing to give bail at a Crimes Court, Maguire was sentenced to one month in prison. He would later be appointed attorney general and chief justice of the Supreme Court.

Meanwhile, the authorities had been looking for Patrick O'Hegarty for some months for promoting the Loan. They finally caught up with him. 'The constables opened fire with carbines on the retreating car, and a lively exchange of shots followed,' reported the *Cork Examiner*. 'None of the police were hit.'[77] Although the car was 'riddled with bullets', the driver managed to keep control of the vehicle, despite having a small portion of his ear blown off and his overcoat pierced in several places. A local doctor, also in the car, was shot through the leg, and another bullet grazed his forehead and smashed through the windscreen. 'Volley after volley was discharged,' recounted Dr Doyle, 'but though the bullets were whistling all round, the car continued its course.' Patrick O'Hegarty was unhurt.

The police gave pursuit on bicycles, as in a Buster Keaton or Harold Lloyd film, but it was no comedy. The car stopped in a nearby village. Shortly after, the police arrived and attempted to arrest the driver, but they were attacked by a hostile crowd with a fusillade of bottles and stones. 'The men jumped into the car and made off. The police again fired. The driver's cap was blown off, and the man reeled. The car wobbled and was nearly wrecked in a ditch, but the driver righted it, and the car disappeared over a rise in the road, followed by a few more shots.'

The following morning the police arrested Dr Doyle, but he was released after being searched. The wounded driver of the car and Patrick O'Hegarty had disappeared.[78] Dr Doyle later said that the occupants of the car were unarmed and denied that there had been an exchange of fire. He claimed that the car passed through the police cordon slowly and had only gone a few yards when the police opened fire.

New weapons

Dublin Castle continued to add more weapons to its legislative arsenal. On 10 October, the *London Gazette* announced that curfew powers had been authorised for use in Ireland under DORA regulations.[79] Although promulgated in London, the curfew order was issued on the recommendation of the Irish executive.[80] If enforced in Dublin, the military would patrol the streets, and anyone caught out of doors without a permit after the hours fixed by the competent military authority was liable to arrest. With Dublin Castle already exercising extensive control of road and rail movements, patrols on the streets of Dublin after dark would be a serious obstacle to Loan logistics.

Lord French also added to his powers under the Crimes Act. The lord lieutenant and the military commander in Ireland signed a proclamation enforcing Sections 3 and 4 of the Crimes Act in Dublin.[81] Special juries could be sworn in and the court venue moved to a location where the attorney general believed that a fair and impartial trial could be held.

Counter-state

Once the Speaker of Dáil Éireann took his seat at 7.25pm on Monday 27 October, the business of the session commenced. Meeting in private in the Oak Room of the Mansion House, which the lord mayor continued to make available despite the prohibition of Sinn Féin in Dublin two weeks earlier, only 28 of the 69 elected representatives were able to attend. Many had been arrested or were on the run, and others were in America and Paris. Michael Collins and Robert Barton had received peremptory requests from the Cabinet not to attend, as they 'must retain their liberty to carry on the work of the Dáil'. Such was the risk of arrest that members whose health would not stand the strain of a term in prison received similar mandatory stay-away requests.

In the absence of Michael Collins, Arthur Griffith told the Dáil that £10,626 of Loan applications had been received, though £30,700 had been promised, and reports had not yet been received from many parts of the country. The Dáil approved the appointment of Donal O'Connor, chartered accountant, as auditor of the Loan.

The most pressing point on the agenda was the establishment of the National Land Bank. Robert Barton had outlined his proposals at the previous meeting in August. Although TDs were supportive of the proposals,

Barton was realistic in his assessment of their response. 'It had a very good reception,' he told his wife, 'but largely due to the suddenness of its appearance, lack of time to criticise and sympathy for me on the run producing anything.'[82] Two months later, the TDs were growing impatient. The threat of agrarian violence was rising and the Dáil government could not afford to spend its political capital and limited financial resources in supporting another land war.[83] Dr John Crowley, TD for Mayo North, said that the situation was 'very urgent' in Mayo.

Arthur Griffith told the Dáil that the bank and the land acquisition scheme were approaching completion. Although Robert Barton had stated that it would take at least six months to get the Bank going, impatient TDs still put forward their own impractical interim solutions. Daithi Ceannt asked for an immediate allocation of funds to purchase land in 'urgent cases'. It was important to show 'that something was being done in this direction', but there was no administrative structure in place to handle the purchase of land; even if there had been, the money was not available. 'We have no idea when we may get the money which is now being raised in America,' Arthur Griffith informed the Dáil. In reply to a motion by James Dolan, TD for Leitrim, to make £200,000 available to the Director of Agriculture, Griffith said that to 'decide at present to devote any definite sum such as £200,000 would be an impossible proposition'.

In the end, the Dáil voted just £1,000 for initial set-up expenses for the bank. Four days after the meeting, on 31 October, Diarmuid O'Hegarty sent formal confirmation to Robert Barton of the approved expenses and requested the Department of Finance to release the funds. Robert Barton received a cheque for £1,000 signed by Michael Collins on 10 November.[84]

In his opening statement, Arthur Griffith highlighted the propaganda gains being made in America, France and Italy. The correspondent of the *Corriere d'Italia* had visited Ireland and had 'completely come over to our side'. Consuls had been established in New York, Paris, Genoa and Buenos Aires 'and were en route for other countries'.

Despite the growing number of consuls, little progress was being made in opening new trade routes because the English government was making 'every effort to interfere with the development of direct trade'. Cables and correspondence had been delayed and suppressed. TDs from Cork, where enterprise activities were most advanced, noted that the American consul in the city had promised to do his best to facilitate direct trading between Ireland and America, and that the provision of return cargoes was a matter of 'immense importance'. Joe McGuinness, who was appointed substitute Director of Trade following the arrest of Ernest Blythe during the raid on 6 Harcourt Street, said that steps were already being taken in this area. The appointment of McGuinness was not optimum, however, as he had his own business to run and could not act on a full-time basis. Attempts were being made to recruit someone to work under him.

The Dáil was informed that the National Commission of Inquiry into the Resources and Industries of Ireland, with Darrell Figgis as secretary, had commenced its investigations and would soon hold public consultations. At an organisational meeting in the Mansion House on 19 September, just eight days after Dáil Éireann was prohibited, Arthur Griffith had told the attendees that the commission was a 'responsible, autonomous and independent body'.[85] This was an attempt to establish the independence of the body from Dáil Éireann in order to lower the risk of its suppression by Dublin Castle.

The commission's credibility was enhanced by the appointment of John O'Neill, a successful entrepreneur, as chairman. He had founded the Lucania bicycle company, which had an exclusive contract to provide bicycles to the Post Office.[86] He set up a car assembly business when tariffs were imposed on imported assembled cars and was credited with having started the business of large-scale car assembly in Ireland.

Early priority was given to the development of the food and power generation sectors and two subcommittees were set up. The food committee was headed by Thomas Johnston, secretary of the Irish Labour Party, and the power generation committee was chaired by Dr Hugh Ryan, a professor of chemistry in University College Dublin.

The Department of Local Government was dealing with issues related to a housing problem, a milk shortage, relief for the elderly and other urgent matters. Confidence was high that Sinn Féin would win control of most of the urban councils and corporations in the upcoming municipal elections, handing much of the real governing power in the country to the counter-state.

The committee responsible for establishing the new courts system had 'met with difficulties', however. Terence MacSwiney said that unionists in

47

his constituency were 'quite willing' to submit cases to the courts if they were guaranteed a fair hearing. A special meeting was planned, as the committee 'was not meeting satisfactorily'.

Detective Sergeant Wharton

On 19 September the first steps were taken to organise the squad on a full-time professional basis. At a meeting in 46 Parnell Square, called by Dick McKee, brigadier of the Dublin Brigade, and also attended by Richard Mulcahy, chief of staff, and Michael Collins, four of the squad were told to leave their employment and to become full-time paid members of the unit.

Nevertheless, the next squad operation was carried out in a reckless rather than in a professional manner. In a failed assassination attempt on a G Division detective, a young female student was shot in the head and two squad members were lucky to survive the engagement. On 10 November Paddy O'Daly and Joe Leonard had been on the lookout for Detective Sergeant Thomas Wharton. On their way to pick up a gun for Leonard, by chance they crossed paths with Wharton in the company of three other detectives.

'I told Joe it would be a pity to let the opportunity pass,' recalled Paddy O'Daly.[87] He knew that one of the detectives was working for Michael Collins, but two men, one unarmed, taking on three experienced detectives in broad daylight was poor decision-making. Not surprisingly, Joe Leonard 'felt very uncomfortable on account of having no gun'.

O'Daly fired at Detective Wharton, who fell to the ground, and then his gun jammed. O'Daly and Leonard had to make a run for it. The other detectives drew their weapons. The friendly detective, showing quickness of thought, made as if to fire but moved bravely into the line of sight between the detectives and the fleeing men.

O'Daly's bullet hit Detective Wharton in the back of the right shoulder, passed through his right lung and exited in front, striking the head of Gertrude O'Hanlon, a student from Sligo, who was walking in front of Wharton.[88] Fortunately, she was not seriously wounded. Detective Wharton survived, though he was left incapacitated for life. A native of Killarney, he had spent almost nine years in the DMP, the last three in the G Division, and had recently been married.[89]

Raid on 76 Harcourt Street

On the morning after the shooting of Detective Wharton, 11 November, Armistice Day, Daithi O'Donoghue walked out of 76 Harcourt Street on his way to the Sinn Féin Bank. It was around noon. As he walked the curve of the street, No. 6 came into view and he could see military lorries parked outside. He immediately turned back to warn those in No. 76 to be prepared in case of a raid. Going to his own office on the first floor, he stowed away money and account books in the secret hiding place and sent word up to Michael Collins in his top-floor office. Then he left the building and headed back in the direction of the Sinn Féin Bank to mingle with the crowd that had gathered outside.[90]

The raid on No. 6 ended surprisingly fast. O'Donoghue followed the military lorries as they left Harcourt Street and turned right along the south side of St Stephen's Green, watching them until they were out of sight. On his way back to the office, he bumped into Brian O'Higgins TD and Fionán Lynch TD at the corner of the Green. They were going to a meeting in No. 76. Deep in conversation as they walked along Harcourt Street, they were just about to enter the building when military lorries came speeding towards them and pulled up outside. The three continued walking past the entrance, 'saved by a matter of seconds'. O'Donoghue left O'Higgins and Lynch at the corner of Hatch Street while he crossed to the other side of Harcourt Street and doubled back to mingle with the crowd that had now gathered to watch the raid on No. 76.

Looking up at the first floor, he saw Paddy Sheehan holding up a sheet of white paper at a window: 'All Hands Arrested'.[91] Soldiers on the roof attracted his attention. He hoped that Michael Collins had escaped by the skylight. Distracted by all that was going on, he did not see Joe O'Reilly approach. 'I was standing on the offside edge of the crowd with my hands behind my back, when I felt someone tapping my hands and pressing a slip of paper between my fingers.' By the time O'Donoghue looked over his shoulder, O'Reilly was slipping away on his bicycle.

Needing to find somewhere to read the note without attracting attention, O'Donoghue walked quickly down Harcourt Street, turned left on to Montague Street and went into the back yard of Corrigan's Undertakers. 'Follow them up, send in food, smokes, mattresses and blankets,

M.C.' A sigh of relief escaped O'Donoghue, knowing 'from the old familiar handwriting' that Mick was safe.

He needed to find out where those arrested were being taken. Retracing his steps back to Harcourt Street, he crossed the road and hired a horse car on Clonmel Street, just in time to follow the military lorries on to St Stephen's Green and down Grafton Street until they stopped at the Bridewell Garda Station behind the Four Courts. 'I arranged with the Four Courts Hotel to supply nine teas right away and nine breakfasts for the morning,' he recalled. 'I still have the receipt for these. I then went across to the Clarence Hotel and I asked them to send in nine mattresses and the necessary bed-clothing.'[92] Finally, he purchased a supply of pipe tobacco, cigarettes and matches. Surprisingly, all of this was allowed in to the prisoners, except for the bedding. O'Donoghue recalled Patrick Sheehan telling him later that he almost cried on account of the bitter cold in his cell.

With his mission complete, O'Donoghue went home to Drumcondra. There was no sign of Lucy, his wife, when he entered the house and the children were in bed. Arriving home later, Lucy was 'astonished' to find him there.[93] She had been told that everyone in No. 76 had been taken to the Bridewell. After putting the children to bed, she had left home with an overcoat, rug and toiletries for him. Through a confusion of names, they found their way to a surprised and very grateful Dan O'Donovan, leaving Lucy believing that Daithi was in a cell.

O'Donoghue found out later what had happened in No. 76 as he watched the raid from across the street. Eithne Lawless had been looking out the window when the military lorries pulled up. She rushed to the front door and 'slipped the Yale lock'. This bought Michael Collins enough time to escape through the skylight, cross the roof of the building and get into the Standard Hotel next door.[94] Meanwhile, the police had gone down to the basement entrance. Bob Conlon was downstairs with Seán McCluskey, the caretaker. 'We delayed the entry of the military by bolting the door and they had to burst it in with their rifles.'[95] McCluskey rushed upstairs to warn the others, but they had already been alerted by Eithne Lawless, who in the meantime had brought sensitive documents down to the bedroom of Mrs McCluskey, who was resting after giving birth. Mrs McCluskey hid the documents under her bed.[96]

Picking up the pieces

Despite the nationwide prohibition of Dáil Éireann in September and of Sinn Féin in Dublin in October, and although he had anticipated raids, Michael Collins had made a deliberate decision to continue to operate the Department of Finance and the secretariat from 76 Harcourt Street in 'a determined effort to take a public stand' to establish the Dáil government as the recognised authority in Ireland.

Although Collins watched closely the reaction of Dublin Castle to any moves he made, the decision to remain carried a hint of arrogance. On the morning of the raid he had even arranged a meeting of TDs, which, according to Eithne Lawless, was summoned 'fairly openly, probably with a view to asserting their right to meet as a government and legislate for the country'.[97] The decision to keep the full complement of staff, and to conduct much of the Dáil business, in Harcourt Street proved costly to the work of the national government and the Loan campaign. Diarmuid O'Hegarty, head of the secretariat, was arrested, along with Dan O'Donovan, who was in charge of the Loan registers, and most of the senior head office staff.[98] Dick McKee was also arrested. The raiders seized mainly Loan-related documents.[99]

The outcome could have been worse, however. Michael Collins had nearly been captured and Daithi O'Donoghue, quickly becoming Collins's right-hand man in finance matters, was lucky not to have been in the building. Those arrested were handed relatively short two-month sentences under the Crimes Act, but the Dáil government had suffered a near-fatal loss of staff at a critical time, especially for the Loan campaign.

After the raid and the loss of so many staff, some must have doubted that Dáil Éireann could ever replace the Dublin Castle administration as the legitimate government in Ireland. Certainly, the odds were stacked against it. The Irish executive had shown its determination to use its substantial legislative weapons—the Crimes Act and DORA—and it had overwhelming military power, which it had yet to let loose. Nevertheless, if there were those who had doubts, they were in a minority.

On the day after the raid, Daithi O'Donoghue went back to Harcourt Street. Seán McCluskey had avoided arrest thanks to Inspector McFeely, who had unexpectedly come downstairs and whispered to him to stay below out of sight. McCluskey suspected that McFeely was working for Collins.[100] Making a sweep of the building, O'Donoghue recovered the account books, gold and banknotes from the hidden storage area in his office and the Loan registers from another secret shelf built by Batt O'Connor. That night he carried all the documents to a safe location, ready to continue the work of the national government again.

With most of the head office staff in prison, O'Donoghue had 'a hectic time trying to keep things going, practically alone'.[101] By day, he and Kate O'Toole worked in a room provided by Cáit (Wyse) Power over the Irish Farm Produce shop on Camden Street. And night after night, sometimes until the morning, he and Lucy worked together in their kitchen, with blankets fixed across the window blinds.

Bill Murray, a Sinn Féin employee, and Kate Gifford–Wilson did much of the Loan registration work from their homes.[102] Kate, whose husband had died in the Spanish 'flu epidemic, had a degree in languages and had worked abroad. Her younger sister, Grace Gifford, the artist and cartoonist, had married Joseph Plunkett in Kilmainham Gaol hours before his execution.

Meanwhile, Michael Collins and Jenny Mason transferred the majority of their work to the home of Eileen Hoey and her mother at 5 Mespil Road, a quiet residential street, where Collins had an existing office.[103] It was also his 'war office'.[104] The Cabinet continued to meet on a weekly basis.

Eithne Lawless continued to work in the almost empty 76 Harcourt Street after the raid. She worked for Michael Collins after Diarmuid O'Hegarty's arrest. Collins was not a regular caller. Instead, he sent a 'methodical' list of instructions through Joe O'Reilly for correspondence and other work that he required to be done, including filling in cheques that had been pre-signed by him and registering Loan certificates.[105] Eithne Lawless took her files home in an attaché case every evening, especially papers that would give clues to Loan subscriber addresses in the country.

New offices had to be acquired and replacement staff recruited. Number 22 Mary Street became the principal office of the Finance Department until its discovery in May 1921.[106] Much of the Loan work was carried out there. Michael Noyk had found the office, which was located over the premises of Hogg Robertsons, seed merchants.[107] One day

Michael Collins spotted Seán McCluskey and Joe O'Reilly coming out of the office onto the street. 'He called us over,' remembered McCluskey, 'and gave us a dressing-down.'[108] Two people were not to come out of the office at the same time.

Eilis Ryan, a Cumann na mBan member and an intelligence operative, was one of the new recruits in the Finance Department working at 22 Mary Street.[109] One day, completely unexpectedly, she received a note from Collins asking her to meet him at the Keating Branch of the Gaelic League. To her surprise, he offered her a job. She had no hesitation in joining the national government at his request, despite having recently received a promotion and giving up 'bright prospects' in her existing job.

The Department of Finance had a second office at 29 Mary Street, close to the corner of Liffey Street and over Geary's milliners and drapers.[110] It had a secret room, which was used to hide books and documents.[111]

As the proceeds of the Dáil Loan started to accumulate, it was necessary to find a safe home for the money.

3. Protecting the money

Man of honour

'One day early in October 1918, we were summoned in batches into the presence of the head of the Land Commission [and] Mr Justice Wylie,' recalled Daithi O'Donoghue.[1] An order had come from the British government that an oath of allegiance should be administered to all civil servants in Ireland. O'Donoghue, a senior member of the commission at the time, assembled his staff for the meeting. Having questioned the legitimacy of the proposal, O'Donoghue asked what was the alternative to taking the oath. 'Instant dismissal', was the reply.

O'Donoghue and his wife Lucy had a young family and a home to maintain in Drumcondra. No one would have questioned his taking the oath. Most nationalist civil servants, even veterans of 1916, did so. Strong arguments were given for swallowing it: an enforced oath was not binding, you could make a mental reservation while taking it, and some priests had said that it was not even morally binding.[2] And there were family, finance and career factors to consider in making the decision.

When called to take the oath in front of his staff, O'Donoghue had refused. A disappointed Judge Wylie summoned him several more times and on each occasion he endeavoured 'in the most friendly manner' to wear down his objection. But O'Donoghue refused on each occasion: 'I naturally had no hesitation in making up my mind'. He could not take the oath because 'the Republic had been proclaimed in 1916'. This was not just loyalty to the nation; there was also something more personal in the decision—loyalty to friends.

Daithi and Lucy O'Donoghue used to frequently attend summer picnics in the mountains hosted by the Wyse-Powers. Over two dozen friends, mainly from the Gaelic League, went on these outings, which were 'very pleasant affairs and were usually held in what was called the Pine Forest on the banks of a stream'.[3] They were a close-knit group of young friends. Patrick O'Keeffe, the secretary of Sinn Féin, married Cáit Wyse-Power, and James Kavanagh, an accountant with Sinn Féin, married Áine Cullen.

Michael O'Hanrahan, a journalist and writer and a senior member of the Volunteers, was a regular on the picnic outings, usually with his brother Larry and his sister Eily. O'Donoghue had become very friendly with O'Hanrahan, who was also a native Wexford man. Both were passionate about the Irish language. Michael O'Hanrahan was executed by firing squad in Kilmainham gaol in 1916. Sunday outings must never have been the same again. O'Donoghue could not swallow an oath to the executioner of his friend.

Not long after the Rising, Patrick O'Keeffe was speaking to a visiting English journalist who was plying him with insistent questions on the aims of the republican movement. Exasperated with the many unsatisfactory answers he was receiving, in the end the journalist asked, 'Mr O'Keeffe, would you at least say what exactly you yourself want?' At this O'Keeffe, with his keen eyes and waspish tongue, banged the desk with his fist and roared: 'Vingeance, bejasus, vingeance!'[4] O'Donoghue and others must have had a similar motivation.

O'Donoghue was formally dismissed from the civil service on 16 December 1918, two days after the general election that saw Sinn Féin emerge as the dominant nationalist political grouping.[5]

So began the journey of the husband, father, bowler-hat-wearing, career civil servant towards being the person to whom Michael Collins and Dáil Éireann entrusted the safekeeping and money-laundering of the funds of the counter-state.

The timing of O'Donoghue's dismissal was serendipitous for the new national government. One month later, he was working as an accountant for the secretariat of Dáil Éireann on a salary of £208. His boss, Diarmuid O'Hegarty, had also refused to take the oath.

In August 1919 O'Donoghue was appointed secretary to the trustees of the Loan.[6] In a normal environment, the role of the secretary would be to assist the trustees in exercising their fiduciary responsibility and in the preparation of accounts. This, however, was not a normal environment, and safeguarding the Loan proceeds required activity that extended well beyond routine fiduciary duty.

The Dáil had appointed three trustees on 19 June 1919, with

responsibility for safeguarding and disbursing the Loan funds. Critically, the trustees were given discretion to bank the money in their own or any other names. Funds could only be disbursed using a hierarchical approval structure, however, at the top of which a vote of the Dáil was required. In the event of the Dáil being unable to meet, the trustees could act on the approval of the Cabinet. If neither were able to meet, the trustees or 'such of them as may be free' could disburse funds on their own authority. The most important mandate given to the trustees was 'to keep the ordinary services going'. The choice of trustees, however, was not optimal for day-to-day decision-making purposes.

The three trustees appointed were Éamon de Valera, president of the Dáil, James O'Mara TD and Dr Michael Fogarty, bishop of Killaloe. In June 1919, the same month in which he was appointed a trustee, de Valera went to America to seek recognition for the Irish Republic and to promote the American Loan. He would not return until December 1920. He was joined in America by James O'Mara in November. Dr Fogarty was only an occasional visitor to Dublin.

James O'Mara, 47, was the owner of a successful bacon-processing business with substantial financial interests in Limerick and London. University-educated, he had succeeded his father as an MP for the Irish Party, but in 1907 he surprisingly resigned his seat and left the Irish Party to join Sinn Féin. Elected as a TD to the First Dáil, he was one of the few politicians to serve in both the House of Commons and Dáil Éireann. He played a key role in the success of the American Loan, at great cost to his family life, his business and even his personal finances (he funded his own expenses). Yet the Irish State largely forgot him. His daughter Patricia Lavelle wrote: 'There was no tricolour over his coffin, no bugles sounded over his grave. No guns were fired in salute but we paid silent tribute to him for all he had done and suffered that Ireland might be free.'[7]

With two of the three trustees in America and the third living outside Dublin, it fell to Michael Collins and Daithi O'Donoghue to guard and release sufficient funds to keep the underground government functioning in all eventualities. Although Arthur Griffith was appointed acting trustee in de Valera's absence, according to O'Donoghue he 'was not at all keen on having responsibility in finance matters, and, in fact the responsibility fell on Micheál Ó Coileáin and on myself'.[8]

O'Donoghue kept Griffith up to speed with a weekly financial statement that he also sent to Collins. Dr Fogarty was kept updated on the status of the Loan using the underground postal service.[9] On the bishop's visits to Dublin, O'Donoghue had meetings with him, sometimes with Collins or Griffith in attendance, when he also gave him detailed accounts.

O'Donoghue set to work putting systems and processes in place to record, control and safeguard the funds. 'Of course, in the absence of the Trustees,' he noted, 'I never parted with nor moved any of the funds without the authority of Micheál Ó Coileáin, nor did I make any banking arrangements without first consulting him.'

Banking the proceeds

Up to the establishment of Dáil Éireann, the funds of the republican movement had been lodged in the Sinn Féin Bank. David Kelly, the manager and sole employee, issued books of unstamped cheques to Sinn Féin, risking heavy penalties if it came to the attention of the British authorities.[10]

Michael Collins introduced a different procedure for the Dáil Éireann funds. Instead of keeping the money in the Sinn Féin Bank, it was deposited into the large commercial banks, but he continued to use the Sinn Féin Bank for cheque payments. 'So Mick when making payments would draw cheques, unstamped, on the Sinn Féin Bank,' said James Kavanagh, 'and then lodge sufficient money to meet these cheques.' Kavanagh thought that this was unfair to David Kelly because 'That system did not bring in much revenue to the bank'.[11]

Collins and O'Donoghue, however, had no option but to use the Sinn Féin Bank in this way. The large gold lettering on the front of 6 Harcourt Street was a beacon for trouble. They could not risk depositing the main Dáil funds in the bank, even if it was legally independent of Sinn Féin and David Kelly was trustworthy. And the large commercial banks would not offer chequing facilities to Dáil Éireann, though friendly branch managers would accept Sinn Féin Bank cheques.

Using this system not only facilitated the day-to-day operation of the Dáil government but was also a useful way of laundering the proceeds of the Loan. Cheques were used to cover staff expenses, office rents, stationery, printing, heating (coal) and other costs. Once the cheques were lodged or cashed by staff and suppliers, the funds were separated from their illegal source and washed into the financial system.

O'Donoghue had to be selective in choosing the commercial banks in which to lodge the Loan proceeds. Of the seven banks quoted on the Dublin Stock Exchange at the time, three had a nationalist disposition—the Hibernian Bank, the Munster & Leinster Bank and the National Bank. This, however, was no guarantee of support for Dáil Éireann. Patrick Moylett, a high-profile and successful Sinn Féin businessman, believed that every bank in Ireland was 'entirely a British bank, with a British, non-Catholic directorship'.[12] Moylett was exaggerating, but nevertheless O'Donoghue had to be careful in his dealings. The decision to use a particular bank or branch came down to personal relationships.

Henry Campbell was the manager of the head office branch of the Hibernian Bank on College Green. The bank was enjoying one of its best years in his ten years as a manager. Commenting on the results released to the stock exchange for the last six months of 1919, the chairman said that the bank experienced a jump in deposits and the business was exhibiting satisfactory expansion.[13]

The Hibernian was founded in 1825 in response to perceived anti-Catholic discrimination by the Bank of Ireland, established in 1783 under royal charter.[14] The Hibernian targeted primarily the Dublin business community, putting it in direct conflict with the Bank of Ireland. The latter blocked the Hibernian's attempt to acquire the right to issue banknotes of its own, even after the Bank of Ireland had lost its monopoly on note issue in 1845.[15] The hegemony of the Bank of Ireland over the Irish banking system continued into the new century. It exercised considerable control over the other Irish banks through the Irish Banks Standing Committee (IBSC), set up by Andrew Jameson, the Scottish-born director of the bank and member of the whiskey family.

One morning in 1914, Seán T. O'Kelly, a Volunteer and a member of the IRB, arrived at Henry Campbell's branch office with a letter of introduction from Patrick J. Little, editor of *New Ireland*. He wanted to exchange a cheque for £1,000 for the same value in gold coin, which was required to fund an arms purchase in Belgium. Little knew Campbell to be a Home Rule supporter with some interest in the foundation of the Volunteers, though if Campbell knew that O'Kelly was a member of the IRB, which was secretly planning the Rising to proclaim the republic, there was no certainty that he would help him.

O'Kelly, who would become the Dáil envoy to Paris and later the second president of Ireland, came straight to the point when he met Campbell. 'I told him that I wanted £1,000 in gold and I told him exactly the purpose for which I required it'.[16] Henry Campbell was amiable and told him to call back at the same hour the next morning, when he gave him a package containing 1,000 gold sovereigns.

Henry Campbell could be trusted with Dáil funds. O'Donoghue opened loan accounts in his College Green branch and also in the Camden Street branch of the Hibernian Bank, where Thomas Read was the manager.[17] The Hibernian branch on Dorset Street accepted Sinn Féin Bank cheques, as did the O'Connell Street and probably Thomas Street branches.[18]

It was the Munster & Leinster Bank, however, that was especially favoured by O'Donoghue and Collins.[19] It was regarded as the most national of the three banks but, according to Liam Cosgrave, Dáil Minister for Local Government, 'their colour of green could never have been described as pronounced as ours was at the time'.[20] Shareholders in the bank were happy in 1919, as it too was about to release strong numbers for the second half of the year.[21] The *Irish Independent*, in its year-end review of the Dublin Stock Exchange, described its balance sheet as in a 'very flourishing condition'.[22]

The Munster & Leinster was the only quoted bank with its headquarters in Cork. Apart from the Bank of Ireland, it was also the only one not established in the wake of the Irish Banking Acts in 1824 and 1825. It emerged out of the liquidation of the Munster Bank, established in 1864, which had collapsed owing to mismanagement and the fraudulent activity of its chairman, William Shaw. Shaw was also the owner of the Lane brewery, which had become heavily indebted to the Munster Bank. Another Cork brewer, J.J. Murphy, came to the rescue and the Munster & Leinster Bank was established. The Lane brewery was amalgamated into Beamish & Crawford in 1901.[23]

J.F. Dawson, the manager of the head office branch on Dame Street, was well known to both O'Donoghue and Collins. On one occasion he helped Collins to dispose of cash taken in a raid on a mail van at Westland Row railway station. A large consignment of banknotes addressed to various banks was seized. Collins issued instructions to George Fitzgerald, an intelligence operative, to send the money addressed to the Munster & Leinster banks to J.F. Dawson. 'I delivered many large parcels on a bicycle,' Fitzgerald recalled, 'and an hour following the delivery I was told that the Manager of the Bank had acknowledged the receipt of the notes to Collins.'[24] He did not know what became of the cash belonging to the other banks.

Dawson also provided support to the Dáil government during the 'Belfast Boycott' campaign, when the Dáil enforced an embargo on goods from Belfast in response to sectarian violence. Michael Staines was appointed director of the campaign and provided support to people moving their accounts from banks headquartered in Belfast. 'I was generally able to arrange matters, principally through Mr Dawson in the Munster and Leinster Bank,' said Staines. 'This had the effect of extending Munster and Leinster Bank business through the six counties.'[25]

O'Donoghue opened Loan deposit accounts in the Dame Street, O'Connell Street and Phibsborough branches.[26]

The southern roots of the bank proved useful for laundering purposes. In September 1919 Michael Collins wrote a Sinn Féin Bank cheque for £2,000 to 'self'. The cheque was cashed in the Limerick branch of the Munster & Leinster Bank, but it was deliberately kept out of the normal cheque clearance process. It should have been sent to the Dame Street head office in Dublin for clearing. From there, the bank's 'runner' would bring it to the Sinn Féin Bank at 6 Harcourt Street for collection. Instead, this cheque (no. 1027), although paid out by the Sinn Féin Bank, bypassed the Dame Street clearance procedure.

The National Bank was less trusted by O'Donoghue. Founded by Daniel O'Connell, it was known as the 'Liberator's Bank' in his honour,[27] and it targeted farmers and businesses outside Dublin as customers. It established its headquarters in London, which enabled it to issue its own banknotes, bypassing the Bank of Ireland's legal monopoly on issuing notes within a 50-mile radius of Dublin. Having its head office in London, however, diluted its nationalist credentials.

Eamon Morkan, a Volunteer and IRB member, had worked in the College Green branch until the 1916 Rising. When he returned from internment, the bank delayed reinstating him to his old position. Morkan was eventually transferred to the branch in Birr. His Volunteer activities did not stop. One Monday morning, after participating in a Volunteer parade the day before, he found an order from the head office in London suspending him from duty. The order requested an explanation of his taking part in an activity that the bank felt was 'prohibited by their rules'. He was suspended for a week and transferred again.[28]

O'Donoghue was selective in his engagement with the National Bank, opening a Loan deposit account in the College Green branch only. He was not the only person reluctant to use the bank. Cahir Davitt, a judge in the Republican Courts, received a monthly salary cheque from Dáil Éireann, which he cashed in the Sinn Féin Bank. He was 'somewhat shy' about lodging the cheques in the National Bank, despite having an account there.[29] Davitt later became the president of the High Court.

Trusted friends

Of course, O'Donoghue could not open accounts in the name of Dáil Éireann or Sinn Féin, even in the supportive banks. Instead, he placed 'some very large' funds on deposit in accounts opened in the names of people friendly to the republican movement, and also opened bank accounts using fictitious names.[30]

'I was told, to my amazement, that at one date I had several thousand pounds to my credit,' recalled Dan MacCarthy. An IRB member trusted by Collins, MacCarthy later provided logistical support during the treaty negotiations in London.[31]

Another name used was that of Julia O'Donovan, a close friend of Michael Collins. Julia was a remarkable woman who regularly put her family, her home and her businesses at risk in support of Dáil Éireann. She was a cousin of Gearoid O'Sullivan, adjutant-general of the IRA, who invited Michael Collins to stay with him in Julia's home at 16 Airfield Road, Rathgar. They stayed for over a month, often working on Loan paperwork late into the evening. Julia also allowed guns to be delivered to her home and to her shop on Rathgar Road. Another shop, on Mespil Road, was used as a covering address for letters. O'Donoghue deposited £4,000 of Loan money in an account in the Munster & Leinster Bank in Julia's name. 'I still have a notification from Mick,' she recalled fondly, 'with a personal note at the end informing me that he had withdrawn the money and thanking me for my co-operation.'[32]

Other names used to open bank accounts included those of Dick Tynan, whose pork butcher's shop on Wexford Street was used as a clearing house for Loan money and literature, and Margaret MacGarry, one of the Dáil's most proactive supporters.[33]

O'Donoghue also gave Loan proceeds to 'trusted individuals' who opened bank accounts in their own names.[34] He handed over 'fairly large sums' of money to these individuals, who acted as sub-trustees. They were liable to Dáil Éireann for interest earned on the accounts (between 1919 and 1920 interest rates moved between 5% and 7%) and were entitled to ample notice before being asked to return the money.

These trusted individuals included Erskine Childers, author of *The riddle of the sands* and future TD. Childers, a truly remarkable individual, was—amongst many other things—English-born, a former intelligence officer in the Royal Air Force, a former clerk of the House of Commons and a recent convert to the Irish cause. Molly Childers, the daughter of a prominent wealthy Boston doctor, also acted as a trusted friend. Other account-holders included Alderman Patrick Corrigan, a member of Dublin Corporation and owner of the well-known undertaker's on Camden Street; Liam Devlin, whose public house on Parnell Street was one of the three 'joints' used as regular meeting places by Michael Collins; George Nesbitt, a trustee of New Ireland Assurance and treasurer of Sinn Féin; and Mrs Davin.

Holding the Loan proceeds in the accounts of private individuals guaranteed greater security for the funds than exists today. Banking confidentiality on private accounts was legally protected at this time and all bank employees took an oath of secrecy. As long as the account was in the name of a private person and the bank was not *officially* informed of the purpose of the account, the funds were secure.

It was not until 1924 that courts in England established limitations on the contractual duty of privacy owed by bankers to their clients.[35] The absence of anti-money-laundering (AML) legislation at this time meant that O'Donoghue and the trusted friends could open bank accounts and move large sums of money without any reporting obligation on the part of the bank.

O'Donoghue opened a mix of different accounts in the three banks to suit the needs of the Dáil government. Some money was placed in ordinary deposit accounts. Large sums in 'one or two banks' were payable on demand or at very short notice for 'emergencies'. Large current accounts were used to meet the regular outgoings of the government departments, some of whom also opened their own bank accounts.

Money from America

Daithi O'Donoghue and Michael Collins were also responsible for laundering the American Loan funds into the financial system in Ireland.

Vera McDonnell had come to Dublin in 1917 to study shorthand and typing in the Underwood School in Leinster Street. She was quickly recruited by Sinn Féin as a stenographer. 'I used to do the cablegrams and codes for the Dáil Éireann Loan to the USA for Daithi Ó Donnchadha and Mick Collins,' she recalled.[36] She also did some typing for Robert Barton in connection with the setting up of the Land Bank.

Corrigan & Corrigan, solicitors, played an important role in laundering the American Loan funds. The firm had been providing legal services to Sinn Féin since its foundation in 1906 and acted 'as a sort of Clearing House' by agreeing to receive particularly large cheques sent from America.[37] A friendly firm of lawyers prepared paperwork linking the funds to a legacy or some other seemingly legal activity. 'Messrs Corrigan would carry out any formalities that might be necessary,' according to O'Donoghue, 'and afterwards transfer the money to the Trustees.' That was only one method of getting the funds to Ireland.

Michael Collins also sent a list of trusted individuals who agreed to receive bank drafts from America. These included Erskine Childers, George Nesbitt and Alderman Corrigan, who had already opened accounts as sub-trustees for the Dáil Loan. Drafts were also sent to Patrick J. Little and John Woods, and to Little Doyle & Woods, solicitors, in which both were partners. Others to receive the drafts included Margaret Pearse.

It was James O'Mara and Harry Boland who organised the issue of the bank drafts on the American side with friendly managers. Drafts were issued for an average amount of £14,500. The first bank used was the National City Bank of New York, and the drafts were drawn in London on the National Provincial & Union Bank of England (2 Princes Street) and in Dublin on the Belfast Banking Co. (College Green). The first draft was for a massive £58,880, payable to Bishop Fogarty, one of the trustees of the Loan. Drafts were also issued by Brown Brothers & Co. (drawn on the Northern Bank, Grafton Street) and the Guaranty Trust Company of New York (drawn on its own branch in London).

Drafts drawn on London banks were sent to the recipients using the address of the Jermyn Court Hotel in Piccadilly.[38] The hotel was used regularly by those on political business in London, including Patrick Moylett and Archbishop Clune of Perth during their failed peace discussions in late 1920, and was where Art O'Brien, Dáil envoy to London, threw 'a hectic birthday party where the champagne flowed'.[39] Private addresses were also used, including the London home of Erskine Childers, which was one of the first addresses used for the transfer of American funds.[40]

As the volume of money coming from America increased, Collins asked Boland to draw drafts only on banks with head offices in Dublin and Cork.[41] From that time the drafts were issued by Kountze Brothers, New York, and drawn on the Munster & Leinster Bank, Dame Street.

James O'Mara, for some time based in Chicago, became concerned that the names on the list sent from Dublin were being overused. 'All the names given from Ireland have been utilised for remittances—some a second time,' he wrote to de Valera in the Waldorf-Astoria in New York. And he asked rhetorically, 'Do you think it safe to continue to cover these names again with drafts?'[42]

O'Mara also appeared impatient with de Valera when he postponed a shipment of American Liberty Bonds to Ireland.[43] These were unregistered bearer bonds that paid interest and returned the capital to the physical holder of the bond. De Valera was concerned that they might fall into the wrong hands. 'The risks seem to me too great without direct authorisation from Ireland,' he replied to O'Mara, and he left the final decision to Michael

Collins: 'We can ask the messenger to find out what is the view of the Secretary of Finance on this'.

The search for reliable couriers was a constant struggle. They had to be trustworthy and brave, and secrecy was vital to ensure that they were not intercepted. 'This will introduce to you X who sails for Ireland on Saturday,' went one letter received by James O'Mara. 'If you have either money or messages to send over X will be only too glad of the opportunity to serve you.'[44]

The courier network operating between Ireland and America had been built up over many years. Individuals sent from Ireland on political and intelligence work brought messages and funds back on return journeys. New York- and Boston-based supporters of the republican movement took jobs on passenger ships above and below deck, to act as couriers and to provide support to those smuggled to America, including de Valera and James O'Mara, who made the journey as stowaways.[45]

Nora Connolly, one of the first couriers used in the early part of the revolutionary period, understood the risks. In December 1915, four years before the first Dáil meeting and aged just 23, she was coming back from America with letters and gold after successfully completing an intelligence mission for her father, James Connolly. She had been told before going to New York that she could be hanged for treason, as would several others connected to the operation, if she was exposed. Nora was not deterred. 'If you think I am fit for such a job,' she told her father, 'I will do the job.'[46]

She was tasked with delivering a personal message to the German ambassador to America, Johann Heinrich Graf von Bernstorf. America had not yet entered the First World War. Nora had memorised sensitive information on the construction of Q-boats, heavily armoured disguised merchant vessels used to lure U-boats into making surface attacks. 'I was given a sheet of paper to learn off by heart,' she recalled. 'There was detail of the construction of Q-ships, and what was being done, where they were being built, what they hoped to achieve with them, what their appearance was.'

Her father came to Liverpool to see her off. On arrival in New York, and after introductions being made, Nora refused to pass the information to the German consul or to military and naval attachés introduced to her. Like a mystery woman in a novel, she was told that if she took the midnight train to Washington, von Bernstorf would see her in the morning. 'I had the whole palaver of military and naval attachés there again,' she remembered. 'Finally, I got to von Bernstorf.' After receiving the information, von Bernstorf stood up and shook her hand. 'Well, it's amazing!' he told her. 'So much information comes to me that must always be bought. This is the first time information is given to me as a present.' Nora had completed her mission of establishing the republican leaders as a credible source of information.

She received coded instructions from her father to return home. 'Your mother is not at all pleased about your being away … so you had better make arrangements to come home as soon as possible.' She was given sensitive letters and gold to carry back to Ireland.

During the journey home, Nora noticed a male passenger watching her. 'He seemed to be always about, wherever I was. I got rather worried.' She learned from a friendly worker on the ship that he was a Scotland Yard detective. Convinced that he was following her, she decided to strike up a friendship with him. She needed to know for sure. After dinner, she went over to the rail where he was standing and they started talking. Without disclosing his profession, he told her that he had been asked to join the ship on the day it had set sail. Nora became frightened because her ticket had been bought on the same day.

She asked him directly why he was on the ship (she needed to know) and he told her that he was a detective. 'My relief was so great that I laughed.' He was not following her for professional reasons. 'I realised I was the only young woman on board, and no wonder he was always in my vicinity.' On arrival in Liverpool, she found a use for her new friend. As they walked towards customs, she linked his arm and gave him her overcoat to carry. The secret letters were in the lining of the coat. 'When I was through, I went to him, thanked him, and took the coat.'

On Nora's return to Dublin, her father brought her to see the military council and she handed over the letters and gold. Her father, James Connolly, the republican and socialist leader, was executed by the British four months later. The critically wounded Connolly gave his daughter one final mission the evening of his execution. 'I remember he said to me—we were talking about various things—he said: "Put your hand under the bedclothes". He slipped some paper into my hand. He said: "Get that out, if you can. It is my last statement".'

Barcelona

Art O'Brien, the Dáil envoy in London, saw an opportunity of lodging Dáil funds in a Spanish bank. He had become friendly with Henry Bradley, an English civil servant,[47] whose brother was a bank manager in the Barcelona branch of the 'Anglo South American Bank'.[48] The bank, originally founded to finance trade in nitrates between Chile and Europe, opened the branch in Barcelona in 1916 as part of an expansion across the country.

O'Brien had worked as an engineer for five years in Spain, after studying civil engineering in Paris and electrical engineering in London.[49] He later turned down an offer to become Ireland's diplomatic representative to Spain. He broached the subject of lodging money in the bank with Henry. Henry's brother agreed to the request and an account was opened in the names of Henry Bradley, Richard Murray and Charles Betrand Dutton.[50] The latter two were prominent in the London Irish community. Dutton, an old business associate of O'Brien's, managed the Dáil Éireann office in Adam Street, off the Strand.[51] He was also assistant secretary of the Gaelic League in London.

At least £878 ($60,000 today) was transferred to the Barcelona branch. The funds were repatriated to the London branch of the Anglo South American Bank shortly after the signing of the treaty.[52] The treaty, which O'Brien opposed, 'had the effect of unravelling his political world and shrouded the rest of his career in controversy.'[53]

Henry Bradley had been awarded an MBE in the 1918 New Year Honours list for his work during the war years.[54] In 1922 he found himself in trouble with the authorities. British police, raiding Art O'Brien's office, found Henry's name on a list. Bradley was given the option of resigning from his post and drawing his pension, but he refused and was dismissed.[55] The Irish government gave him a job handling insurance compensation claims, and later he managed the patents office and the office of Gaeltacht industries.

4. Building a bank

Dummy corporation

In the Dáil meeting on 20 August 1919, Alderman Tom Kelly asked Robert Barton whether the 'machinery of British Law' was to be used in the establishment of the Land Bank. As treasurer of the Sinn Féin Bank, Alderman Kelly knew the importance of being legally compliant to avoid suppression by Dublin Castle. He also asked Barton whether any provision had been made for the contingency of the seizure of the money by the English government. No reply was minuted, but Robert Barton was addressing both issues and they would require some innovative solutions.

An illegal counter-state government investing over £200,000 ($13.5m today) as seed capital to establish a legally compliant commercial bank presented a challenge.[1] The money had to be invested without the authorities identifying Dáil Éireann as the main shareholder. Fortunately, the counter-state was not short of legal and accounting expertise.

'By way of camouflage a fictitious company was formed, bearing the name of Natland Limited,' according to Daithi O'Donoghue, 'whose members were, *mar dh'eadh* ['Yeah, right!'], to put up the cash required to establish the bank.'[2]

The full name of the dummy corporation was the Natland Co-operative Society Limited. Professor Arthur Clery, a lecturer in property and contract law in University College Dublin, agreed to allow his home address to be used as the registered office of the society. Professor Clery was also a judge in the Republican Courts.[3] The Natland directors held a number of meetings, and fictitious minutes were produced to disguise the true nature of the business.[4] Donal O'Connor, chartered accountant, and Patrick McGilligan TD helped set up the society.[5] McGilligan would later become attorney general and Minister for Finance, as well as a professor of constitutional and international law.

Momentum

The first meetings to establish the new bank took place in the downstairs study of the home of Edward Stephens at 38 Upper Leeson Street. The study opened on to the garden at the back. 'In the autumn of 1919,' recalled Stephens, 'I was approached by Lionel Smith-Gordon ... to ask me whether I would join in organising a co-operative bank, ... and whether I would allow my house to be a meeting place for those engaged in the organisation.'[6]

Stephens, a young barrister and a nephew of J.M. Synge, was brought in to provide momentum for the start-up. Smith-Gordon was the manager-designate of the bank but lacked the practical skills to set up a new business. Barton could not attend all the meetings while on the run and needed someone to help with the groundwork. He put together an experienced advisory committee from different backgrounds, including Batt O'Connor, his friend and an experienced property developer.

Lionel Smith-Gordon was born in England and educated at Eton and Oxford. He married the daughter of Senator Duncan Fletcher of Florida, who became Lady Smith-Gordon when Lionel inherited his father's title. He arrived in Ireland in 1912 from Canada, where he had been a professor at the University of Toronto.[7] He became secretary to Sir Horace Plunkett, founder of the Irish Agricultural Organisation Society (IAOS), with whom he had an 'intimate connection' in business affairs.[8] He resigned from the IAOS to become manager of the Land Bank.[9]

Smith-Gordon, an academic rather than a businessman, earned his appointment more for his personality, background and connections than for any leadership, efficiency and organisational skills. When Patrick Moylett, the outspoken Sinn Féin businessman, learned of Smith-Gordon's role, he could not understand how 'That man, who had no qualifications whatever, was made managing director of the Land Bank'.[10] Moylett claimed that under Smith-Gordon the Irish Agricultural Wholesale Society (IAWS) had lost at least £250,000 and that the Co-operative Wholesale Society in England had to write off £100,000 of debt owed to it by the IAWS.

Moylett claimed to have been the first person to propose setting up a bank. According to Moylett, Éamon de Valera and Arthur Griffith had asked him to put forward a plan for a national loan that was under consideration.

The plan he proposed advocated the setting up of a bank. 'I think it was the first that was heard of it.'[11] Of this confident businessman, who was comfortable in political, legal and media circles in both Dublin and London, Michael Collins would later say: 'I fancy him to be a man who thinks nobody can tell him anything'.[12]

Bringing Edward Stephens on board, however, was a good decision by Smith-Gordon. Momentum grew and the National Land Bank was registered on 2 December under the Industrial and Provident Societies Act 1893. The registered office given was 5 Harcourt Terrace, the home of Smith-Gordon. The job of building a banking business could now commence. Batt O'Connor left the organising committee at this stage, as 'he was more concerned with bricks and mortar than with banks.'[13]

The Dáil Cabinet voted set-up expenses of £10,000.[14] On 15 December Michael Collins sent Barton a cheque for £1,200 for the 'accountant and organiser', probably the fees of Donal O'Connor and Edward Stephens.[15] Barton sent copies of the proposed rules governing the bank to a number of people, including Diarmuid O'Hegarty in Mountjoy prison. O'Hegarty replied on 29 December, thanking Barton and including his comments.[16]

Meanwhile, Smith-Gordon spent much of the crucial set-up time out of the country. On 12 December he went on a fact-finding mission to Switzerland and Italy to study methods of extending credit to co-operative farming societies.[17] He did not return until mid-January.

5. Bring it to me in gold

Gold exchange network

On 6 March 1920 the *Irish Times* reported on the 'sensational rise' of the British pound against the US dollar in New York, which caused a great deal of excitement in the markets. The pound had risen over 1% to $3.60 and, indeed, had risen 7% over the previous week. A market rumour was doing the rounds that the United States was going to buy the West Indies as a way of settling the large debts owed to it by Great Britain.[1] Another and more credible rumour, coming from New York, was the expectation of a large shipment of gold to be sent by England to America. Gold reserves were crucial to underpinning currency exchange rates.

Smart traders in London, however, were far from confident about the outlook for the British pound.[2] The currency had been on a downward trajectory against the dollar since the end of the war. The recent strength of the pound was unusual. Michael Collins shared the same negative outlook for the pound as the London traders.

Collins needed to protect the purchasing power of the Loan proceeds against the dollar, in particular to fund the purchase of arms in America. He needed to build a gold reserve. The only way to do that was to get new subscriptions in gold or to convert some of the proceeds into gold sovereigns. Gold coins were scarce, however, though some sovereigns still remained in circulation, despite the British government having withdrawn them at the beginning of the war and people keeping them as souvenirs.[3]

On the same day as the *Irish Times* report, Michael Collins added a special request to a circular to Loan organisers. 'I would ask you to get all the gold you can,' he wrote. 'It is once and a half as useful to us as English paper currency. When dealing with such a country as America ... gold is as valuable as it was formerly.'

'Bring it to me in gold, Batt,' Collins said to Batt O'Connor, when he went to him with Loan subscriptions. 'I obeyed,' O'Connor recalled. 'I got shopkeepers and business men whom I knew, to hoard every sovereign and half-sovereign which came into their hands, and I exchanged the notes for the gold from time to time.' That was the beginning of the gold exchange network.[4]

Collins instructed Mary Woods to stop going to Cumann na mBan meetings and to give the impression that she was getting 'cool and careless'.[5] With Batt O'Connor as an intermediary, her new role in the revolutionary movement was 'to get safe houses [and] carry out espionage', and generally to do anything that O'Connor instructed her to do. She secured one safe house on St Mary's Road, telling the owner that it was for her 'delicate sister who wanted to be near the Church and her doctor'. She also recalled other work she did for Collins. 'Another of my activities for Mick Collins was collecting gold in exchange for notes. On account of my husband's business and in other ways I was able to procure a lot of gold which I handed to Batt O'Connor.'

Oliver St John Gogarty, the well-known medical doctor, poet and conversationalist, was part of the network of gold-collectors. Batt O'Connor was one of his patients, and 'To him I gave whatever gold I could come by for his reserve'.[6] A larger-than-life character, Gogarty featured as the fictional Buck Mulligan in James Joyce's *Ulysses*.

Patrick J. Little was also part of the network. He regularly received sums of money in gold from John Burke, a solicitor, which he handed in to the 'Dáil Loan office'.[7]

Joe Kinsella, a lieutenant in the 4th Battalion of the Dublin Brigade and an intelligence officer, had agents in banks and shops exchanging paper notes for gold coins. He exchanged up to £20 into gold every week, which he handed over to his brigade intelligence officer.[8] Much of the gold found its way to the New Ireland Assurance head office. Frank Thornton recalled Daithi O'Donoghue collecting the gold that had been deposited during the day. 'He was escorted either by myself or by Tom Cullen on all occasions.'[9]

Eilis Ryan, whom Michael Collins had recruited into the Department of Finance, also participated in the gold exchange network. She had met Collins, Diarmuid O'Hegarty and Liam Archer at meetings of the Gaelic

League in 1915 and they became good friends. In between keeping a full-time job and maintaining an active social life, she found time to participate in the 1916 Rising, to act as an intelligence agent and to join the Cumann na mBan executive. Attached to a First Aid unit during the Rising, Eilis tended the wounded under 'deafening' rifle fire and at constant risk of stray bullets.[10] She crossed paths with O'Hegarty and Archer in the Church Street area towards the end of the fighting.

In her early intelligence work, Eilis built a close relationship with the intelligence section working in the General Post Office. There were two groups, one monitoring postal activity in the sorting area and the other in the telegraph section. Liam Archer was a member of the telegraph section. Eilis carried intercepted military, police and government correspondence to GHQ Intelligence 'with as little delay as possible'. Messages in cipher were first decoded by Archer, using cipher keys provided by Collins. Eilis later married Seán O'Connell, who headed another intelligence group operating in the telegraph office at Kingsbridge.

As part of what she called the 'Dáil Loan gold collection', Eilis collected gold coins and brought them to Daithi O'Donoghue, who gave her the equivalent in notes and silver, which she gave back to the donors. She rented a room from the Misses Heffernan, who were also attached to the intelligence section in the Post Office. The Heffernan sisters collected 'quite a lot' of sovereigns and half-sovereigns through their work in the Post Office and from their network of friends.[11]

Gold was also arriving into head office as Loan subscriptions. Martin Finn, a medical student and a section leader in the 1st Battalion of the Dublin Brigade, passed on 25 gold sovereigns to James Kirwan, the publican on Parnell Street, who gave them to Michael Collins. 'The Dáil Loan … had been floated at the time,' Finn remembered, 'and the success of which was the concern of every member of the Movement.'[12] Going on the run delayed his medical studies, but he eventually completed his final medical examination and became Command Medical Officer, Army Medical Corps, Eastern Command.

Margaret MacGarry and her daughter Maeve, active supporters of Dáil Éireann, helped in collecting Loan proceeds in gold. Both were also active in the suffragette movement. At one protest meeting, a group 'attacked us and treated us most brutally', recalled Maeve.[13] The MacGarry home played an important role during the period. 'When the Dáil Loan campaign was started, people—priests principally—came from the country with their collections. My mother collected quite a lot of gold.'[14] No. 5 Fitzwilliam Square also hosted Cabinet meetings and was an important message clearing-house for Michael Collins and Diarmuid O'Hegarty.

Gold coins received at the Department of Finance office were securely sealed in small tobacco tins, each flat tin containing either £250 or £500 in gold. Once the tobacco tins had been filled, O'Donoghue brought them to Corrigan's Undertakers on Camden Street and handed them to Peter Corrigan, who buried them at the back of the premises 'at dead of night'.[15] Only four people knew where the gold was buried: Peter Corrigan, his brother William, Michael Collins and O'Donoghue himself.

6. Battle preparation

Lines drawn

Lord French and Macpherson completed their circle of suppression in Ireland on 25 November, when Sinn Féin was prohibited throughout the country.[1] It had been ten weeks since the prohibition of Dáil Éireann, six weeks since Sinn Féin was proclaimed in Dublin and two weeks since the raid on 76 Harcourt Street. Lord French issued an order prohibiting Sinn Féin in 28 new counties and four cities, adding to the previous proclamations in Dublin, Cork, Tipperary and Clare. The order included the very definitive statement, 'This means that all Ireland is now proclaimed'.

The prohibition of Dáil Éireann in September had already changed the perspective of many Sinn Féin leaders regarding the inevitability of military conflict. Each successive repressive step since had reinforced that view. Richard Mulcahy, chief of staff, had placed the army on an offensive footing as a direct response to the prohibition of the Dáil, which 'made it natural that there would be clashes'.[2] GHQ authorised local units to organise aggressive attacks against police barracks to build up the supply of arms.[3]

In London Lloyd George, finally engaging with the Irish question, struggled to reconcile the competing political demands of Sinn Féin (independent republic), unionists (no change in the constitutional arrangement of the United Kingdom), 'Ulster' unionists (six- or nine-county northern parliament) and moderates on both sides (single Home Rule parliament), whilst also ensuring that London retained control over military and foreign affairs, taxation and banking. A twelve-man Irish Committee issued its first report on 4 November. It expressed a preference for a two-parliament solution, one for the three southern provinces and one for Ulster, together with a Council of Ireland composed of members of the two Irish parliaments.

There was, however, an inherent contradiction between the recommendation of the Irish Committee in London and the suppression policy exercised by Dublin Castle. *The Times* questioned how Lloyd George hoped to introduce a southern parliament in which Sinn Féin would, 'for a time at all events, be an important, if not a dominant force', while at the same time prohibiting Sinn Féin.[4] The paper was concerned that the motivation behind the decision to prohibit Sinn Féin was 'something worse than ineptitude and more dangerous than futility'.[5]

A two-parliament recommendation for Ireland did not make sense, unless Dublin Castle hoped to crush Sinn Féin before the southern parliament was summoned. In fact, that had been the Castle's plan for months. When Lord French prohibited Dáil Éireann in September, he wrote to Bonar Law that 'we are really at war'.[6]

The Dublin correspondent of the *Daily Express* had an inside line to Castle politics: 'It is believed that the proclamation suppressing Sinn Féin … marks the opening of a vigorous campaign on the part of the Irish Government for the suppression of crime and outrage during the coming winter months'.[7] In other words, Lord French and Macpherson were ready to step up their campaign of oppression, but they would not have it all their own way.

On 19 December the squad, led by Michael McDonnell, attacked a convoy of cars carrying Lord French on the ten-minute drive between Ashtown train station and the viceregal lodge in the Phoenix Park.[8] Lord French survived the attack but Martin Savage, a young Volunteer, was shot and killed.

The attempted assassination of Lord French sent shock waves through Ireland and Britain. French was the highest British official in Ireland, the hero of the Second Boer War and the man 'who inspired his immortal army to hold the rocking line at Ypres', as the *Irish Times* put it.[9] Cardinal Logue sent a telegram to Lord French. 'Have just heard of dastardly attempt. I heartily congratulate Your Excellency on miracle escape.'[10] The *Irish Independent* called it 'A Deplorable Outrage'.[11]

The attack marked a turning point for Lloyd George in London. On 22 December, three days after the attempt on Lord French's life, he warned that 'any attempt at secession will be fought with the same determination, with the same resources, with the same resolve as the Northern States of

America put into the fight against the Southern States. It is important that that should be known, not merely throughout the world, but in Ireland itself.'[12]

Meanwhile, Lord French, who had already been preparing for battle and was shaken by the attempt on his life, was determined to crush Sinn Féin in one final strategic move—the mass arrest, internment and deportation of the entire Sinn Féin leadership across the country. His rationale was simple: deportation of a few hundred of its leaders would finish the Sinn Féin 'criminal organisation'.[13]

Secret committee

A week before the ambush at Ashtown, Lord French was sure that the extremists were 'getting stronger and more arrogant in every direction'.[14] Angry and frustrated with the intelligence services, he believed that the secret service was 'simply non-existent. What masquerades for such is nothing but a delusion and a snare.'[15] He was equally scathing about the police. 'The DMP are simply demoralized and the RIC will be in the same case very soon if we do not act quickly to set our house in order.'

French had established a secret committee to report and make recommendations on the police intelligence services, and to develop a plan to 'place matters in Dublin and the country on a proper footing'.[16] The four committee members were Walter Edgeworth-Johnstone, chief commissioner of the DMP, T.J. Smith, the acting inspector general of the RIC, Sir John Taylor, the assistant under-secretary, and Alan Bell, a hard-line elderly resident magistrate and former RIC detective who had transferred to Dublin from Armagh.

Joseph Byrne, the Catholic head of the RIC, was a noticeable absentee from the committee. Byrne was unlikely to back the hard-line policy to be espoused by the other committee members. He had opposed the introduction of martial law and the recruitment of war veterans into the police force. Lloyd George paid him a backhanded compliment when he said that he was not sure whether Byrne had 'lost his nerve' or had 'simply the intelligence' to recognise that the task in Ireland was a hopeless one.[17] Lloyd George needed a commissioner 'of less intelligence and more stolidity'. Lord French forced Byrne to take one month's holiday and T.J. Smith was brought in from Belfast as acting inspector general of the RIC.

In a report dated 7 December, the secret committee set out a plan of legal and extra-legal actions to take back the initiative from the 'Sinn Féiners'.[18] The recommendations in the report constituted a secret battle plan. Dublin was the 'storm centre'. It was 'absolutely essential that all the resources of the Government should be used in the Metropolis to break down and destroy' the IRA.[19]

The secret committee recommended (i) appointing an outside special assistant commissioner to work full-time on political work and revitalise G Division; (ii) sending an agent from America, already closely connected to the republican movement in that country, to operate outside the RIC and DMP chains of command; (iii) sending tradesmen to Dublin to join trade unions to gather information; and (iv) setting up a covert counter-assassination force to protect G-men as they walked the streets.

The covert force was to be recruited from young RIC men from the country 'of courage and determination, good shots, men accustomed to city life'. Operating independently of the DMP, the recruits would lodge together in pairs in various parts of the city. Secretly tracking G-men as they walked the streets about their work, the undercover force was to shoot anyone who dared to attack. 'We are inclined to think that the shooting of a few would-be assassins would have an excellent effect. Up to the present they have escaped with impunity.' Anxious for results, the committee thought that this should be implemented as soon as possible.

Lord French also sought the support of Basil Thomson, head of the Directorate of Intelligence in London, and asked him 'to run the Irish secret service from London'.[20] Thomson had at least one undercover agent operating in Dublin who had already met Michael Collins.

A revitalised G Division under a new assistant commissioner, undercover agents infiltrating the Sinn Féin organisation at the highest level and implementation of the covert actions recommended by the secret committee were three key elements in Lord French's battle plan. But to implement the mass arrest and deportation of several hundred Sinn Féin leaders he needed committed leadership, secrecy and, most of all, manpower. This was not a job for the police force, which already could not cope with the increased number of 'outrages'.[21] Tactically, Lord French needed military support to carry out an operation of this scale.

Stopping short of introducing martial law throughout Ireland, which was politically sensitive, counter-insurgency powers were handed to the British military under DORA regulation 14b, 'Restrictions on, or internment of, Persons of Hostile Origin or Associations'.[22] Responsibility for policing operations against 'perpetrators of outrages' was passed from the police and magistrates to the military. As Lord French put it, 'the military take the initiative and the police follow'.[23]

The military were given the power to search individuals and buildings for arms, explosives and seditious literature. Lord French was determined to defeat Sinn Féin: 'a large number of men must be arrested and deported, or else we must have martial law'.[24] As a harbinger of things to come, Alderman Tom Kelly TD, a highly respected member of Dublin Corporation and the treasurer of the Sinn Féin Bank, was arrested without cause and interned in Wormwood Scrubs.

The counter-state was also readying its forces. Army GHQ was ready to play a more offensive role and GHQ Intelligence was increasing its operational capability. Liam Tobin and Frank Thornton had left their jobs in New Ireland to take up full-time intelligence roles. They were joined by Tom Cullen, whose 'loyalty, discretion and bluff common sense Collins valued highly'.[25] This management triumvirate, under the strategic direction of Collins, was determined to build a professional and élite intelligence unit, though it was still an inexperienced group towards the end of 1919 and had never faced the full capability of British Intelligence.

The squad was also an unproven unit. On 29 November Detective John Barton was shot and killed. The attack, carried out by two separate sections of the squad, operating independently, resulted in a 'friendly fire' incident, with one unit caught in the crossfire of the other.

David Neligan, one of Collins's agents within the G Division, described Barton, who was from Kerry and unmarried, as 'easily the best detective in these islands'.[26] Larry O'Neill, the nationalist lord mayor, offered a special expression of sympathy, praising Detective Barton 'as a great asset to the City of Dublin, and his loss will be hard to replace'.[27]

The civilian arm of the counter-state continued to operate through November and December, albeit in more difficult circumstances. Although the Dáil had not met since 27 October, the Cabinet convened weekly in secret. The Department of Finance and the secretariat staff no longer worked in a spacious Georgian building on Harcourt Street. Instead, they worked from home or in offices over shops and businesses on narrow, busy retail streets.

Most of the senior staff, including Diarmuid O'Hegarty and Paddy O'Keeffe, were in prison, but despite the increased risk of discovery and arrest motivation and morale were high. The Sinn Féin organisation, despite being prohibited, was preparing for the municipal elections, in which it expected to win control in a majority of councils and corporations.

7. New Year's message

On the morning of Thursday 2 January 1920, David Kelly was in the Sinn Féin Bank at 6 Harcourt Street. Around midday, a police inspector and two constables arrived at the bank. The inspector had been instructed to enforce a closure order on the building that had been issued by the competent military authority. Kelly explained to the inspector that the building was owned by the Sinn Féin Bank, a properly registered company carrying on business with the other banks across the city, and that the closure order was invalid. He said that he did not have the power to close the bank without consulting his shareholders.[1]

The inspector went upstairs to serve the closure order on Joe Clarke, the caretaker, who lived on the top floor with his wife and three children. As usual when police called, Joe was not at home. He was a Sinn Féin candidate for Dublin Corporation in the municipal election. In his absence, the inspector read the notice to his wife and asked when she could leave. Mrs Clarke said that she could not answer the question. After the inspector took note of this, he made his way to the near-empty No. 76 on the same street. Seán McCluskey, the caretaker there, was still living in the basement flat with his wife and young family. The inspector read the same notice, but Seán said that he was unable to leave as he could not find another house.

At 2.30pm Michael Staines, treasurer of New Ireland Assurance, was receiving cash from one of his agents in the head office at 56 Sackville (now O'Connell) Street when three military lorries thundered across O'Connell Bridge and came to a sudden halt at the corner of Bachelor's Walk. Armed soldiers jumped from the lorries and took up positions in front of the shop of Kapp and Peterson, pipe manufacturers.[2] The business had been founded by the Kapp brothers, German immigrants, who were later joined by a Latvian named Charles Peterson; patents awarded to the company in the 1890s had revolutionised the pipe-making sector.[3] Detectives, accompanied by a large number of uniformed policemen, entered the building and went up to the New Ireland offices overhead.

Michael Staines was pointed out to the inspector in charge by a detective. After waiting until Staines had finished dealing with the agent, the inspector informed him that he had been instructed to search the offices thoroughly. Staines asked for the inspector's name and requested a receipt for anything removed from the office. The inspector, perhaps afraid, refused to give his name but agreed to provide receipts.[4] He had reason to be cautious. As well as being a Sinn Féin TD and a member of Dublin Corporation, Staines was a senior member of the Volunteers, a 1916 veteran and an 'excellent soldier' according to Batt O'Connor.[5] His home had been raided in the nationwide searches in September following the proclamation of the Dáil. The police examined books and documents, but surprisingly left the New Ireland offices after just twenty minutes.

At 3pm, half an hour after the raid on New Ireland, two lorries of military and police pulled up outside the home of Batt O'Connor at 1 Brendan Road, Donnybrook.[6] Batt had built the twelve houses on the road, which he named in honour of the patron saint of his native Kerry. Robert Barton had stayed here after his escape from prison the previous March. Michael Collins had slept in the house on two or three occasions but no more, as 'it was too dangerous a place for him'.[7] Mrs O'Connor was at home alone with her five children. The soldiers remained outside while the police searched the house, but they left empty-handed.[8]

Over the weekend, the first of the new year, Dublin was free of raids and generally quiet. The only notable events were the ongoing barmen's strike for Sundays off and a pay rise (though many pubs remained open) and a protest against the new motor permits organised by the drivers' union.[9] Interviewed by the *Irish Independent*, David Kelly said that he was going to resist the closure order, stressing that the Sinn Féin Bank was a legitimate business.[10] Arthur Griffith was quoted in the Monday papers distancing himself and the Sinn Féin party from the operations of the bank.[11]

The IRA, however, ensured that the opening weekend of the year was far from quiet in Cork. On Saturday five police barracks were attacked, including Carrigtwohill, which was captured after a four-hour gun battle. Richard Mulcahy, chief of staff, had authorised Tomás MacCurtain and Terence MacSwiney to carry out the first sanctioned large-scale engagement by the counter-state. MacSwiney had been especially anxious to step up military activity, after Cork's failure to participate in 1916.

On 7 January the police returned to 6 Harcourt Street, but this time accompanied by a large military force.[12] Arriving in the Sinn Féin Bank shortly after the raid had commenced, David Kelly was told that orders had been received to close up the bank. Kelly asked whether the police or the military authorities had issued the closure order. This caused confusion among the police and army officers, who apparently did not know the legal authority under which the order was issued. A DMP inspector and a number of military officers withdrew to confer. They did not take long to make up their minds; they ignored the question and gave the order to board up all the interior rooms in the building, including the Sinn Féin Bank.

A large crowd had gathered outside to watch the raid. To their delight, Mrs Clarke appeared at a top-floor window. When the police and military were finished, they nailed shut the front door of the building. The Clarke family could still enter and leave by a back entrance. Number 76 Harcourt Street was also visited by the raiding party and given the same treatment. The McCluskeys could access their living quarters through the basement.

The inspector and the military officers told David Kelly that they believed that an application to have the bank reopened would be granted. The Sinn Féin organisation was clearly the target of the raid, not the Sinn Féin Bank. Kelly, quick to go to the newspapers, highlighted the injustice of the decision, calling the action of the police and military tyrannical and illegal. He said that he had no intention of making an application to reopen the bank, which was accepted by other branches of the administration: 'the Inland Revenue authorities are willing to take two pence upon each of the bank's cheques, and the income tax authorities are willing to take income tax'. Indignant and defiant, he said that he would carry on the business at 3 Harcourt Street.

Dublin Castle described the raids as a sequel to those on the previous Friday, because the closure orders had been ignored. Sinn Féin said that the raids were part of Dublin Castle's policy of disrupting its preparation for the municipal elections.

A second raid on the New Ireland Assurance headquarters on the same day was no sequel. It had a different purpose. Fifty soldiers—accompanied by no policemen—jumped from their lorries onto O'Connell Street with fixed bayonets. The raiding party did not climb the stairs to the New Ireland offices over Kapp and Peterson's shop. Instead, a party of soldiers with crowbars proceeded straight to cellars at the back of the building.[13] Portions of the floor were dug up and waste-paper sacks turned inside out.[14] The soldiers withdrew empty-handed after half an hour.

Michael Staines attributed the raid to business jealousy and trade rivalry.[15] He told the *Evening Telegraph* that he had information that at least one prominent member of the Masonic Order had worked hard to bring the business to the attention of Dublin Castle.[16]

Staines may have had genuine concerns that sharp business practice played a part in the raids. New Ireland was taking market share from the incumbent 'foreign companies', as Staines described his competitors. The business had been a huge success in its first two years of operation. In 1919 premium income rose almost 450%, and membership had increased 900% from 2,000 to 20,000.[17] Nevertheless, Staines also had other reasons to be concerned by the increasing number of raids on the business.

Most of the staff of New Ireland had dual roles. Maura O'Kelly was a logistics specialist in the head office. 'Not alone did she fit in dealing with the Dáil Loan,' according to Frank Thornton, 'but also was always ready to receive parcels of arms [and] ammunition and have them sent to their proper destination.'[18]

The work was not without risk. The previous morning, James Hoey, one of its insurance agents, was arrested on his way to work. Immediately deported, he was given no opportunity to say goodbye to his family, whom he had left that morning just like any other day. James, a candidate in the Bray Urban Council election, was a well-known Sinn Féin activist who had been in prison previously.[19] The *Evening Herald* compared his treatment to that of Thomas Kelly and warned that what had happened to Alderman Kelly and Mr Hoey 'might happen to any one of us any day'.[20]

Joe O'Doherty, the inspector for the Ulster region and a member of the Dáil, was on the run. A warrant for his arrest was issued in December for soliciting Dáil Loan subscriptions at a meeting in October at which £40 was collected.[21] Five policemen had been admitted to his home by a servant shortly after nine in the morning. Joe was having breakfast in his upstairs bedroom. When he arrived at the top of the stairs, one of the detectives in the hallway read the warrant for his arrest. Joe had a brief conversation in Irish with the servant, who told the detective in English that she was going to get some heavier clothing for Mr O'Doherty. Joe returned to his room to finish his breakfast. Waiting for some minutes and running out of patience, the policemen asked Margaret O'Doherty, a medical doctor, when her husband would be ready. She replied casually that he had gone out the back. The policemen hurried to the rear of the house, just in time to see Joe disappearing over a wall.

New sheriffs in town

The raids early in the new year were accompanied by several actions taken by Lord French to implement his aggressive new strategy against the republican movement.

On 5 January Detective Inspector William Forbes Redmond had been officially appointed assistant commissioner of the DMP, tasked by Lord French with reorganising and revitalising the G Division. Efficient, energetic and hands-on, he had famously organised a fleet of motorcars and lorries to bring a force of 200 policemen to Galway from Belfast at the start of the 1916 Rising.[22] He had arrived in Dublin from Belfast three weeks earlier, on 20 December, the day after the assassination attempt on Lord French, which was probably no coincidence.[23]

Inspector Redmond was married and had two daughters. His late father had founded a timber merchant's business in Belfast, which was run by one of his brothers. Another brother managed the family business in Newry.[24] Redmond had joined the RIC as a cadet and had risen to the rank of assistant commissioner and head of the detective department in Belfast. He played golf, tennis and badminton, and was well known as a motorcar enthusiast.[25] Motivated and brave, he had left his family and the relative calm of his native Belfast to move to Dublin, where four detectives had been shot, three fatally, in the previous five months. Redmond proved to be a formidable opponent for Sinn Féin.

On 7 January General Boyd received operational instructions from Army GHQ to prepare a list of officers and prominent members of the Irish Volunteers and other individuals responsible for outrages.[26] Boyd had just been appointed commander of the newly created 'Dublin District' command.[27] As the competent military authority in the district, he was responsible for implementing DORA regulations in the city.

The major round-up demanded by French was planned for Saturday 24 January, but this was later postponed by a week. Operational procedures for the day were clear. Sinn Féin leaders suspected of complicity in an outrage were to be detained under a 'Detention Order'. An application would then be made for a warrant to deport and intern any person regarded as 'dangerous'. Ironically, those against whom there was any actual evidence of an offence were to be handed over to the civil authority.

A few military officers had been running small intelligence operations on their own individual initiative.[28] These were used to supplement the weakened intelligence units of the RIC and DMP. In Dublin, Major Hill-Dillon had at least one undercover agent working on the ground.[29]

Just before the year's end, Lord French had asked Alan Bell to establish a special inquiry into the attempt on his life at Ashtown. Alan Bell had been transferred to Dublin as a resident magistrate. He also acted as an adviser to Lord French, including participating in the secret committee. The inquiry into the Ashtown ambush propelled Bell into a front-line investigative role, a role that the near-retired magistrate and former RIC inspector relished.

On 30 December he had launched the inquiry into the Ashtown ambush under Section I of the Crimes Act, the first 'Star Chamber' to be set up since the power was reintroduced in Dublin.[30] Having secured a room at the Children's Court, he sent a memo to John Taylor, assistant under-secretary, requesting that the DMP 'should furnish me with the full names and addresses of any persons who they have reason to believe can give me some material evidence'. He said that care should be taken to furnish the full names and addresses accurately, 'so that there may be no error in the issue of summonses', which he requested to be served personally on suspects. Alan Bell knew the importance of attention to detail in these matters. The memo was passed on to Edgeworth-Johnstone, chief commissioner of the DMP, who in turn directed it to the superintendent of the G Division.

8. Alan Bell

Alan Bell was born in King's County (Offaly) in 1857, the son of Revd James Bell, a Church of Ireland minister from Banagher.[1] A cousin of the family, Arthur Bell Nicholls, had married Charlotte Bronte.[2] Bell joined the RIC officer cadets in 1879 after coming second in the cadet examination, rather than following family and cousins into a church, medical or military career.[3]

Alan Bell had spent much of his 40-year career fighting political crime, mainly connected to land agitation, first as an RIC district inspector during the Land War and subsequently as a resident magistrate. He began his career as a detective in 1879, just twelve years after the Fenian Rising and in the same year that the Land League was established. The first edition of the Crimes Act was passed in Westminster in 1881, the Protection of Persons and Property (Ireland) Act. Bell had been using the Crimes Act to suppress political agitation for longer than most of the Sinn Féin leaders had been alive.

Friends and colleagues described the 62-year-old Bell as a 'very quiet, studious gentleman' who had 'very little interests outside his duties and domestic life'.[4] He was known for his 'goodness and kindness to the poor'.[5] Older members of Sinn Féin, and former adversaries during the land agitation, did not share the same good opinion of Bell. He was intelligent, ruthless and did whatever was required to secure a conviction, including bribery and witness coercion. Bell despised the republican movement, 'a menace to the maintenance of the peace; recruited from the rowdy element of the population and under no proper control'.[6]

Not my brother's keeper

Bell's arrival in Dublin was not a secret. On 8 November the *Irish Times* quoted a magistrate in Portadown thanking Bell for his service after 'having been called to a more important sphere of duty in the Metropolis'. On 22

November, in the personal section of the same paper, it was announced that the lord lieutenant 'has appointed Mr Alan Bell, RM, to be a Resident Magistrate for the County of Dublin'.

Dr James Bell, his brother, was a doctor in the prison where many of the 'German Plot' internees had been detained. Josephine MacNeill, the fiancée of Pierce McCann, who died from influenza, praised Dr Bell as 'a singularly fair-minded man, without bitterness, very kind and sympathetic'.[7] On the night McCann died, Dr Bell told her that the government 'was as responsible for Pierce's death as if they murdered him'.

Bell's arrival in Dublin may or may not have come to the attention of GHQ Intelligence, which was still only building up its capabilities. Charlie Dalton only joined the group in February 1920. One of his jobs was to monitor the society columns of newspapers to trace the movements of prominent people.[8] Even if it was known, Michael Collins would not have been unduly concerned about the appointment of an elderly magistrate, even one with a prior reputation. It just confirmed the continuation of the same oppressive tactics employed over the previous months.

Alan Bell appeared equally unconcerned about taking an appointment in Dublin, despite the risks. He had spent the previous four years as resident magistrate in Portadown, performing additional duties in Belfast.[9] It was here that Bell became acquainted with Redmond and T.J. Smith, the acting commissioner of the RIC, then chief commissioner in Belfast. Although Bell had never been posted to Dublin, his wife Ellen had been raised in a three-storey Georgian building on Waterloo Road. They now lived near Dalkey, a coastal village about 14km from the city centre. Bell commuted by tram to Dublin. As a precaution, he had an RIC escort from his home to the tram stop. He was met at Trinity College by a G-man, who escorted him to Dublin Castle or the Police Courts.[10]

Craughwell prisoners

As a young RIC sub-inspector, Bell had quickly found himself at the centre of a political storm following the murder of Peter Doherty in November 1881. In Galway, between May of that year and June 1882, eight people were murdered within the geographical triangle formed by the towns of Loughrea and Athenry and the village of Ardrahan, each approximately 20km from the other.[11] In the centre of the triangle lay a small village called Craughwell.

Bell brought James Morrissey to trial for the murder. Morrissey's family had been active in boycotting activities. The local resident magistrate complimented Bell for his 'untiring zeal and intelligence' in gathering 'minute circumstantial evidence' in an environment of 'widespread terrorism'.[12] The Crown prosecutor, however, did not agree. He threw the case out for lack of evidence.

Bell, under pressure to deliver a conviction, set his sights on Patrick Finnegan from Craughwell, who was already interned under the Crimes Act on suspicion of murder and for attending a Land League meeting. Five others were also arrested in January 1883. Patrick Finnegan had not killed Peter Doherty, but Bell unearthed an 'approver', the equivalent today of a suspect who turns State's evidence, who admitted to participating in the murder and was willing to testify against Finnegan.[13]

Newspapers made allegations of police harassment and witness bribery. Bell was accused of coaching witnesses, and inconsistencies were found in depositions.[14] In court, Margaret Raftery, the wife of an informer who had turned against her husband, accused Bell of falsifying her witness statement: 'Mr Bell wrote down that I said my husband was not in until six o'clock, and I said that was not true; I don't know if it was corrected; I told them it was not right. Mr Bell wrote down more than I said, and I told him so.'[15]

Despite his coercive actions, Bell failed to secure a conviction against Patrick Finnegan, because in his view there were 'only seven good jurors on the panel'.[16] A second trial was ordered, but this time the odds were stacked against Finnegan. The court hearing was moved to Sligo and a 'special jury' was sworn in under the Crimes Act. The all-Protestant jury arrived at a murder verdict, but only after receiving considerable guidance from the judge. Alan Bell was promoted to district inspector.

Diplomatic incident

While investigating the murder of Peter Doherty, Alan Bell also made his most famous arrest and created an international diplomatic incident. On 10 August 1882 he arrested Henry George, an American political economist and hugely popular writer and speaker who was in Ireland covering the activities of the Land League for the *Irish World* newspaper.[17] The arrest of George in Athenry for barely credible reasons forced the British into issuing a written apology to the American government. After the incident, Henry George received a personal invitation to visit the US secretary of state. Many in the British establishment supported the arrest and believed that no apology should have been made. Bell was making a name for himself among hard-liners, and his reputation was further enhanced during the Parnell Commission which commenced in 1888.

Piggott forgeries

Richard Piggott, an Irish journalist, had forged letters in the handwriting of Charles Stuart Parnell, the nationalist leader in the House of Commons, appearing to condone the 'Phoenix Park Murders', the fatal stabbing of the chief secretary and under-secretary in 1882. *The Times* eagerly published the letters, a move which many nationalists believed was deliberately timed to influence the passing of the Crimes Act 1887, an update to the 1881 legislation.[18]

At the parliamentary inquiry established to examine the accusations against Parnell and the wider events surrounding the case, Alan Bell appeared as a witness at the tenth session. The *Belfast Newsletter*, calling him the 'most capable witness of the day', was impressed with his refusal under intense cross-examination to be backed into a corner. The cross-examiner 'had now tackled one who had all his wits about him'.[19]

Providing background to the land agitation problem, Bell informed the inquiry that tenant evictions caused 'a great deal of boycotting, intimidation and outrage', and that bailiffs had to be under permanent guard when discharging their duties.[20] Bell's cross-examiner was Sir Charles Russell, a renowned barrister, an Irish Catholic and a future lord chief justice of England. Later in the inquiry Russell would raise the case of the Craughwell prisoners and the murder of Peter Doherty, where 'two men were tried, and found guilty, but there was no evidence even of membership of the Land League'.[21]

Ruffian hireling

Bell spent much of the 1890s anonymously serving as a district inspector in Mallow, until an outbreak of land agitation in Mayo in 1898, organised by the newly formed United Irish League (UIL). Bell's experience was required and he was appointed a resident magistrate in Mayo.[22]

The UIL had been founded in January 1898 in Westport by William O'Brien, a nationalist MP, journalist and social reformer, who had been imprisoned a number of times under the Crimes Act. In 1900 John O'Donnell, an MP elected for the UIL, described Bell as 'a ruffian hireling, backed up by an idle band of police-bloodhounds, who instead of preserving law and order have been let loose upon the people ... in a manner unworthy of any Government officials'.[23]

Another MP, Conor O'Kelly, who was elected for the UIL in North Mayo, was arrested on a charge of illegal assembly under the Crimes Act. Prior to his arrest, according to the *Connaught Telegraph*, 'Mr Conor O'Kelly was followed and dogged all day in a most insulting and irritating manner'.[24] His arrest and sentencing to two months in prison in a Crimes Court where Alan Bell was one of the two magistrates was discussed in the House of Commons and received extensive newspaper coverage. Bell remained in Mayo until his move to Portadown in 1915.

Bell's transfer to Dublin in late 1919 was his first appointment in the capital. Lord French needed his extensive experience in dealing with political crime.

9. Counter-state progress

Bank building

At 8.30pm on Wednesday 7 January, the same day that General Boyd received instructions to prepare his arrest list, the directors of the National Land Bank held their first general meeting at 5 Harcourt Terrace, the home of Lionel Smith-Gordon, who had still not returned from his fact-finding mission to Switzerland and Italy.[1]

Under the guidance of Robert Barton and the direction of Edward Stephens, the banking start-up was making good progress towards opening. Stephens informed the directors that a search for suitable premises for the bank was under way, that they had 'gone carefully' into the exact procedures to be followed in making loans for the purchase of land and that the necessary forms for carrying out the transactions had been drawn up.[2]

Four establishment figures had been chosen as directors to add credibility to the new financial institution in the eyes of the public: Sir Henry Grattan-Bellew, a descendant of Henry Grattan; Erskine Childers, a well-known novelist; Edward Stephens, a barrister and nephew of Synge; and James MacNeill, chairman of Dublin County Council and a brother of Eoin MacNeill TD. MacNeill was the only director from a working-class Catholic background. He would later become governor-general of the Free State. Not everyone, however, agreed with the choice of directors. Patrick Moylett was 'very annoyed' when he learned their names. 'Every bank in Ireland from the date they were founded in 1824 or 1825 was, and is, entirely a British bank, with a British, Non-Catholic directorship,' he railed. '... I could not see why a country which was 90% Catholic should have 90% Protestants in the bank.'[3]

On the same evening the following week, the directors were informed that No. 68 Lower Leeson Street had been acquired by the bank. Michael Collins had sent a cheque for £850 to Robert Barton to cover the cost of the premises.[4] The directors discussed staffing arrangements, the equipment required (typewriters, stationery, books and forms) and the building fit-out (strongroom, safe, telephone system).[5] A subcommittee was formed to perform weekly cash checks. The share register was opened and the prospectus and promotional circulars were discussed.

Lionel Smith-Gordon, who had returned from his overseas travel the day before, presented his report to the board. The trip had been plagued with setbacks: a large number of public holidays in Italy at the time, unusually bad weather and a false report of the death of Horace Plunkett.

Switzerland and Italy offered few lessons for Ireland. Swiss small farmers usually owned their own land; Italian farmers rarely owned the land that they farmed but they did not aspire to ownership. In Italy, Smith-Gordon saw that there had been some success with a collective farming model. An expensive and unsuccessful collective farming experiment was carried out under his recommendation. Unlike in Ireland, however, Italian farmers had an established culture of communal rights of cultivation and profit-sharing. Michael Collins later informed the Dáil that £6,675 was a 'special amount' put aside for an experimental operation on one farm. He added rather pointedly that 'The Director of Agriculture will, *no doubt*, have something to say on this subject'.

On 21 January the directors discussed new banking arrangements with the IAWS, an offer of a £20,000 deposit and loans to fishery co-operatives. It was agreed to change the registered office to 68 Leeson Street.

The directors were anxious about the large cash balance held by the bank pending the issue of loans for land purchases. Although investment by the Dáil was cloaked using a dummy corporation, 'the fear existed that the monies might be identified by the British authorities as belonging to Dáil Éireann and confiscated'.[6] After several weeks of looking at alternative proposals, the directors settled on placing the money on deposit in co-operative societies in England.[7]

The IAWS, which acted as agent for the banking departments of these societies, facilitated the transfer of the funds to twenty co-operative banks, mainly in the north of England.[8] The directors believed that the money was out of reach of Dublin Castle, because the British authorities would hesitate to antagonise the powerful English co-operative movement. The directors also liked the solution because the interest rates paid on co-operative society deposits were higher than the corresponding rates in the commercial banks.[9]

Barton continued to meet Michael Collins almost every evening in Cullenswood House in Ranelagh, where Collins had an office and Richard Mulcahy, chief of staff, had his home.[10]

Collins personally recruited the caretaker of the bank. He moved Seán McCluskey and his family from 76 Harcourt Street to 68 Leeson Street. He needed a trusted person on the ground.

Local election victory

Meanwhile, on 15 January, the eagerly anticipated municipal elections, the first since 1914, had taken place. The poll offered the first opportunity to gauge the support for Sinn Féin—now a prohibited organisation throughout Ireland—since the landslide win in the general election thirteen months previously. The Labour party, which had stood aside in the general election to ensure a strong republican victory, fielded its own candidates.

Dublin Castle introduced proportional representation for the first time, believing that it would reduce the Sinn Féin/Labour seat count on councils and corporations. In 1918 Sinn Féin had won 70% of the seats with less than 50% of the vote in the general election.

National political issues took precedence over local ones during the campaign, though it was a non-political issue that dominated doorstep discussions in the cities. An ongoing shortage of coal, caused by poor distribution infrastructure between the mines and the ports and not helped by the motor permit strike when the coal did reach Ireland, caused a fuel famine.[11] Law and order issues were less of a concern in Dublin than in the rest of the country. Speculation that Joseph Byrne, the Catholic inspector-general of the RIC, was about to be dismissed was a boon to Sinn Féin.

After the votes were counted, Sinn Féin and Labour had won 31% and 22% respectively of the 1,816 seats, and their combined seat total gave them control of nine of the eleven corporations, including Derry. Wexford Corporation had a Labour majority and Belfast remained under unionist control. Cork and Limerick corporations immediately pledged allegiance to Dáil Éireann, and Dublin followed on 3 May.

In Dublin Sinn Féin had captured 45% of first-preference votes. Labour had polled 12% and nationalist candidates 14.5%.[12] Unionists, who polled 27% nationally (securing 20% of the seats), secured only 1% of the vote in Dublin, after many candidates and voters defected to the Municipal Reform Association (MRA), set up to tap into middle-class concerns across the political divide. The MRA and Independents secured 24% of the first preferences in Dublin.

Alderman Tom Kelly, interned and in poor health, topped the poll in his constituency and was unanimously elected lord mayor of Dublin.[13] When Dr McWalter, a nationalist elected as an MRA member of the corporation, called Sinn Féin the most infamous tyranny from which Ireland ever suffered, laughter erupted in the chamber. Nevertheless, Dr McWalter continued: 'Still, if a man be an honest man and a good corporator, I think that the fact that he is a Sinn Féiner should not deprive him of the honour of being Lord Mayor of Dublin'.[14] The sole unionist on the corporation also voted for Tom Kelly.

Larry O'Neill, the outgoing mayor, had nominated Alderman Kelly for the position and the nomination was seconded by William O'Brien, leader of the Labour party. Larry O'Neill put on record the events surrounding the Alderman's arrest:

> 'His home was surrounded in the early hours of a winter's morning, without any summons, without any warrant, taken from his family, guarded by military with fixed bayonets, thrown into a military wagon, placed on board a warship at Kingstown, landed at Holyhead, railed to a distant part of England, detained by the authorities without charge, without any trial, treated worse than the most abominable criminal, and left lingering, as he is a delicate man, in an English jail perhaps to die.'[15]

In Waterford Dr Vincent White was elected mayor by 24 votes to four, a stunning victory for Sinn Féin in the 'Redmondite' city. In 1918 Dr White had lost a by-election and general election to Captain William Redmond, son of the deceased John Redmond. Patrick O'Mahony, the provincial organiser of the Dáil Loan in Munster, was particularly satisfied with Dr White's victory.[16]

O'Mahony had provided security for Sinn Féin at the by-election in March 1918. Captain Redmond had the support of a powerful local group called the Ballybricken Pig Buyers Association, which organised and controlled the sale of pigs to the bacon factories in Waterford.[17] 'We were being sniped at from Thomas's Hall,' O'Mahony recalled, 'principally by shot-gun pellets which wounded some of our men.' He drafted extra Volunteers into the city. 'I led an assault on this place, took it, and held it during the period of the Election.' Dr White had to be hospitalised after being attacked on his way to the polling station. Following Captain Redmond's victory in the general election, members of the Ballybricken Pig Buyers Association paraded from the courthouse to their base in Ballybricken and burned an effigy of Dr White. Just over a year later, Sinn Féin supporters raised the tricolour over Waterford Town Hall.

The 1920 municipal elections were a much calmer affair across the country. The only serious incident reported was in Cork on polling day, when one man had his forearm broken by a revolver bullet and another was stabbed in the thigh during a collision between Sinn Féin supporters and demobbed soldiers.[18] Sinn Féin complained that policemen tore down election posters, that promotional literature was held up in the Post Office and that an election telegram from Éamon de Valera in America was not transmitted until after the poll.[19] The only reported arrests were those of James Hoey, the New Ireland agent and candidate in Bray, and Fred J. Allan, an election organiser in Dublin.

At all costs

The election had stretched the organisational capacity of the republican movement to the limit, and at the Loan campaign's expense. On 17 January the Department of Finance issued a circular, signed by Michael Collins, announcing an extension of the closing date for Loan subscriptions to 1 May, owing to time spent on voter registration and election campaigning.[20]

Voter registration was a complicated process. As early as November, the RIC reported that Sinn Féin activities, 'so far as they came openly under notice, were mainly devoted to registration of voters in the revision courts, and to promoting the Republican or Dáil Éireann Loan'.[21]

The extension of the closing date, however, was clearly not due only to time spent on voter registration and election campaigning. There was another reason why only £30,000 had been subscribed to the Loan by mid-December, necessitating the issue of the circular in mid-January.[22] Although Collins remained confident of reaching his target of £250,000—progress had been slow but sure and 'in the neighbourhood of £100,000' had been promised—he had written to de Valera in December that 'the main enemy objective is directed to secure the failure of this enterprise'.[23] Dublin Castle was succeeding in its attempt to suppress the Loan. Collins added that 'Advertising is impossible practically, meetings are impossible practically, movements of prominent Sinn Féiners are greatly interfered with'.[24] Arrests, restrictions on road and rail transport, and the loss of most of the head office staff were taking a toll. Collins wrote that 'The arrests at the Dáil Offices were a very serious handicap from a routine point of view'.

In the New Year, Collins struggled to convey to de Valera the intensity of Dublin Castle's campaign: '[You] can scarcely conceive the limits to which the English have carried their repressions and suppressions against this Loan … and with a renewed determination and savagery'.[25] He believed that the enemy must 'at all costs prevent our getting the necessary funds'.

'His military and armed police smashed up meetings called to support the Loan. They suppressed newspapers, and removed their machinery, if mention were made of the Loan. Prospectuses and literature were seized in the Post Office where discovered. Everywhere all through the country our workers were held up at the point of the bayonet and searched, in some cases three and four times in one day. Official action denied us the use of motor cars, searches and hold-ups denied us the advantages of even horse-vehicles and bicycles. Our people, in distributing leaflets and prospectuses, had to use the by-ways, and not infrequently had to cross country to avoid the enemy forces. Men were put in jail for requesting applications, and men were put in jail for making applications. People found in possession of documents relating to the Loan were put in jail, and the entire male Head Office Staff was put in jail as an "Illegal Assembly". The Head Office itself was closed by military force.'

Across the country it was the Loan organisers and workers who were the victims of oppressive measures. Joe McGinley, arrested in December for promoting the Loan, was manacled and surrounded by at least half a dozen RIC constables—with batons ready to draw—during his trial.[26] He was given a five-month prison sentence. TDs making fund-raising tours of their constituencies had to be given armed escorts when holding secret Loan meetings.[27]

Owing to the increased suppression measures employed by Dublin Castle, the distribution of marketing material and the collection of subscriptions 'had to be done quietly, unassumingly, and with much labour'. Collins complained to de Valera that 'the combination does not appear to appeal to several people'. The demand for hard work featured in almost all of Collins's correspondence regarding the Loan. Not every Loan committee was delivering. He grumbled to Terence MacSwiney, one of the best organisers, that 'if you saw some of the particulars we were supplied with they would simply drive you mad'.

Terence MacSwiney's work ethic was not in doubt. In December Collins told him that it was 'very refreshing to have such a satisfactory account from you … It shows what work and energy will do.'[28] Although they were never great friends, MacSwiney's work ethic ensured Collins's respect. MacSwiney was more sombre, intellectual and romantic than Collins, but he had also worked for sixteen years in a warehousing and distribution business, starting as a fifteen-year-old entry-level clerk.[29]

MacSwiney had a huge capacity for work and was known for demanding rigorous control of finances in his activities. Working closely with Seán Nolan, MacSwiney built a robust Loan organisation structure in his constituency, creating five 'sub-executive' areas. He told Collins that 'we are laying our lines so well that if anything happens to the two of us the work will go on successfully'.[30]

This level of planning and organisation did not exist in every constituency. If the Loan was to reach its target, an improved performance was required across the country. When setting the revised closing date, Collins wrote that no later date can be fixed and that the Dáil Cabinet expected 'a very strenuous effort' on the part of all workers in order to make the Loan a success.[31]

American newspapers

On the same day that Collins issued the circular, Éamon de Valera launched the American Loan in New York. As part of the marketing campaign, de Valera was given the freedom of the city by Mayor Hylan.[32] According to Reuters, it was announced at an event in the Lexington Opera House that $2.5 million (£625,000) had been subscribed in New York alone.[33] This was a vastly inflated amount leaked to the correspondent for propaganda purposes. Reuters noted the presence of James O'Mara, 'a member of the Irish Parliament', and another Sinn Féin leader, adding 'How they reached New York is not known'.[34] James O'Mara had made the crossing as a stowaway on a transatlantic liner.

Éamon de Valera embarked on a nationwide promotion tour backed by an extensive press advertising and postering campaign. Under the efficient management of James O'Mara, he attended mass meetings attracting thousands of supporters. Wide newspaper coverage of the events ensured a continuous news cycle for the American Loan. The support of the Catholic Church was pivotal to the funding campaign. The *Daily Mail* reported that the sale of 'Irish bonds' in churches was 'almost universal now throughout the States'.[35]

A major propaganda coup was scored when Dr Harty, archbishop of Cashel, sent a letter and a cheque for £50 to de Valera, 'the trusted representative of the Irish people'. Dr Harty released his letter to the Irish media.[36]

> 'Ireland is in a state of political and industrial bondage. Our Press is muzzled, our fairs and markets are stopped, our exhibitions of industries are prohibited, our national games are barred, our literary and musical festivals are proclaimed; even princes of the Church are asked to guarantee that they are not criminals before they are allowed to use their motor cars ... our elected representatives are not allowed to meet in our Irish Parliament, and some of them have been deported in British gunboats.'

The launch of the American Loan presented a unique challenge to the censorship policy in Ireland. In the general public's eyes, there was only one Dáil Loan. Every newspaper report on the success of the American campaign in the Irish papers was an advertisement for the Loan in Ireland. Dublin Castle had another censorship problem: what to do with American newspapers, carrying advertisements for the American Loan, arriving into Dublin every morning for distribution throughout the country. Unable to order the suppression of American newspapers, the Irish executive seized them at the General Post Office, carried them to Dublin Castle, cut the wrappers and searched the contents before releasing them for distribution.[37]

Commission prohibited

With the election out of the way, the Dáil government could again focus on building up the civil administration and implementing the constructive programme. A three-day open hearing of the Commission of Inquiry into the Resources and Industries of Ireland, headed by Darrell Figgis, was publicly announced to take place in Cork on 21 January. The first day of the hearings was scheduled to begin at 11am in the City Hall.

Dublin Castle had tolerated the existence of the commission. Suppression of the body, which had neither military nor political attributes, presented a challenge for the Irish executive. The first public session of the commission had been held at the City Hall in Dublin on 2 December 1919. Experts from different sectors of the food industry, including David Houston, a consultant on agricultural bacteriology, appeared at the hearing, held over six days. The published minutes for the first three days alone came to almost 200 pages.

That first hearing took place at a particularly sensitive time, just three days after the shooting of the widely respected Detective Barton. And being held in the City Hall, 100 metres from Dublin Castle, the hearing was particularly aggravating to the authorities. Dublin Castle censored its proceedings. The *Daily News* called the censorship action 'inconceivable stupidity', adding that it strengthened the conviction of Sinn Féiners that the object of the authorities was 'to prevent … the development of Irish industrial resources'.[38]

A commission delegation, including John O'Neill and Darrell Figgis, had been prohibited from addressing Monaghan County Council in

November. Two unionist members of the council wrote a joint letter to a local paper in protest at an agenda item to receive a deputation from the 'Sinn Féin Commission of Inquiry'.[39] In the House of Commons, the attorney general for Ireland justified the decision to block the delegation on the grounds that the commission was 'appointed by Dáil Éireann, the so-called Parliament of Ireland ... [which] was suppressed by Proclamation under the Criminal Law and Procedure Act'.[40]

Dublin Castle, nevertheless, had permitted the first public hearing to go ahead in Dublin. Holding a public hearing in Cork, however, in view of the increased raids and arrests in the New Year and less than three weeks after the attacks on five police barracks in the county, was a provocative move. Darrell Figgis, secretary of the commission, was never likely to cancel the event. Standing down was not in his nature, and suppression of the meeting would provide substantial propaganda benefits.

The 37-year-old Figgis was a controversial figure in the republican movement, tolerated by few and disliked by many. A prolific writer and journalist, he was well read in English and French literature. His red hair, red pointed beard, green eyes—usually complemented by a ginger tweed lounge suit and a moss green velour hat—and commanding manner gave him a striking appearance.[41]

An inner confidence frequently extended to arrogance. 'I knew him well, and, despite his failings and oddities, almost because of them perhaps, I liked him,' recalled Kevin O'Sheil. 'I have known many egotists in my time, but never a man with such an immense, overwhelming, unshakeable belief in himself and in his intellectual and physical prowess.'[42] Although intellectually and physically vain, he was not without courage in both areas. One of those who tolerated Figgis was Arthur Griffith, which explains his appointment to the commission.

On the morning of the hearing, Darrell Figgis and Liam de Roiste TD arrived early at City Hall. The main entrance on Burgh Quay was blocked by a large party of policemen, who prevented them from entering the building. Figgis was not deterred so easily. He arranged for the commission members to enter the building through a side entrance. The meeting started on time. It took the police an hour to realise that they had been tricked. The head constable and his men entered the building, located the room and ejected everyone onto Burgh Quay.

Figgis waited outside the front of City Hall for the arrival of the lord mayor of Cork, who was escorting a Labour Party delegation from England on a fact-finding tour of Ireland. On their arrival, Figgis made a number of attempts to enter City Hall but was pushed back by the police.[43] The Labour delegation issued an official statement later: 'Why a body of men should be harassed in pursuing such an inquiry is a thing the [delegation] ... cannot understand, unless it be part of a deliberate policy calculated to hinder development of Irish Industries'.[44]

Denied access to City Hall, the hearings were held in secret over three days in the School of Art, the Chamber of Commerce and other locations throughout the city.[45]

10. One month to get Collins

Ashtown investigation

Alan Bell was making progress in his Crimes Act or 'Star Chamber' inquiry into the ambush on Lord French in Ashtown, where Martin Savage had been shot dead and Dan Breen wounded in the leg. Bell had the full resources of the DMP available to him, and he worked closely with the new assistant commissioner, Redmond, to whom he forwarded specific questions and requests. Bell wrote to Lord French that through Redmond he could make inquiries that he 'should not care to entrust to the G Division'.[1]

The squad left a long trail of evidence after the attack because they could not use cars to get to Ashtown. The unit, supplemented by Dan Breen and others, cycled to the ambush point. The motor permit regulation had the desired effect of limiting the use of cars in 'outrages'. No squad member could apply at a police station for a permit that required a name and photograph. With the Drivers Union on strike, almost no cars were on the road, and even driving a commandeered vehicle exposed the squad to attention from the police.

The evidence path commenced with the body of Martin Savage. Without motor transport, Michael McDonnell made the difficult decision to leave his body in Ashtown. When one of the bicycles broke down on the way back from the ambush, they commandeered another bicycle from a man named Michael Donoghue, promising to return it to a designated location in the city that evening. And Dan Breen's wounded leg left a blood trail, despite his best efforts to stop the flow by tying a bootlace round the end of his trousers.

The DMP swiftly identified the body of Martin Savage from a bank lodgement slip in his pocket and confirmed his movements prior to the ambush. Savage had left 137 North Strand Road, where he was employed as a grocer's assistant, to lodge money for his employer in the National Bank on College Green. Inspector McFeely interviewed bank officials at the branch. In a typed report dated 15 January, McFeely noted that Savage had lodged money at 11.30am on the morning of the ambush. Employees of the bank were unable to confirm whether any other person was with him at the time.[2] McFeely sent the report to Redmond, who forwarded it to Alan Bell.

On 9 January Bell had sent a memo to Redmond requesting that a summons be served on Michael Donoghue, whose bicycle had been found at the corner of Talbot Street and Gardiner Street. On the following day, Bell sent another request to Redmond for the names and addresses of any persons who had seen the bicycle being dropped. 'Very careful inquiry has been made into this,' Redmond replied the same day, 'but so far, no person can be found who saw ... who left the bicycle.' Meanwhile, a boy named Henry Leane had been located who could possibly identify the wounded Dan Breen. Bell reported to Lord French: 'The boy Henry Leane has since seen the man who passed him on a bicycle supported by another man ... where the boy saw signs of blood on the track'.[3]

So close

Meanwhile, Redmond was settling into his temporary accommodation in the Standard Hotel on Harcourt Street while waiting for living quarters in Dublin Castle. His wife remained in Belfast and their two daughters were returning to school in England after the Christmas holidays.[4] Every morning and evening he made the fifteen-minute walk between the Standard Hotel and Dublin Castle. He chose not to have an escort. Newly arrived in Dublin and dressed more like a stockbroker than a policeman, he could walk in Dublin in relative safety.[5] He took one precaution, however, in a city where four detectives had been shot: he wore a bulletproof steel vest.[6]

Immediately upon his arrival, Redmond called a meeting of the G Division staff. Known for his own energy and efficiency, he warned those present that they had one month to get Michael Collins and those responsible for the shootings or else he would order them to resign.[7] In

December the British had identified Collins for the first time as the key person in the republican movement while de Valera was in America, and as the man responsible for ordering the shooting of detectives. The late recognition of Collins's importance was not confined to the British. Even Joe Slattery, a member of the squad, did not know that Collins was the 'heart of things' until he received orders to shoot Detective Hoey in September.[8]

It was through Basil Thomson, head of the Directorate of Intelligence in London, that the true nature of Collins's role had been uncovered. On the day of the Ashtown attack, Basil Thomson wrote to Lord French informing him of 'definite and trustworthy information that Michael Collins is directing the murders of Policemen; that he has attained such a position that his friends say the Police dare not touch him, and that if any attempt was made to arrest him it would precipitate a Rising in Ireland'.[9]

Redmond managed to convince the G Division detectives that Collins was not untouchable. His warning to the detectives at their first meeting and the arrival of his own men from Belfast reinvigorated the detective division.[10] 'After that there were constant holds-up by detectives in the city,' recalled Paddy O'Daly, 'some of them very harmless, but some of the detectives became very active.'[11]

For Redmond, the key to getting Collins was John Charles Byrnes, a former British soldier who had been recruited into British Intelligence by Basil Thomson. Operating as John Jameson, he had arrived in Dublin on 6 December with a letter of introduction to Michael Collins from Art O'Brien, the Dáil envoy in London. Byrnes had convinced O'Brien of his supposed anti-establishment credentials, his willingness to provide arms to the IRA and his ability to sow discontent among British Army personnel in Ireland.

Byrnes travelled to Dublin posing as an employee of Keith Prowse, a theatre ticket broker, convincing Art O'Brien that this position gave him ready access to army barracks.[12] (Keith Prowse still organises group travel packages to cultural and sporting events.) Two days after arriving, Byrnes was introduced to Michael Collins. According to Basil Thomson, Byrnes 'saw a man described by his lieutenant as the greatest man Ireland has ever produced, far greater than De Valera'.[13]

Redmond and Byrnes worked on a plan to entrap Michael Collins.[14] On 16 January Byrnes had arranged a lunchtime meeting with Collins at Batt O'Connor's home on Brendan Road. Redmond decided to have him arrested at that meeting and personally organised the raiding party.

On the morning of the raid, Redmond posted a plain-clothes detective on the corner of Morehampton Road and Brendan Road. Redmond himself was in a military lorry with the raiding party on Waterloo Road, about 700 metres away. After the meeting, Byrnes left the house accompanied by Liam Tobin. Collins remained inside. Byrnes and Tobin headed towards the tram to return to the city centre.

When the military lorry came speeding up Morehampton Road, the plain-clothes detective unexpectedly signalled the driver to stop. In the mistaken belief that it was Collins rather than Tobin who had left the house with Byrnes, he told Redmond to abort the raid. Redmond ordered the lorry to turn around.

Meanwhile, Byrnes and Tobin had arrived at the tram stop and climbed to the top deck of the next tramcar. They had both seen the man leave the top of Brendan Road; Tobin had no reason to be suspicious, while to Byrnes it signified that the raid was about to take place. At the next tram stop, Tobin saw the same man speaking to a police officer and noticed soldiers jumping into lorries. The writer Frank O'Connor, Collins's biographer, described the reaction of Byrnes and Tobin as they watched events from the Waterloo Road tram stop:

> 'Tobin took fright. "If they turn to the left it'll be Mick they're after," he said to Jameson. From the top of the tram they looked back eagerly. The convoy of soldiers and police wheeled to the right! Jameson's thoughts on this occasion must have been such as lie too deep for tears. One can only guess at his bewilderment and consternation when he saw his great chance [of getting Collins] thrown away.'[15]

Redmond must have been white-hot with rage when he learned of the detective's mistake. He arranged another raid on the same location for the following day. Byrnes may have told him that Collins lunched there on a daily basis. Redmond did not know it but the raid was destined to fail. James MacNamara, a detective in the G Division, got word to Collins of the impending raid.

Redmond again led the raiding party. Mrs O'Connor, home alone with the children at 1 Brendan Road, opened the door. Frank O'Connor described the scene:[16]

> 'She found herself faced by a drawn revolver. Redmond brushed in past her and, levelling his gun, flung open the dining-room door. His disappointment was bitter when he saw a clear table covered with a strip of green baize—not a sign of lunch, much less of Collins. Unable to believe his eyes, he rushed upstairs, and when he came down his chagrin and rage were visible to all. His eye lit upon a picture of a group of Dáil delegates; he wished to take it; she begged him not to, telling him he could get a small reproduction for a copper. Decently enough, he withdrew and said he would not trouble her again.'

Redmond, frustrated and humiliated, returned to the house that evening to listen at a window in the hope of overhearing something.[17] Ironically, he brought Detective MacNamara with him.

Redmond learned nothing new that evening but he was not giving up on capturing Collins after coming so close. He organised a raid on Cullenswood House, where Collins had a basement office and Richard Mulcahy and his wife lived in a top-floor flat. He must have had good information, perhaps provided by Byrnes. The raid was set for 20 January. If successful, he would capture Collins within one month of his arrival in Dublin, as planned. Collins, having again been forewarned about the raid, is reported to have said, 'If we don't get that man he'll get us, and soon'.[18]

End of the road

On Wednesday 21 January, around 6.30pm, Assistant Commissioner William Charles Forbes Redmond was fatally shot as he approached the Standard Hotel on Harcourt Street. Dressed in civilian clothing, he had a walking stick in his left hand while his right hand was clasped round an automatic pistol in his overcoat pocket.[19] He did not have time to draw the weapon.

GHQ Intelligence and the squad prepared and carried out the assassination with a new attention to detail and precision. The intelligence unit had even warned Collins not to trust Byrnes but, disregarding their advice, he had gone ahead with the near-calamitous meeting in Batt O'Connor's house.

Having learned of Redmond's arrival in Dublin from an agent in Belfast, GHQ Intelligence had started to build a file on him immediately, but they had no description of Redmond. As no one in Dublin could identify him, Frank Thornton was sent to Belfast to obtain a photograph.[20] With the aid of Sergeant McCarthy from Kerry, who was stationed at the Chichester Street police barracks, Thornton stole a picture from the files in the detective inspector's office.

Once Redmond had been identified, his movements were tracked round the clock. James MacNamara had informed GHQ Intelligence that Redmond was staying in the Standard Hotel. Tom Cullen was sent to stay as a guest in the hotel to record Redmond's movements,[21] monitoring his time of leaving and returning to the hotel and his evening and night-time activity.

On the evening of his death, Redmond left Dublin Castle around 6pm. Five separate teams of the squad were positioned along his route to the Standard Hotel. It had become a matter of urgency to remove him. Michael McDonnell was in charge of the operation. On a busy Wednesday evening in Dublin, and even with five assassination teams in place, it was difficult to isolate Redmond among the crowds.[22]

Redmond evaded the first squad unit, positioned outside the gates of Dublin Castle. He walked by the second unit at the corner of Dame Street and South Great George's Street. The third and fourth teams were waiting at either end of Grafton Street but none of them had the opportunity to take a shot. Paddy O'Daly was part of the last three-man unit, positioned at the beginning of Harcourt Street, less than 100 metres from the Standard Hotel. When he had complained about being part of the last team, expecting the job to have been completed before Redmond got that far, Michael Collins had told him that 'the goal-man often gets as much of the ball as any of the team'.[23] O'Daly shot Redmond in the head. Although O'Daly did not know it, Redmond was not wearing his vest that evening.

Redmond had very nearly succeeded in capturing Collins, which would have been a massive propaganda victory for Dublin Castle and a devastating—possibly even fatal—blow to the national government.

11. Stalled

Redmond's death was a crushing blow to Lord French. The revitalisation of G Division was an integral part of his plan to defeat Sinn Féin. Two days after the shooting, he was interviewed by a French journalist. He blamed the troubled situation in Ireland on the youthful post-war demographics of the country. 'The principal cause of the trouble,' he told the French newspaper, 'is that for five years emigration has practically stopped. In this country there are from one hundred thousand to two hundred thousand young men from eighteen to twenty five years of age who in normal times would have emigrated.'[1] In addition, with no conscription in Ireland, fewer of those young men had been used as cannon fodder for generals like Lord French during the war.

Lord French's problem was not only an excess of young men in the country. He had also gravely underestimated the determination, passion and intelligence of all the men and women of whom his enemy consisted. Later he would admit that 'we are up against a powerful conspiracy—something more than the "scallywags" we thought'.[2]

In the same week that Redmond was shot, Charlotte Despard, Lord French's sister, attended a sold-out event organised by the Irish Self-Determination League at the Royal Albert Hall in London. Despard, a well-known socialist, suffragette and Sinn Féin supporter, was seated next to Eva Gore Booth, sister of Countess Markievicz. A collection for the Dáil Loan was handed around, and press reports noted that Despard 'watched this distribution with the most evident satisfaction'.[3]

Round-up

Lord French hoped for better success from the military. On 26 January, General Boyd received final instructions from GHQ for the mass round-up of Sinn Féin and IRA leaders. Separate instructions were sent to the military commanders in the 5th Division (midlands and west of Ireland) and the 6th Division (south of Ireland). Five days later, in a massive operation commencing from early morning on 31 January, raiding parties left their barracks in darkness. Soldiers in full equipment, under the direction of local police, raided homes across the country, mainly between 3am and 5am.

The *Saturday Herald* was the first newspaper to cover the story: 'Big Round Up, Military and Police Make Many Arrests, EARLY MORNING RAIDS, Sinn Féin MP Amongst Those Taken in Dublin'. Dublin Castle spun the success of the raids by issuing an official list of the names of 58 people detained as being members of illegal organisations, including many 'known to be members of the so-called Irish Republican Army'. No MP or TD was listed among the names.[4] It was later established that Robert Barton had been recaptured by accident during the raids, almost a year after his daring escape from Mountjoy.

Despite the capture of Barton—a huge loss to the Dáil government— the raids were a spectacular intelligence failure. As more information filtered out to the media, it became apparent that none of the Sinn Féin leaders were sleeping in their homes that night. Dublin Castle and the military were made to look foolish, while the estimation of their opponents was rising: '… the result [of the raids] is that once more the prestige of the Government has had a fall,' wrote the editor of the *Irish Independent*, 'while everyone is speaking of the ability of the Sinn Féin intelligence staff'.[5]

Dublin Castle was forced to deny that the raids were connected with the election results when it became known that two Sinn Féin members of Dublin Corporation had been detained. The most embarrassing arrest was that of a William Tobin who was mistaken for Liam Tobin, deputy director of GHQ Intelligence. The press knowingly alluded to this case of mistaken identity without openly identifying Liam Tobin's intelligence role.[6]

The military had underestimated the intelligence paralysis within the police forces.[7] Local RIC men could give little reliable information beyond a statement that so-and-so was 'a bad boy' or 'a bad article'.[8] Target lists were completely out of date and had to be taken over by military intelligence officers, who were scarce on the ground. Military intelligence had to take sole responsibility for determining the 'IRA status of the person it was proposed to arrest'.[9]

On the eve of the raids, Robert Barton had attended a Cabinet meeting in the house of Mrs McGarry. He noticed Michael Collins leaving the room for a few minutes when handed a note by Joe O'Reilly. When the meeting finished, Collins informed the Cabinet that a round-up was planned. Mrs Ceannt's house, where Barton was staying, was not on the list.[10] On Collins's instructions, Barton went to the homes of four TDs, including his neighbour Richard Mulcahy in Cullenswood House, to warn them not to sleep at home.

Barton's capture was accidental, random and just plain bad luck. That night, the military went to capture Richard Mulcahy at 4 Oakley Road, the official address of Cullenswood House, but there was no number on the door. They searched up and down the road looking for No. 4. Mrs Ceannt lived at 44 Oakley Road, and one of the door numbers had fallen on the ground. Mistaking the house for No. 4, it was raided and Barton was taken.

Michael Collins felt Barton's absence profoundly. 'Since last I wrote you the worst thing that has happened is the arrest of Barton,' he wrote disconsolately to de Valera. 'He is an irreparable loss to us.'[11] They had become great friends over the previous year; both were on the run, both were setting up new enterprises and they were meeting almost every evening. Most of all, it was the loss of a confidant for Collins: 'I am smarting under a feeling of great personal sorrow, as we had been in such close association on pretty well all things during the past difficult year'.[12]

Robert Barton was tried by court martial in Dublin on 12 February at Ship Street. Collins organised a rescue while Barton was being transferred back to Mountjoy prison, but this time his information source was not good, as the military lorry intercepted was not carrying him.[13] Barton was deported to Portland Prison and remained confined until shortly before the truce.[14] He was bitterly disappointed at being taken. 'I had barely got the Land Bank legislation through the Dáil, premises taken, staff appointed and its programme under way.'[15]

Staines targeted

On the day after Barton's court martial, Michael Staines, treasurer of New Ireland, had a lucky escape from a military raid on his family home at 63 Murtagh Road, near the Phoenix Park, where he lived with his father, sister and younger brother. The military arrived in lorries about 5am, took covering positions and surrounded the house. The noise of the lorries had woken Staines, however, and the period taken to set up the security perimeter gave him sufficient time to make a getaway. The soldiers made an intensive search of the house and they did not leave empty-handed. Seventeen-year-old James Staines was arrested, taken away in a military lorry and kept in solitary confinement for five days in Mountjoy.[16] A friend of Michael Staines, interviewed later that day by the *Freeman's Journal*, said that he was 'very indignant' at the arrest of his younger brother. The teenager was given a one-month prison sentence for possessing 'seditious documents'.[17]

Cleaning agents

Three undercover British agents were operating on the ground in Dublin in early February 1920. Within six weeks all three were dead. Byrnes, after a brief interlude in London following the shooting of Redmond, surprisingly returned to Dublin. In an ironic twist, it was Redmond who had sealed his fate.

In a careless moment, when dressing down members of G Division in frustration at their failure to get Collins, Redmond let slip information that inadvertently pointed to Byrnes as an agent. David Neligan was at the meeting with Redmond. 'It was extraordinary, he said, that we, who knew Dublin so well, could not catch Michael Collins.' Redmond contrasted their failure with 'a man who had only just arrived from England [who] had managed to meet him more than once'.[18] James MacNamara reported the comments to Collins. The timing matched Byrnes's arrival in Dublin.[19]

GHQ Intelligence already had their doubts about Byrnes. Tom Cullen had distrusted him from their first meeting.[20] It was decided to lay traps for Byrnes and he fell into the very first one.[21] 'Suffice to say that following other incidents which happened,' according to Frank Thornton, 'it was finally decided that Jameson was a spy and as such would have to be shot.'[22] Jack Byrnes, alias John Jameson, was shot on 2 March 1920.

Walter Long, First Lord of the Admiralty, told the Cabinet in London that Byrnes was 'the best secret service man we had',[23] although, according to Michael T. Foy, this may have had less to do with Byrnes's ability than with Long's desire to emphasise the seriousness of the situation in Ireland.

Meanwhile, a second agent had presented another serious threat to Collins. Timothy Quinlisk was handsome, charismatic and confident. When he returned to Ireland after the war, he was also poor. The 23-year-old had fought with the British Army, and after being taken prisoner by the Germans he had been recruited into the Irish Brigade by Roger Casement. Collins, thinking that he could make use of Quinlisk, who spoke German and French, initially funded him on his return to Ireland.

Instead of using his natural advantages to build a career, Quinlisk used them to avoid work. Collins had found him a job in New Ireland Assurance, but that did not last long.[24] 'He was always immaculately dressed,' according to one acquaintance, 'and one would have said that with his good looks, his self-assurance and general bonhomie he would have got anywhere. He liked to give the impression that he was in on all of Mick Collins's secrets.'[25]

Quinlisk soon became a nuisance to Collins, who cut his funding. The discarded Quinlisk wanted revenge. 'The scoundrel Michael Collins has treated me scurvily,' he wrote to Dublin Castle, offering himself as an informer, 'and I now am going to wash my hands of the whole business.'[26]

GHQ Intelligence, inevitably, found out about Quinlisk's contact with the Castle. When exposed, he claimed that he was operating as a double agent but this explanation failed to dispel distrust. A trap was laid by feeding him false information that Collins was going to be in Cork on a certain day. Soon after, Liam Archer, working in the telegraph section of the Post Office, deciphered a message from the inspector general of the RIC to the county inspector in Cork. The message, probably passed on by Eilis Ryan, said that Collins would be in a hotel the following night and that he 'would probably be armed, was dangerous, and should be captured dead or alive'.

Quinlisk went to Cork and ingratiated himself with a senior Volunteer officer. He told the suspicious officer that he was from GHQ and had a special message for Michael Collins, which could only be delivered personally.[27] The Cork Volunteers set their own trap. Quinlisk failed the test and was shot in a field on 18 February.

Sergeant Fergus Bryan Molloy of British Military Intelligence had arrived in Dublin with a letter of introduction to Michael Collins. He had spent months ingratiating himself with senior Sinn Féin leaders in Mayo, where he had relatives.[28] Denied immediate access to Collins, he was met by Liam Tobin, who, taking an instant dislike to him, did not even disclose his own name.

A dangerous espionage game was played by Tobin and Molloy over a number of meetings, as each tried to establish the other's true identity and purpose. Each meeting exposed Tobin to capture by Molloy's military handlers. There was 'a certain amount of shadow boxing going on …,' according to Richard Walsh, 'and it proves Tobin's ability and courage in dealing with Molloy that he survived this episode.'[29] Molloy was finally exposed as a spy, probably by Lily Mernin, who typed intelligence reports for Major Hill-Dillon at Dublin District Command headquarters.[30] According to Frank Thornton, 'a large amount of the credit for the success of Intelligence' was due to her work.[31]

One evening, about 6pm, Vinny Byrne trailed Molloy down Grafton Street. 'We made several attempts to get him,' Byrne recalled, 'but, owing to the large number of people in the street, it was very difficult.' They followed Molloy into Wicklow Street. He had to be stopped before reaching the Central Hotel, which was occupied by the British military. Michael McDonnell and Jim Slattery shot him at the corner of South William Street. Jim Slattery remembered that people 'started shouting and made attempts to stop us getting away'.[32] It is possible that they were mistaken for undercover British agents after a week of shootings in Ireland. Like a professional assassination team should, Tom Keogh and Vinny Byrne, who were covering the shooters, drew their guns and dispersed the crowd, enabling McDonnell and Slattery to get away.

Stalled

'The murder of Mr Redmond has been a great set back to us,' Alan Bell wrote to Lord French towards the end of February.[33] Without the support of Assistant Commissioner Redmond and a functioning detective division, his Star Chamber inquiry into the ambush on Lord French had stalled.

Bell had no formal role in either the DMP or the RIC, and his only official standing was as a resident magistrate.[34] He had directed requests relating to the Ashtown inquiry through Redmond, whose men, brought in from Belfast, performed the most sensitive field investigative work. Bell did not trust G Division with these enquiries, and the detectives that Redmond had brought from Belfast had hurriedly left Dublin.[35] 'I feel very much disappointed I am not making faster or more important progress in the Ashtown case,' he wrote to Lord French. 'It is a dreadfully uphill piece of work.'[36]

Bell continued to act as a special adviser to Lord French and as his conduit to the intelligence agencies. He had operational control over some constables on the beat, maybe an allocated resource from the DMP. He wrote to French that 'in the course of their moving about my men have picked up a good deal of useful information which leads to raids'.[37] He passed this information to General Boyd. He was also in communication with Edgeworth-Johnstone, chief commissioner of the DMP, and Major Hill-Dillon in military intelligence, as well as developing a relationship with Basil Thomson, director of intelligence in London.[38]

No progress was being made on his core investigation, however. Bell was not close to arresting any member of the squad, and the investigation presented no threat to Michael Collins (unlike Redmond's work). Bell apologised to Lord French: 'I only wish Your Excellency had better reason to be satisfied with what has been done'.[39]

Bell took on an unofficial role next to the official police and military investigations into the shooting of Redmond. He began investigating a separate line of enquiry from a lead provided by Saunderson, Lord French's private secretary.[40] A man had phoned the vice-regal lodge claiming to have information. Bell was convinced that the man was telling the truth, though he would only give evidence before a court martial.[41] Although Bell was kept up to date on the progress of police and military investigations into the Redmond shooting, he played a limited operational role.

And, like the Ashtown inquiry, the investigation was going nowhere. General Boyd had information that he *hoped* could lead to the identification of the assassin.[42] Edgeworth-Johnstone and Hill-Dillon had interviewed Frank Leopold, a member of the air force stationed at Baldonnell Aerodrome, but had ruled him out as a suspect in the Redmond case (and also from any involvement in the Ashtown ambush).[43] The investigation into the Redmond shooting had also stalled.

Bell was engaged in other investigative work, but it was at a very early stage. He told Lord French that his Ashtown inquiry raised matters 'which are useful in other directions'.[44] He was in contact with a person in a prominent position in the Dublin dockyards, an area which he believed would be a 'happy hunting ground' for Sinn Féiners.[45] He was also 'on the track' of a Sinn Féin escapee from Mountjoy.[46] He even continued an investigation into Frank Leopold, despite the DMP's ruling him out as a suspect in both the Ashtown and Redmond cases. Bell believed that there were 'one or two points in the matter which require further inquiry', because his men had information that Leopold attended Sinn Féin meetings when on leave in Dublin.[47] Nevertheless, none of these leads looked like ever getting close to Michael Collins or to members of the intelligence unit or the squad.

Loan update

Meanwhile, Dáil Loan funds had continued to accumulate: '... all the attempts have signally failed,' Michael Collins wrote assuredly to de Valera on 10 February, '... to prevent the people knowing the terms of the Loan and the attempts to prevent them subscribing'.[48]

Two constituencies had provided the benchmark for others to follow. Collins used these to motivate or embarrass the rest into action. West Limerick had raised £10,000 and was 'by no means finished yet', and MacSwiney's Mid-Cork had raised £5,000, despite being 'remote and mountainous, with no town of any size'. Collins was sure that the figures 'assure final success to our efforts here'.

Three weeks later, however, Collins was much less sure of reaching the Loan target, although not on account of the suppression tactics of Dublin Castle. There had been more attempted arrests and convictions, but these were more of a nuisance than anything.

James Hayes addressed a public meeting in support of the Loan in Sligo on 2 February. According to the *Sligo Champion*, he 'had a number of narrow escapes from capture during the past few weeks'.[49] On 11 February Timothy Daly was sentenced to two months in prison at a Crimes Court in Bandon for soliciting subscriptions.[50] Daly, described by the Crown solicitor as 'a responsible businessman', was found with seven subscription receipts and copies of the prospectus in his possession. On 25 February Thomas Reilly was remanded in custody in Cavan 'on a charge of posting up Republican loan notices'.[51]

Collins's biggest problem was that not everyone was pulling their weight. 'If you saw the bloody pack down there, & their casual, indefinite, meaningless purposeless way of carrying on', he wrote to Cathal Brugha.[52] The Loan deadline was approaching. Collins had only one shot to ensure the success of the Loan, one more opportunity to motivate the Loan workers. He had to seize the moment. Failure was not an option.

On 6 March he issued a strongly worded special circular to all Sinn Féin officers and a covering letter to the members of Dáil Éireann, which also included a statement of the amounts of the Loan received by constituency. Applications totalling only £98,124 had been received at head office. This did not include monies promised or held locally pending safe passage to Dublin.[53] 'From the total amount received,' Collins wrote in the covering letter, 'you will see that a very considerable effort is still necessary in order that the enterprise may be the success it ought to be.'

Collins asked the TDs to personally address an 'urgent letter' to those recently elected to the borough and urban councils, to get their active co-operation for the next few months. He also reminded them that there was a chief organiser for each province if they had any issues that needed addressing. 'But the Ministry make this final appeal to you to re-double your efforts in aid of the Loan.'

In the special circular, Collins made it clear to the Sinn Féin officers that the Loan was 'one of the immediately pressing duties'. To stress the message, the circular opened with an exhortation, written in bold type, from Dr Fogarty, bishop of Killaloe, that 'we must not in this great National enterprise fall behind our American friends. It will be a shame to do so.'

The circular praised the best-performing constituencies, including West Limerick and Mid-Cork. The performance of Terence MacSwiney's Mid-Cork constituency was remarkable. It had submitted applications for £5,117—75% more than Cork city (£2,914) and 350% greater than the average of the eleven Dublin constituencies (£1,136). 'If you were living in one of the above areas,' pressed Collins, 'redouble your energies; if you are not, then make your district good as they are.' In a pointed rebuke to organisers in underperforming constituencies, he added: 'Remember these amounts were not realised by any magic formulae, they are the results of hard work and ceaseless endeavour.'

The circular asked the Sinn Féin officers to call a 'special meeting' if the next meeting of the local organisation was more than two weeks off. 'But above all,' he added in bold lettering, 'don't put this circular in your pocket and forget about it.' Collins was pulling no punches.

New strategy required

By the end of February it was clear to Lord French that a new strategy of attack was required against Sinn Féin. He had failed in his core strategy of arresting and deporting hundreds of the Sinn Féin leaders. Alan Bell was making no progress in his criminal investigations; Assistant Commissioner Redmond, although having come close to capturing Collins, had been shot. G Division was not fit for purpose as an investigation unit, and no impression was being made in stopping subscriptions to the Dáil Loan. Reports of the funding success in America were concerning.

Time was running out and his options were limited. The DMP and RIC were ineffective against the republican movement. Military options were few without effective intelligence support, but personnel were still low on the ground. Introduction of curfew could reduce the number of 'outrages' but it would have less impact on the political advancement of the republican movement. Basil Thomson, director of intelligence in London, had sent only one agent to Dublin. It would take considerable time to find and train new ones.

One possible option was linked to Alan Bell's past. As an RIC district inspector in 1889, he had reported to Dublin Castle on the funding activities of the 'Plan of Campaign', a land agitation strategy backed by a fund-raising campaign to support evicted tenant farmers. William O'Brien was one of the organisers. In his reports, Bell emphasised the success of the church-gate subscriptions to the fund: 'the movement has been taken up strongly by the Catholic clergy who have generally assumed the direction and leading parts in local collections'.[54]

Fearing confiscation of Land League funds, the money had been moved to Paris for safekeeping by Patrick Egan, treasurer of the Land

League. The funds were first banked with Monroe and Company, its banker in Paris. New money raised in America often never reached Ireland. It 'came first to London, was transferred to Paris and ended up back in America, being invested in American railway bonds and never having been in Ireland'.[55]

If Lord French could not arrest the Sinn Féin leaders, he could choke off their funding, finally putting an end to Dáil Éireann and its constructive programme. He asked Bell to go after the Dáil Loan funds in the banks.[56]

12. And so it begins

Financial raids

On 27 February, at 12.30am, two military lorries filled with armed soldiers roared down an otherwise eerily quiet Westmoreland Street.[1] A curfew was in place in Dublin. A *New York Times* journalist wrote, 'For five hours after midnight Dublin was dark and silent as the grave'.[2] Dublin Corporation had turned off the streetlights in protest at the curfew order. 'The silence was almost appalling in its completeness.'

The lorries stopped outside Kildare House, 13 Westmoreland Street. The soldiers entered the building and proceeded straight to the office of Donal O'Connor & Co., Chartered Accountants and Auditors. Spending over an hour and a half on the premises, they made a thorough examination of documents and removed some papers.[3]

Donal O'Connor was the auditor of Dáil Éireann and auditor of the Dáil Loan, and he had helped to set up Natland, the dummy corporation used to disguise Dáil Éireann's investment in the National Land Bank. The battle for the Dáil government funds had commenced.

O'Connor was born near Kenmare in 1872. Raised by his mother after his father's early death, he moved to Dublin and qualified as a chartered accountant in 1909. He was a senior member of the Gaelic League and the Celtic Literary Society and a collector of rare books and manuscripts.[4] He also found time to lecture in accounting in the National University.[5] When Michael Collins moved to Dublin from London in advance of the 1916 Rising, Donal O'Connor allowed him to 'go into his office, so that he would have an objective'.[6] From that time Collins involved O'Connor in all his financial decisions.

Half an hour after the raid on O'Connor's office, a separate raiding party of military and police arrived at 6 Harcourt Street. The only occupants of the building were Joe Clarke, now a member of Dublin Corporation,

Mrs Clarke and their three children. The interior rooms and front door had been boarded up. The Sinn Féin Bank had moved to No. 3.

Mrs Clarke was woken by violent banging on the front door.[7] Leaning out of a top-floor window, she told the military officer, whose soldiers had failed to break through the door, to go to the back of the building. The front door had been nailed closed. Not waiting for Mrs Clarke to open the back door, the soldiers broke it down, rushed upstairs and met Mrs Clarke on her way down. There was no sign of Joe Clarke. The officer in command ordered a search to be made of the building. A soldier shouted that he had seen Clarke on the roof. A corporal was sent out armed with a revolver with instructions to use it if necessary, but Clarke had escaped.[8]

The military entered the abandoned rooms of the Sinn Féin Bank and smashed open the safe.[9] David Kelly still used the safe, despite having moved the front office of the bank to No. 3. It was the first raid on the building in which the legal independence of the Sinn Féin Bank was not respected by the authorities.[10]

A separate raiding party then entered 3 Harcourt Street by breaking in the door.[11] They removed books and documents from the Sinn Féin Bank, and seized £8,370 in cash, deposit receipts and gold.[12] All the office equipment, including the typewriter, was taken.

David Kelly vented his outrage to the press. 'I was carrying on a legitimate banking business, trading with all the banks in town,' he declared to the *Sunday Independent*. 'This place has never been a political concern.'[13] He was determined to carry on trading. 'Despite all handicaps, victimisation, and unfair treatment,' he added, 'it is business as usual here again.' He told the journalists that he had instructed the bank's solicitor to issue proceedings for the recovery of the books and money. The legal threat was not empty.

The Sinn Féin Co-operative People's Bank Ltd issued a writ against Colonel Edgeworth-Johnstone and Lieutenant-General Sir Frederick Shaw, military commander in Ireland. David Kelly, the manager of the *Sinn Féin* Bank, was suing the two most senior security officials in the British administration! The writ claimed the return of documents and the £8,370 forcibly removed from the bank.[14]

Kelly engaged Corrigan and Corrigan, solicitors, who instructed two barristers: Tim Healy, a former Home Rule supporter and one of the few King's Counsel barristers prepared to represent Sinn Féin, and James

Murnaghan, the son of a former nationalist MP. The plaintiff asked the court for an immediate injunction restraining the defendants from parting with the funds. In the House of Commons, John Davison, a well-briefed English Labour Party MP, raised the injustice of the seizure of the funds with the attorney general for Ireland.[15]

Four days later, the military spent half an hour searching the offices of New Ireland Assurance.[16] No documents were seized. As the soldiers left the building, a group of young people attempted to block them from mounting their military lorry. During a brief scuffle, the tin hat of one of the soldiers, who were carrying rifles with fixed bayonets, was knocked off. The soldiers brought their rifles to their shoulders and made ready to fire. A serious incident was averted when the officer in charge ordered guns to be lowered. One of the soldiers on the lorry provocatively waved a tricolour at the crowd. He had taken the flag from the New Ireland offices. A young man rushed forward, grabbed the flag from the soldier and carried it in triumph through the cheering crowd.

Shortly after midnight, military and police had arrived at the home of William O'Brien, founder of the United Irish League and old adversary of Alan Bell.[17] In darkness, the 68-year-old was ordered out of bed, arrested and deported without trial to England. O'Brien was a member of Dublin Corporation and secretary of the Irish Labour Party. A former MP, he had stood aside in favour of a Sinn Féin candidate in the 1918 election.

Military parties raided 30 homes across the city that night. An official statement said that 35 bombs and two revolvers were recovered.[18] Thomas Hunter, TD for Cork North East and a member of the IRA, was also arrested. He was a business partner of Peadar Clancy in a tailoring shop on Talbot Street provocatively called 'The Republican Outfitters'.

The *Irish Independent* published a withering indictment of government policy in response to the raids. 'Drastic measure after drastic measure has been tried; each has ended in failure.' The paper depicted the Irish executive as an 'autocratic, arbitrary junta of Junkers', comparing the rulers of the country to the landowning aristocracy who staffed the Prussian army.[19]

The *Freeman's Journal* blamed the escalating crisis in Ireland on domestic British politics in London. 'If this country were not the dedicated victim of the British Party System ... there would long ago have been a complete change of men and methods in the government of Ireland.'

In the House of Commons, some liberal MPs challenged the suppression measures being employed in Ireland. In a heated debate on legislation to make permanent the Defence of the Realm Act, Colonel Penry Williams said that it was 'a political crime to inflict the injustice which the bill contained on the people of Ireland'. Captain Wedgwood Benn said that the bill put 'a murderous instrument into the hands of the Irish administrators'. Macpherson, the chief secretary, was outraged. 'I would not be surprised if, after some remarks made in this debate, to-morrow, the lives of many loyal officials are in danger.'[20]

13. Bank inquiry

Subpoenas

Four days after the raids on the offices of Donal O'Connor and the Sinn Féin Bank, on Tuesday 2 March Henry Campbell, manager of the Hibernian Bank on College Green, received an unexpected visitor. He was personally handed a summons by a police sergeant. He had been commanded to appear before Alan Bell, Resident Magistrate, at the Police Courts on Monday 8 March at 11 o'clock.[1]

Campbell was one of ten bank managers issued with a summons that day, five from the Hibernian Bank and five from the Munster & Leinster Bank, each directed to attend a 'Star Chamber' inquiry established under the Crimes Acts.[2] The sergeant asked Campbell to confirm his attendance at the appointed date and time.

A criminal inquiry into banking operations in Ireland was an antagonistic and controversial move, even by Dublin Castle standards. Curfew, censorship, raids and internment were the standard responses expected from the Irish executive. News of the inquiry spread rapidly through the financial and legal communities in Dublin.

The documents seized in the raids on the offices of Donal O'Connor and the Sinn Féin Bank provided sufficient evidence for Alan Bell to issue the subpoenas. The two-page summons referenced an offence committed on 31 October, when 'persons' unlawfully received contributions for Sinn Féin and Dáil Éireann at Harcourt Street. The date meant nothing to Campbell, or to any of the other managers summoned. The offence was a red herring. A Crimes Act inquiry could only be established on receipt of a sworn statement from the police that an offence had actually taken place within the previous six months.[3]

On reading the second page of the summons, Campbell saw that the inquiry was much broader in scope than a single offence. He was commanded to produce documents and records relating to '*any* dealings and transactions' between his bank and Sinn Féin and Dáil Éireann, including '*all* Books of Accounts'. The documents requested included telegrams, letters, notes of telephone messages and any securities held by the banks on behalf of Dáil Éireann or Sinn Féin.

Daithi O'Donoghue had opened Loan accounts in the College Green branch, some of which were 'very large'. This implies deposits of up to £20,000 (over $1m). Campbell may have known that money in these personal accounts was held in trust for Dáil Éireann, but since he had not been *officially* informed that the accounts were opened as trustee accounts, they were protected by client confidentiality rules—unless, of course, Alan Bell could prove otherwise.

Four days later, the National Land Bank announced itself on the financial stage through a series of advertisements in the Saturday editions of the *Irish Independent*, the *Freeman's Journal* and the *Irish Times*.[4] There was probably never a good time to launch a bank illegally funded by a counter-state government, but four days after ten bank managers had been summoned to appear before a criminal inquiry into the banking sector was not ideal.

Reading the *Irish Times* on Saturday morning, and turning to page four, Alan Bell must have viewed with disbelief the large advertisement on top of the page: 'THE NATIONAL LAND BANK LTD founded to secure for the benefit of the Irish people the use of Irish money in Ireland and to establish a financial centre for the development of their interests'. And the promoters of the new bank had been good enough to provide the names of the four directors and of Lionel Smith-Gordon, secretary and manager.

Michael Collins must have considered postponing the bank's launch. The seizure of documents from the offices of Donal O'Connor concerned him, and the pending bank inquiry presented a new and still undetermined threat to Dáil funds, including those invested in the Land Bank. Collins became more cautious. He delayed dealing with a $200,000 bank draft that James O'Mara had sent from America 'owing to a certain Banking Inquiry that was going on here',[5] but he did not postpone the Land Bank launch.

Renewed agrarian tensions may partly explain the decision. An urgent solution was required to prevent political and financial capital being lost to a new land conflict. Delaying the launch would expose the Dáil government to the risk of losing credibility with the people. TDs were impatient for the launch of the bank.

Moreover, even if Collins had wanted to stop the launch, it might have been too late to pull the advertisements. The subpoenas were served on the bank managers just five days before the newspapers were published. And if it was not too late, pulling the advertisement from the *Irish Times* would confirm suspicions of a formal link between the bank and Dáil Éireann. The *Irish Times* would have been sure to inform Dublin Castle that the advertisement had been pulled.

Michael Collins did not know that Alan Bell was already aware of plans to set up a bank.[6] His prepared questions for the inquiry included asking bank managers about accounts in the name of Robert Barton. Lionel Smith-Gordon's name was written under that of Robert Barton in his financial notes.[7]

Remarkably, it took five days for news of the bank inquiry to break in the newspapers. On Sunday, the 'stop press' edition of the *Evening Telegraph* reported that steps were being taken to compel Irish banks to disclose the character and condition of '*all or any* of their clients'.[8]

The vague nature and broad scope of the inquiry suggested by the report caused disquiet in business circles. Dublin Castle moved quickly to clarify that the inquiry was more limited in its scope. The *Irish Times* was 'officially informed' that the inquiry had been set up in connection with the seizure of documents of the Sinn Féin Bank and for the purpose of 'eliciting the relations to be existing between certain Irish banks and the Sinn Féin organisation'.[9] The inquiry was to be 'strictly private'.

The nationalist backlash against the inquiry was swift and aggressive, across all sections of the community. The *Freeman's Journal* called it one of the most 'sensational and far-reaching encroachments by the Irish Executive on the traditional rights of the citizens',[10] and said that to 'destroy the confidence of the public in the safety and secrecy of bankers' books is a matter which everyone, despite his political views, must deeply deplore'. A letter from an unnamed bank manager, published under the title 'The Importance of Secrecy in Banking Matters', said that profound surprise and indignation would be created in business circles.

A 'prominent' Irish bank official told the *Irish Independent* that the objective of the inquiry must be to investigate income tax evasion on bank deposit interest. 'It was absolutely necessary for banks to observe the strictest secrecy regarding their customer's business.'[11] Asked whether there was a link between the inquiry and the Dáil Loan, he replied that it was outside the range of possibility: 'That money, if it reached the banks in this country at all, would, he presumed, be lodged in the names of individuals, and could not be traced'.[12]

The Catholic Church sent a pre-emptive warning to Dublin Castle through a member of the clergy quoted in the *Freeman's Journal*. 'It would be a monstrous thing if it was sought to interfere with any funds belonging to churches, no matter of what denomination,' he commented, 'and should there be any attempt, there would be an outcry which would not be forgotten by the present ruling powers for some time to come.'[13] *Omertà* was expected from God's bankers in Ireland.

In the House of Commons, Captain Redmond, the nationalist MP for Waterford who had defeated Dr White in the 1918 general election, asked the chief secretary whether he was aware of the 'resentment expressed by the whole commercial community at this inquiry'.[14] Macpherson replied that he was not aware that any resentment had been expressed and that he did not apprehend that the future of banking would be in any way affected. That view was shared by the Dublin correspondent of the *Times*, who reported that the commercial and trading community did not share the 'alarmist view' of the nationalist press as regards the threat to public confidence in the banking system.[15]

The Institute of Bankers sat on the fence. 'The Institute,' according to a senior member, 'did not try to influence or interfere in the policy of the directors.'[16]

Henry Campbell deposition

On the morning of Monday 8 March Henry Campbell arrived at the Police Courts.[17] Every precaution was taken to ensure the privacy of the proceedings.[18] The police were stationed at the entrance to the building. More policemen were in the main hall to prevent access to the chief magistrate's room, where Bell was conducting the depositions. Journalists waiting outside made unsuccessful attempts to obtain the names of the witnesses.[19]

In advance of his deposition, Henry Campbell had been advised by the bank's legal representatives that banking secrecy rules held primacy over Crimes Act legislation. He had been instructed by his bank's directors to adopt a firm approach.[20] Journalists in front of the Police Courts noticed that Campbell was not holding any books or records when he arrived. He was accompanied by the bank's solicitor.[21]

At 11.00 Campbell entered the chief magistrate's room. Alan Bell noticed the absence of files and folders. The tone for the deposition had been set. The inquiry started with procedural questions. Bell asked Campbell to confirm the address of his bank, that he was the branch manager and how many years he had been in the position. Campbell clarified that he was the manager of the *office*—College Green was the head office. He had been manager for over ten years.

Bell's next question was critical to the success of his deposition strategy. The first twelve of his prepared questions depended on an affirmative reply.

'In the course of your business, have you, or had you, within the past six months any account with what is called "Dáil Éireann"?'

'No,' replied Campbell.

Campbell asked to be represented by counsel. Bell replied that nobody was allowed in the room, other than the shorthand writer. He repeated his opening question, 'You say, in the course of your business your bank has had no account with Dáil Éireann?'

'No,' replied Campbell.

On further questioning, Campbell confirmed that he did not have an account with either Sinn Féin, the Sinn Féin Bank or any persons representing themselves as trustees of those organisations. His monosyllabic replies were politely obstructive. Bell needed to move on to a different line of enquiry.

'Has your bank been in the custom or habit of *cashing cheques* drawn on the Sinn Féin Bank?'

Here Campbell was on less firm ground. He could not deny under oath that his bank cashed Sinn Féin Bank cheques, because it did, but as the manager of the head office, with large volumes of transactions processed daily, he could claim ignorance of the fact. He gave a longwinded and rambling answer.

'I could not tell you, because a cheque might be lodged to some man's account … we would have no record in the office … you know they go through in hundreds every day; they might go through on the Sinn Féin Bank or anywhere else in Dublin, and I would not *know* about it.'

Sensing a weakness, Bell repeated the question twice more, forcing Campbell to change his answer: 'I do not *believe* any cheque had been cashed.' Bell now had the upper hand. In an admonishing tone, he asked, 'It should not have been done if it was?' Campbell was indignant: 'There is no necessity to add that, because in the ordinary course of business it would not be done without my authority'. Further probing questions and uncooperative replies raised the level of ill feeling on both sides. And then Bell asked, 'Can you say whether your Bank has an account in the name of a man called *Michael Collins*?'

The question presented Campbell with a dilemma. Under oath, he could not deny the existence of an account, if one indeed existed. 'I would not like to say that from memory,' he answered. 'I would have to go up and look it up.' He deflected the question by referring to the scope of the inquiry: 'That is not a name in connection with *certain* societies'. Bell repeated the answer back to Campbell in a tone indicating a question. Campbell replied: 'That is quite right. It would be too *dangerous* for me to speak from memory.'

It was an unusual choice of word for the risk associated with the potential breach of bank secrecy rules. Maybe there was nothing for Bell to read into the remark. Campbell may merely have meant that by replying without looking at his books he would put his banking career at risk, but perhaps he was hinting at something. Maybe an intimation of concern for his personal safety (even if not true) would deflect Bell away from the question.

Bell did not take the hint, if one was intended. 'In order to ascertain whether you have an account in your Bank in the name of Michael Collins, what reference would be necessary?'

Campbell deflected again to the scope of the inquiry. 'Are these *individual* names covered by your summons?'

The repeated reference to the scope of the summons angered Bell. 'I have only asked you *one* name and that name is relevant to the summons.' The temperature in the room went up a degree. Bell asked the question a fourth time. Campbell replied that he would have to check his books to ascertain whether an account for Michael Collins existed. Asked why he did not bring any documents, he replied that 'with regards to the summons … I have none of those accounts … and therefore I brought down no books'.

The reference once again to the scope of the summons incensed Bell. He quoted word for word the requirement to produce all books of account in any way relating to the prohibited organisations 'or persons on behalf of the said organisations, or any of them, or any committee or body constituted by or acting in privity with them, or any of them, which now are in your power, possession or procurement'.

'You say there are no such documents?'

Campbell was annoyed by the tone of the question. 'I cannot say who are privy, or who are mixed up in the thing at all in any of those societies; but we have nothing that shows in any way *any connection with those societies.*'

Bell had been setting a trap. He picked up a cheque and motioned towards Campbell. It was a Sinn Féin Bank cheque drawn on the Dáil Éireann account and signed by 'Míceál O'Coileain'. This proved a *connection* between Michael Collins and Dáil Éireann. Bank secrecy rules no longer applied to an account in his name if he was acting in trust or on behalf of the body.

'Will you take that cheque in your hand and just look at it, please, cheque 2080, Sinn Féin Bank. Can you tell me whose signature that is?'

'No.'

'You see the signature of the drawer?'

'Yes. I do not know it.'

'Do you know what the name is?'

'No. I do not know Irish.'

Bell knew that it was implausible that Campbell did not recognise, even in Irish, the signature of Michael Collins, well known as the Minister for Finance in the Dáil government. He changed the line of questioning again.

This time he showed an unusual interest in the way cheque 2080 was cleared by the Hibernian Bank. Cheques cashed or deposited into Hibernian branches were sent to Campbell's College Green office for clearing with the other banks. Sinn Féin Bank cheques were physically carried to Harcourt Street by a 'runner' and presented to David Kelly. The runner received money matching the amount on the cheque, which was marked as paid. Bell asked for the name of the runner, but Campbell said that he would have to refer to his books to get the name of the man working that day.

Bell then presented four Sinn Féin Bank cheques in quick succession, each drawn on the Dáil Éireann bank account and signed by Michael Collins. He asked Campbell to confirm that they had been cleared in the same way. Perhaps he was building a case that receiving funds on cleared cheques on the Dáil Éireann account was the equivalent of 'receiving contributions', the wording of the offence said to have occurred on 31 October.

Bell asked only one other question about the five cheques that he presented to Campbell, one of which was payable to Eamon Fleming, the Dáil Loan organiser in Leinster. Campbell said that he did not know the payee name.

Bell moved the questioning to accounts in other people's names.

'Can you tell me if there is an account in your Bank in the name of Darrell Figgis?'

'I do not think so. I have too many accounts to venture to say a word, I do not think so.'

'Can you say from your recollection, without reference to your books, whether you have an account in the name of R.C. Barton?'

'I do not think that it is likely. Where you have thousands of accounts I would like to refer to books.'

Campbell was stretching credibility. An account in the name of Robert Barton would have stood out among the 'thousands of accounts'—a former British Army officer turned 'Sinn Féiner', elected TD, Director of Agriculture for Dáil Éireann and a famous prison escapee.

'Or could you say with reference to an account in the name of Alderman Thomas Kelly?'

Campbell confirmed that Kelly had a *personal* account in his name.

'I do not want to ask you about any private account, of course. So far as you recollect you say that that account in the name of Alderman Thomas Kelly is in his own name, and not a trustee account?'

'I cannot say whether it is not or it is, beyond that the man has an account with me.'

Asked the same question again to his annoyance, Campbell replied curtly, 'I know nothing about the account only that he has an account with me; I know nothing further about the account.' The stage was set for a final confrontation.

'Would you cash on sight any cheque drawn by Alderman Kelly?'

Campbell interpreted the question as a slight on the character of the alderman, who was not only one of the most respected politicians in the country but was interned in England and known to be in poor health.

'That is a question!'

Bell backtracked by suggesting that he was referring to cheque cashing limits: 'Within the amount of his account?'

But Campbell had had enough.

'I cash a great number of cheques without ever looking up things at all, if I think they are ordinary straight men—straight in commercial dealings.'

The deposition ended.

While Campbell was being deposed, news came through of another raid on the Sinn Féin Bank. David Kelly found the door of 3 Harcourt Street barricaded when he arrived to work that morning. Between 1am and 2am, a party of military engineers and policemen had barricaded the internal and external doors of the building.[22] Kelly gave no interview to the newspapers this time.

Christopher Tierney deposition

Christopher Tierney was next on Bell's witness list that morning. He presented a different challenge from Campbell. Tierney had been manager of the O'Connell Street branch of the Hibernian Bank since 1888; over 30 years of service with the bank had commenced during the Land War.[23] He was of the same vintage as Bell and did not have to show the respect that a younger man might offer to a near-retired resident magistrate.

He also had firsthand knowledge of Bell's activity during the Land War. The Hibernian Bank had been closely associated with the Plan of Campaign. At one point the bank extended a £7,000 overdraft facility to the organisation.[24] Tierney still supported nationalist activity. His branch cashed Sinn Féin Bank cheques and held accounts for Darrell Figgis and the Commission of Enquiry.[25] It was probable that 'trusted friends' had opened Dáil Loan accounts in the branch.

The deposition proceeded along similar lines to Campbell's, until Bell asked Tierney whether he cashed Sinn Féin Bank cheques in his branch. Unlike Campbell, who avoided a direct answer, Tierney denied outright cashing the bank's cheques. Of course, Bell next handed cheque 2080 to Tierney. A stamp on the back clearly showed that the cheque had been lodged to an account in his branch. Tierney claimed that he had never seen the cheque before.

Bell then asked him three times whether he recognised the signature on the cheque. To Bell's obvious disbelief, Tierney denied knowing Michael Collins's name. He admitted that the cheque was lodged to the account of Andrew S. Clerkin and sent to the College Green branch for clearance. Andy Clerkin was a coal merchant who supplied coke to the IRA for bomb-making.[26] As the deposition progressed, Tierney's answers became casual and offhand.

'Can you tell me have you any account in your bank with a person called Michael Collins?'

'I do not remember. The name is not familiar to me. Can you give me his address?'

Bell pointed to the address of the Sinn Féin Bank on the cheque. '*That* address would probably find him'. Tierney replied matter of factly, '6 Harcourt St., no, no such account'.

'Have you any account in your bank in the name of Darrell Figgis?'

'Not personally. We have an account in which the name of Mr Darrell Figgis appears with others, called *a committee of something*, the Development of the Resources of Ireland, I think.'

'Do you know in whose name or names is that account?'

'I really cannot tell you from memory, but I know Mr Darrell Figgis's name is one. There are three names to the account. I really forget the particular title of the account.'

Tierney's answer was more implausible than Campbell's not knowing whether he had an account in the name of Robert Barton. The co-account holders were John O'Neill, the successful businessman and chairman of the commission, and George Nesbitt, a trustee of New Ireland Assurance and treasurer of Sinn Féin. In reply to another question, when Bell referenced

O'Neill and Nesbitt by name, Tierney could 'not recollect' without reference to his books having a joint account in their names. Tierney did not know that Bell knew from documents seized that O'Neill and Nesbitt held accounts in trust for Dáil Éireann in the O'Connell Street branch.[27]

Bell exhibited none of the frustration that he had shown with Campbell when deposing Tierney. He knew that it was pointless.

Bell asked whether he had brought his ledger.

'Oh, no; I did not bring it, it is a very big book.'

'Have you any account in your branch in the name of R.C. Barton?'

'I cannot say, I do not recollect that name; it is not familiar to me. I am sure I have not.'

'*Of course* if you had your ledger you would be able to say at once?'

'But I could almost say definitely, the name is not familiar; if I had the ledger *I would tell you at once.*'

Before the deposition ended, Tierney denied having accounts in the names of Robert Barton, Arthur Griffith, Michael Collins (the third time asked by Bell) and Ernest Blythe.

Thomas Read deposition

Thomas Read, manager of the Camden Street branch of the Hibernian Bank, was due to appear in front of Bell at 1pm, but Tierney's deposition took much less time than the expected hour.[28] Read had been the branch manager for fourteen years. Daithi O'Donoghue had also deposited 'some very large' Loan funds in this branch.

The deposition began badly for Read. Asked whether he had any account with persons purporting to be trustees of Dáil Éireann, his reply was wordy and rambling.

'Not officially—I mean to say I have no knowledge of them—I could not answer that question more directly than that. What I wish to convey is, I have no *official* knowledge they are trustees.'

Campbell and Tierney had replied 'No' to the same question. Bell asked the obvious follow-on question: 'Have you any *personal* or *private* knowledge of any persons being trustees of any of those organisations?' Read's answer was loaded: 'Not to swear to'.

The Sinn Féin Bank
during (above) and
after a raid (left).
(Source: National Library
of Ireland, via RTÉ, 'Cradle
of the Irish Republic—A
Journey through 6
Harcourt Street')

Cancelled cheques on the Sinn Féin bank signed by Michael Collins (Mícheál O'Coileain & Mícheál O Coileain). (Bureau of Military History)

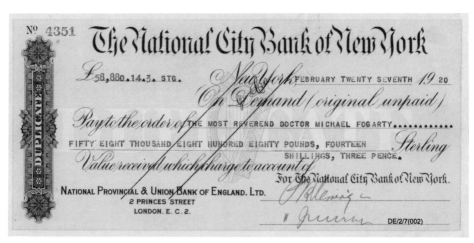

New York bank draft. (Source: Dáil Éireann Files, NA DE 2/7, 002)

Loan promotional film. (Source: Irish Film Institute (https://ifiplayer.ie/historical-material-republican-loans/))

D A I L   E I R E A N N   L O A N.

NETT AMOUNTS RECEIVED AT HEAD OFFICE AS ON 14th SEPTR. 1920.

CONNACHT.

GALWAY:	Connemara ..	1564:13:4
	East	4588: 0:0
	North	4989: 5:0
	South	3295:10:0
LEITRIM:	....	5087: 7:2
MAYO:	East	5613:10:0
	North	4021: 5:0
	South	7057: 0:0
	West	5073: 0:0
ROSCOMMON:	North	4606: 0:0
	South	4667: 0:0
SLIGO:	North	3566: 0:0
	South	3668: 9:6

TOTAL : £57,797: 0:0

MUNSTER.

CLARE:	East	13609: 4:6
	West	7713: 0:0
CORK:	City	12067: 0:0
	East	6519:15:0
	Mid	7237: 2:6
	North	6497: 0:0
	North East.	3787:10:0
	South	4876:15:10
	South East.	2086: 0:0
	West	4350: 0:0
KERRY:	East	5154:10:0
	North	9000: 0:0
	South	3104: 2:0
	West	8571:15:0
LIMERICK:	City	5684:10:0
	East	31875: 0:0
	West	17385: 0:0
TIPPERARY:	East	4862:10:0
	Mid	2907: 6:6
	North	4245: 0:0
	South	4458: 0:0
WATERFORD:	City.......	636: 5:0
	County	4550: 0:0

TOTAL: £171,177: 6:4

LEINSTER.

CARLOW:	....	3383: 5:0
DUBLIN:	Clontarf ...	2204:10:0
	College Gn..	2101: 5:0
	Harbour	1657:10:0
	Pembroke ...	2580: 0:0
	Rathmines ..	1235: 0:0
	St. James'..	1455: 0:0
	St.Michans..	2780:15:0
	St.Stephens.	2270:10:0
	St.Patricks.	2161:10:0
	North Co....	1370: 5:0
	South Co....	2125:10:0
KILDARE:	North	2381:10:0
	South	3445: 0:0
KILKENNY:	North	2912: 0:0
	South	5281:10:0
LONGFORD:	....	5802: 0:0
LOUTH:	....	2575: 5:0
MEATH:	North	1902: 4:0
	South	2262: 0:0
OFFALY:	....	9198: 1:6
LEIX & OSSORY:	....	10030:12:6
WESTMEATH:	....	4660: 0:0
WEXFORD:	North	3280:10:0
	South	4457: 0:0
WICKLOW:	East........	819: 4:6
	West	3713: 0:0

TOTAL: £87,444:17:6

ULSTER.

ANTRIM:	Belfast ...	2355: 6:6
	East & North	196: 0:0
	Mid ....:	162: 0:0
	South	427: 0:0
ARMAGH:	Mid	527:10:0
	North	322:10:0
	South	1665: 0:0
CAVAN:	East	4215:14:8
	West	3211: 5:0
DERRY:	City	1376: 0:0
	North	772:10:0
	South	713: 0:0
DONEGAL:	East	1022: 0:0
	North	885: 0:0
	South	1333:10:0
	West	673: 0:0
DOWN:	East & Mid..	2672: 0:0
	South	1845:10:0
	West	199: 0:0
FERMANAGH:	North	1768: 0:0
	South	1458: 0:0
MONAGHAN:	North	2457:18:0
	South	5705: 0:0
TYRONE:	North East .	2307:10:0
	North West .	1466:10:0
	South	1561: 0:0

TOTAL: £41297:14:2

GRAND TOTALS

CONNACHT	57,797: 0:0
LEINSTER	87,444:17:6
MUNSTER	171,177: 6:4
ULSTER	41,297:14:2
Cumann na mBan	801: 0:0
BRITAIN & FRANCE	11,647: 8:0
	£370,165: 6:0

Loan receipts by constituency prepared by Michael Collins. (Source: Dáil Éireann, NA DE 2/7, 062)

Dáil Éireann

Self-Determination and Loan Accounts

1st MAY, 1920, TO 31st DECEMBER, 1920.

DUBLIN, *7th April*, 1921.

To the Members of Dáil Eireann.

GENTLEMEN,

Having audited your Books for the eight months from 1st May, 1920, to 31st December, 1920, I send you herewith certified copies of the Self-Determination Fund and the Loan Account for that period.

SELF-DETERMINATION FUND

At 1st May, 1920, there was a balance on hands of £30,343 10s. 10d. The Receipts to the 31st December, 1920, came to £12,241 19s. 5d., making a total of £42,585 10s. 3d. The items of receipt are composed of Subscriptions, £11,842 18s. 8d., and Interest, £399 0s. 9d.

The Disbursements for the period amounted to £13,324 0s. 7d. There were, in addition, sums amounting to £18,732 seized, and these are shown on this side. The balance to the credit of the Fund at 31st December, 1920, was £10,529 9s. 8d.

LOAN ACCOUNT.

The Balance on hand at the 1st May, 1920, was £146,294 0s. 0d. The Receipts for the period amounted to £356,208 8s. 3d., making a total of £502,502 8s. 3d. The items of receipt are composed of Subscriptions, £347,844 9s. 9d. ; Refund from Local Government Department, £1,300 ; Earnings from Departments, £908 5s. 7d. ; and Interest, £6,155 12s. 11d.

The Disbursements amounted to £279,176 13s. 2d., of which £200,000 represented Investments, and £35,309 9s. 0d. sums advanced as Loans, leaving the balance on hands at 31st December, 1920, as £223,325 15s. 1d.

SUMMARY OF BALANCES AS AT 31st DECEMBER, 1920.

	£	s.	d.
Self-Determination Fund, Cash on hands	10,529	9	8
Loan Account, do.	223,325	15	1
Amount advanced out of Self-Determination Fund prior to 1st May, 1920, repayable	300	0	0
Amount advanced out of Self-Determination Fund to 31st December, 1920, repayable	300	0	0
Amounts advanced out of Loan Account prior to 1st May, 1920, repayable	27,005	0	0
Amounts advanced out of Loan Account to 31st December, 1920, repayable	35,309	9	0
Investments out of Loan Account	200,000	0	0
Making a Total of	£496,769	13	9

The apportionment of Expenditure as between Self-Determination Fund and Loan Account has followed the lines already laid down. The Interest accrued in the respective Accounts has been calculated with reference to the balances standing at the beginning of each Account.

I am,

Gentlemen,

Yours faithfully,

D. O'CONNOR.

Audited Self-Determination and Loan Accounts. (Source: NA DE 2/7, 015)

Daithi O'Donoghue.

(Source: Bureau of Military History, an album entitled 'Nine people who were prominent in the movement for independence 1916–1921')

Alan Bell RM. (Source: *Freeman's Journal*, 13 March 1920, p. 5 (www.irisharchives.com))

A business-like Michael Collins. (NLI)

Read admitted to having a joint account in the name of Patrick Gleeson, a board member of the Sinn Féin Bank, and Patrick Morgan, but he claimed privilege on personal accounts to avoid giving more details.[29] Morgan was a well-known dentist and his private home was used for Dáil Cabinet meetings.[30] He had also been a member of the original management committee of the Sinn Féin Bank. Bell said, 'You know there is no such thing as privilege in a criminal proceeding?', to which Read coolly replied, 'Well, of course I am not well up in the law'. He had regained his composure.

Read also claimed privilege on another account in the names of Alderman Kelly and Patrick Gleeson. Bell believed that the account held funds in trust for Dáil Éireann. Losing patience, he asked, 'How can you describe an account as "personal" when it is in the name of two persons as trustees?' Read replied, 'It is not in the name of two persons as trustees at all, it is a joint account. It is a purely joint account in two names.'

Read claimed that he had no 'personal recollection' of cashing cheques drawn on the Sinn Féin Bank, but 'if a good customer came in with a cheque on the Sinn Féin Bank we would cash it for that customer'. He also denied having an account with Michael Collins, Arthur Griffith, Robert Barton, Ernest Blythe and Darrell Figgis.

During Read's deposition, unlike those of Campbell and Tierney, Bell asked questions on specific transactions, in particular deposits of £4,000 on 31 January and £2,017 on 13 February. Bell's line of questioning implied that he knew that a cheque for the latter amount was used to open the joint account in the name of Patrick Gleeson and Patrick Morgan.[31] Bell did not believe Read when he said that he could not remember what sort of cheque was used to open the account. He asked no further questions and no further depositions were taken that day.

Media attack

On the morning after the first day of depositions, the *Freeman's Journal* continued to attack the inquiry. Alan Bell found himself thrust into the media spotlight. Discovering that Bell's name did not appear in the legal directory, either as barrister or solicitor, the paper concluded that 'He is, therefore, a gentleman without legal training'.[32] Describing the issues in the inquiry as going to the 'foundations of the nation's financial and commercial structure', it deplored the fact that 'Mr Alan Bell ... may decide the great issues'.

The *Irish Bulletin*, the propaganda organ of Dáil Éireann, also went on the offensive against the inquiry. Under the heading 'Who is Alan Bell?', it described him as acting as an 'Agent-Provocateur' during the Land War, accused him of being the 'secret agent' of the *Times* in the Piggott forgeries case, and claimed that since then he had been used 'in many shady ways by the English Spy System in Ireland'. It accused Dublin Castle of bringing Bell to Dublin 'to assist in the concoction of conspiracy charges against the Republican Leaders'.[33]

Continuing the attack the following day, the *Bulletin* described Bell as 'a notorious English secret service agent poorly disguised as a magistrate' and claimed that the objective of the inquiry was as much to destroy the credit of Irish banks as to seize republican funds.[34]

The *Evening Standard* made a bold claim. According to its Dublin correspondent, the intention to set up the inquiry was known in Sinn Féin circles for more than a week and '... steps would have been taken to remove from the banks any money held on behalf of Sinn Féin'.[35]

The accountant

Bell's next move took everyone by surprise. Revoking the outstanding subpoenas on the remaining seven bankers, he had a summons served on James Davidson, an accountant in the Dame Street branch of the Munster & Leinster Bank. This strategic repositioning of the inquiry echoed later moves by mob investigators.

The inquiry resumed on the morning of Thursday 11 March, after a two-day break. James Davidson entered the chief magistrate's room at 11.00.[36] He was accompanied by the bank's solicitor, who was refused entry to the room.[37] Unlike the previous depositions, it was Davidson who spoke first.

'Before we go any further I am instructed by my directors to protest against being called upon to disclose any particulars about the affairs of the clients of the Bank without the instructions of these clients.'

Bell made no acknowledgement of the remark. Calling an accountant to the inquiry was not the only change he had made. Over the previous two days, he had requested information in advance on specific transactions, and during the course of the deposition he asked Davidson, 'Have you found anything at all in your bank which would explain a transaction of a thousand pounds having come from your bank, whose destination was Paris?'[38]

Seized documents persuaded Bell that a sum of £1,000 for the use of the Dáil envoys in Paris had been advanced to Art O'Brien, whom he knew to be connected to the London office of Dáil Éireann.[39] He believed that the Munster & Leinster Bank had made the advance on 24 May 1919.[40] He further believed that four days later the £1,000 was refunded by a cheque drawn on the Sinn Féin Bank signed by Michael Collins.[41] These supposedly linked transactions occurred almost four months before Dáil Éireann had been prohibited, but Bell was not going to let a technicality get in the way of his investigation.

Bell had a particular interest in Paris. The first financial entry in his notebook was a reference to a communication between the American Express Bank in Paris and an unnamed bank in Dublin concerning the 'Republican Loan'.[42] He also noted that the Hewett shipping agent on D'Olier Street acted as an agent for American Express in Paris. The Hewett name came to Ireland with French Huguenot refugees during the reign of Louis XIV. Bell had detailed knowledge on the activity of Seán T. O'Kelly and Charles Gavan Duffy, the two Dáil envoys in Paris, whom he knew were staying at the Grand Hotel, Boulevard des Capucines.[43] His notebook also made reference to the 'chargé d'affaires' for the 'Irish Republic'.

Bell may have believed that some of the Loan proceeds were hidden in the city, as the Land League funds had been. He knew that an advertisement for the Dáil Loan had been placed in the Paris edition of the *Chicago Tribune*.[44]

The Davidson deposition proceeded at a deliberate and methodical pace. Bell asked Davidson to take a cheque in his hand. As Davidson did so, he reminded Bell, 'You have a note of the protest I made'. Bell again made no acknowledgement of the comment. He believed that the cheque he had handed to Davidson was used to refund the advance of £1,000 given by the Munster & Leinster Bank to Art O'Brien.[45]

Step by step, Bell guided Davidson through the details of the cheque, asking him to confirm each item as he proceeded. Davidson provided the minimum of information. He confirmed that the cheque was deposited into the account of a client of the bank but without volunteering the name.

The deposition continued down a laboured path of technical questions and single-word replies on the recording and clearing of the cheque. Suddenly, almost as if to catch Davidson unawares, Bell asked, 'Can you tell me to whose account that money was deposited?'

Davidson admitted that the cheque was deposited into an account in the name of 'Mr Michael Collins'. He volunteered no further information. Bell asked whether the account still existed. Davidson deflected, 'I could not say without looking up [the books]'. The atmosphere in the room changed.

Bell moved the questioning to the advance of £1,000.

'If a statement was made in a properly ordered account that one thousand pounds was advanced by Munster & Leinster Bank, head office, on the 24th May, 1919, could you say from what you have been looking up whether that statement was *true or false*?'

Davidson deflected the question again by saying that he would need to look up the books of account, and by asking Bell whether he meant the head office in Cork or his office in Dublin. Bell had to repeat the 'true or false' question three times. Exasperated, he finally asked, 'So far as you know, on your oath, is there any explanation at all of that statement?'

Davidson had had an explanation all the time. He just had not volunteered it. On the date in question, his bank had issued a draft for £1,000 drawn on the National Provincial & Union Bank of England in London, made payable to Art O'Brien. Technically, Davidson could justify not disclosing the information earlier, as it was not an advance and did not involve the head office in Cork, as Bell assumed.

Davidson had brought an important document relating to the draft. He would not hand it over to Bell but he verbally gave him the details: 'I have in my hand a requisition note of draft on demand for one thousand pounds, payable in London, in favour of Art O'Brien by David O'Donoghue, 3 King Edward Terrace, Drumcondra, dated 24th May, 1919; it would be inconvenient to part with this document.' Davidson may have regretted disclosing Daithi O'Donoghue's name. When Bell repeated

Davidson's words back to him, and asked whether he had taken it down correctly, Davidson said, 'I can say we drew a draft on London in favour of Art O'Brien on that day. I would prefer to have it put that way.'

The deposition ended with Davidson confirming details of a second matter on which Bell had requested advance information. Bell tried to appear as if he was disinterested in the item and could barely remember what he had requested. It was a cheque for £1,000 payable in favour of Richard Mulcahy, chief of staff. Mulcahy had been a top-tier target for arrest for a number of months. Bell was certainly not disinterested.

Time to act

Meanwhile, Michael Collins wanted to know more about what was going on in the inquiry. He turned to his good friend, Michael Noyk, who was a solicitor, legal adviser and fixer for Dáil Éireann. Devoted and trustworthy, Noyk met Collins practically every night in Vaughan's Hotel. He was the logical person to turn to for information on the inquiry. 'One day a message was brought to me by either Tobin or Cullen to find out something about the Crimes Act,' recalled Noyk. 'The exact message was not very clear.'[46] Seeing Liam Tobin on top of a tram, he asked what exactly was required of him. The instruction relayed later from Collins was clear: 'Mick wanted me to get in there and find out what was happening'. That was easier said than done. Noyk proceeded to the Police Courts and tried to gain access to the inquiry. Not surprisingly, he was not allowed to enter the room.[47]

On the following Sunday, Noyk met a cross-looking Collins in Vaughan's. 'That is a nice way you carried out your duty.'[48] Noyk began to explain the difficulty of the task but, before he could finish, Collins reached out and grasped his hand warmly. 'A great feature about Michael Collins,' remembered Noyk, '… was that he did not like excuses when a project was suggested, but it was a different matter if the project could not be carried out.'

There were other ways to find out what was happening in the inquiry. Despite its being held in private, information started to leak to the press. After the first session on Monday, newspapers knew that the bank managers had claimed privilege to refuse to disclose information on personal accounts.[49] Following Davidson's deposition, they were aware that only one witness was called that day and that he was not one of those originally summoned.[50]

Through legal and banking sources, and contacts in the Police Courts, journalists likely knew more about the proceedings than was being printed. If so, this information was being passed to Collins. 'Nearly all my colleagues on the editorial staffs were sympathetic,' recounted Michael Knightly, a friendly journalist in the *Irish Independent*, 'and helped the movement in no small way.'[51]

Michael Collins and Daithi O'Donoghue, of course, had other sources of information—men like J.F. Dawson in the Munster & Leinster Bank, who was one of the seven managers to have his subpoena revoked. Maybe even the shorthand writer during the depositions was working for Collins.

Certainly, if Collins knew that Bell was asking questions about accounts in the names of Patrick Gleeson and Patrick Morgan, and about specific transactions relating to those accounts; and questions about bank transfers made to Art O'Brien in London and about cheque payments to Richard Mulcahy; and most of all, if Collins knew that Bell had the home address of Daithi O'Donoghue, he would need to act.

Meanwhile, the opening of the head office branch of the National Land Bank at 68 Leeson Street had to be postponed, but not because of the inquiry. The bank had failed to do sufficient pre-launch planning, and its complicated mechanism for issuing land loans had not been fully explained to the public. The full impact of the loss of Robert Barton in the raids at the end of January had become evident.

Where loans were urgently required and much of the preparatory work had been completed, Dáil Éireann stepped in to fill the gap. The Cabinet agreed to provide an immediate loan of £4,500 to the West Carbery Co-operative Fishing Society for the urgent purchase of a boat.[52] Loan approval was subject to receiving personal guarantees from members of the society.

14. Are you Mr Bell?

There was no sitting of the inquiry on Friday, the day after Davidson's deposition. People in banking circles believed that 'the last has been heard of the investigation'.[1] Some even said that the inquiry had 'signally failed in its purpose'.[2] The inquiry did not sit for the following two weeks either. Collins must have wondered what Bell was planning.

Under the Crimes Act, Bell had the power to recall the witnesses within three months of their deposition. Before doing this, he would need to find a way to force bank managers to release their account records and to break through privacy rules on personal accounts. He may have been preparing lists of specific transactions to be investigated, as he had done for the Davidson deposition. This would take time. After the success of the raids on Donal O'Connor's office and the Sinn Féin Bank, he may have been planning another series of raids. He may also have been arranging for Daithi O'Donoghue to be followed from his home, or even to be arrested and interned.

Bell had multiple options at his disposal to disrupt the financial activity of Dáil Éireann, as Michael Collins would have known. He could depose David Kelly, manager of the Sinn Féin Bank, or have him interned in England with his brother. He could apply to have the Sinn Féin Bank shut down; he had proof that the bank held an account for Dáil Éireann and had issued cheques drawn on that account. He could instruct the directors of the Hibernian Bank and the Munster & Leinster Bank to stop clearing Sinn Féin Bank cheques, or at least cheques issued on the Dáil Éireann account.

Bell knew that the military were planning the biggest night of raids ever for Friday 26 March; perhaps he had even selected some of the targets. In advance of those raids, but not connected to them, four unexplained murders took place within five days. The country, in particular the people of Cork and Dublin, were on edge. An atmosphere of gloom filled the country. Rumours were rife. Many felt that the country was slipping out of the control of the authorities.

In the early hours of Saturday 20 March, Tomás MacCurtain, lord mayor of Cork and local IRA commander, was shot at home by men with blackened faces. His wife and five frightened children, aged from ten months to ten years, were in the house. Sources close to Dublin Castle, including some newspapers in London, said that MacCurtain was shot as a traitor by fellow Sinn Féiners. The real killers were rogue RIC officers. A few hours before the shooting, Constable Joseph Murtagh had been shot on the streets of Cork. He was off duty and in civilian clothes.

The following Monday evening, Michael Cullen, aged 22, and Ellen Hendrick, aged eighteen, were shot by a British army officer in Dublin.[3] Michael was a van driver and Ellen was a domestic servant working in Rathmines. The official account of the shooting, issued only to the *Irish Times*, said that a man and woman were killed by revolver shots, with no reference to military involvement.

> 'At 9.30 o'clock last [Monday] night 120 soldiers of the Royal Berkshire Regiment were coming from a performance at the Hippodrome and were singing "Rule Britannia" and "God Save the King", which the crowd resented. A conflict took place between the crowd and the soldiers in the neighbourhood of South Richmond Street, in the course of which a man and woman were killed by revolver shots. One other civilian was injured by a bullet but not seriously—in the right wrist. One soldier was shot through the chest, and four other soldiers were wounded by missiles. At 11 p.m. all was quiet. None of the soldiers were armed.'[4]

A second statement, issued later, provided more details, including that ten shots had been fired by the military.

> 'A call for assistance was received in Portobello Barracks, and a patrol was sent out. On reaching Portobello Bridge it was found necessary to assist in the extraction of the soldiers returning from the Hippodrome. The crowd then attacked the patrol with missiles, and fired shots at it. The officer, having previously given

warning to the crowd to disperse, fired ten rounds and charged the mob. Three persons were seen to fall, and the mob was ultimately driven towards Kelly's Corner and down Fade Street. Fire was again opened on the patrol in Fade Street, and the mob was finally dispersed.'[5]

Chief Secretary Macpherson received cheers of approval in the House of Commons when he told MPs that the troops had opened fire on the crowd.[6] There were immediate calls for an inquiry owing to the 'amazing discrepancy' between the official versions of what happened and the unofficial versions reported in the press.[7] The city was in an 'excited' state after the shooting. It was feared that the previous 'excellent' relations between the military and the citizens of Dublin would be disturbed by the wild charges being made on both sides.[8]

On the following day, the military were confined to barracks until curfew, to the relief of many people.[9] Macpherson announced a military court of inquiry into the shooting.[10] It was later learned that the inquiry would not hear evidence from civilian witnesses and that the proceedings would not be open to the press.[11] The people would have to wait until the official inquest to have any hope of getting the real story.[12]

Adding to people's concern, on Wednesday evening a young man was shot dead by three men walking down Wicklow Street. The unidentified body ignited more rumours, and the sense of gloom in the city increased. This was, of course, the body of Fergus Bryan Molloy, the military intelligence agent, but to the citizens of Dublin it was another unexplained shooting. The funerals of Michael Cullen and Ellen Hendrick took place the following day. More speculation circulated on the true nature of their killings.

Meanwhile, the lord mayor of Dublin, Larry O'Neill, faced a more mundane though nevertheless serious problem. The business of the finance committee, the most important in Dublin Corporation, had come to a standstill, because it no longer had the necessary quorum to hold meetings. Alderman William Cosgrave, who was arrested on Thursday, became the fourth member of the committee interned by the Irish executive. He had received a message not to stay in his house but took the risk of remaining, as his wife was ill.[13]

The inability to call meetings of the finance committee had a negative impact on the housing and public health work of the corporation. With no one else to turn to, O'Neill wrote a letter to Prime Minister Lloyd George, with the opening explanation: 'When in a dilemma as to the proper authority to approach, it is a very safe procedure to adopt to approach those who are in authority over all'.[14] The arrest of William Cosgrave, chairman of the finance committee, posed a particular problem for the lord mayor. He explained to Lloyd George that the irony of the arrest was that a meeting was planned to strike a new rate for the city and to adopt the Financial Report, which had been written by Alderman Cosgrave.

O'Neill also informed Lloyd George of the 'very precarious state of health' of Alderman Kelly. Reports had also come from Wormwood Scrubs that William O'Brien had a bad cold and that his health was deteriorating while on hunger strike.[15] The news added to the gloominess in the city.

At the end of one of the most trying weeks for the people of Dublin, Alan Bell might have been one of the few Friday morning commuters looking forward to arriving at work. As soon as he reached Dublin Castle, he would get an update on the more than 50 raids that the military had planned for the night before. On the list of targets were the homes of Richard Mulcahy, Liam Tobin and Batt O'Connor.[16] He had a copy of the *Irish Times* and a downstairs seat on the tramcar, which was good, as he had a bad cough and showers were forecast. It was usually only younger men who sat upstairs in the open air.

Bell had 40 minutes to read the paper before arriving at College Green. The news pages were filled with post-war geopolitical headlines: reports on the threat of civil war in Germany, challenges to concluding a peace agreement with Turkey, a starving population in Austria, and misery and suffering across the Central European states.

On the domestic front, the paper reported on the three policemen injured in Kerry when their barracks was bombed and burned to the ground—the two-hour siege had been planned 'in the usual elaborate way'—and on the shooting of Michael Cullen and Ellen Hendrick, reported under the byline 'attacks on soldiers', as well as on further evidence presented at the inquest into the murder of the lord mayor of Cork. Two important political headlines concerned the Home Rule debate in Westminster and the 'crushing' new rate burden that was expected to be set by Dublin Corporation.

It would take Bell the full tram journey to go through all the news stories in the paper, but he did not make it to College Green that morning. The main news headline in the *Irish Times* the following day was 'ANOTHER SHOCKING CRIME IN DUBLIN'. 'MR ALAN BELL, R.M., SHOT DEAD'. 'DRAGGED FROM A TRAMCAR AT BALLSBRIDGE'.

First attempts

Alan Bell had survived an assassination attempt almost every day that week. Michael McDonnell and Vinny Byrne were waiting for him the previous Saturday.[17] GHQ Intelligence had received information that Bell would be travelling to the Four Courts by car that afternoon. An intelligence officer posted on Grattan Bridge identified Bell's car by raising a handkerchief and pointing as it passed. McDonnell and Byrne were waiting at the corner of Chancery Street; McDonnell was ready to throw a specially made grenade bomb, so big that he had to carry it in his hands wrapped in brown paper with the pin exposed. The car crossed the bridge, but instead of continuing onto Chancery Street it turned and went up the quays.

On the following day, Jimmy Slattery and Vinny Byrne were positioned outside the Olympia Theatre on Dame Street, watching for Bell to emerge from Dublin Castle. Instead, they became the watched. A man coming out of the Castle gave them 'a very hard look'.[18] The same man doubled back by a circuitous route and emerged again from the Castle a few minutes later, accompanied by a second man. Slattery and Byrne moved up Dame Street towards Trinity College. After confirming that they were being followed, they decided to find a suitable location 'to have a go' at their pursuers. Before they got the opportunity, however, their tail had turned back. 'So all went quiet for that day,' recalled Byrne. 'Of course, we reported the whole matter to our senior officer, Liam Tobin.'[19]

Information was then received that Bell was living in Monkstown. Six members of the squad drove the ten kilometres from the city centre in a recently acquired Ford van. After Ashtown, bicycles would no longer be used on long-distance jobs. Arriving at Bell's home, they saw a car outside and five or six G-men standing about. 'So, if we were to have a go,' recounted Byrne, 'it would mean a bit of a scrap.'[20] The job was called off, to Byrne's disappointment.

Three days into the pursuit of Bell, the squad still did not know that he commuted by tram to the city every morning, and even doubted the information when it was given to them.[21] 'Though Collins maintained an efficient intelligence service,' David Neligan pointed out, 'it had blind spots like all such proceedings.'[22]

Neligan had been informed that Bell was escorted by RIC officers from his home to the tram every morning and was met in College Green by G-men, who escorted him to his office in Dublin Castle or to the Police Courts. The only time when Bell was unaccompanied was on the tram itself. Neligan's informant was one of the G-men who met Bell at the tram stop in College Green. Neligan informed Tim Kennedy, an accountant with Kerry County Council and a brigade intelligence officer, who was close to Michael Collins.

It was understandable that GHQ Intelligence did not have much information on Bell or his movements. In his investigations prior to the banking inquiry, Bell had operated independently of G Division, keeping his own office in Dublin Castle and using Redmond as his conduit to the detective unit. The inquiry into the Ashtown ambush, set up under the same Crimes Act legislation as the banking inquiry, had not been covered by the newspapers.

In later recriminations after Bell's shooting, Macpherson, speaking in the House of Commons, blamed the 'venomous attacks in a certain section of the Dublin Press'.[23] Edward Carson said that the *Freeman's Journal* had 'hounded this man down'. The paper had even published a picture of Alan Bell, identifying him as 'conducting the Star Chamber Inquiry into the business of Irish banks'.[24]

Either GHQ Intelligence did not see the picture in the *Freeman's Journal* or they needed a more recent photo, but they requested Michael Knightly, an *Irish Independent* journalist, to acquire one. 'I was asked to get a photograph of Mr Bell,' he recalled. 'The best I could do was a newspaper picture and this I supplied to Headquarters.'[25]

With the newly acquired information on Bell's movements, squad members 'scouted' the College Green area for a few mornings. A detective, the same one who had followed Slattery and Byrne on Dame Street, stood in the same spot each morning. 'If Bell did not get off the tram, this man moved off to the Castle,' Byrne recalled, 'so the scent was getting hot.' Finally, a plan was made to grab Bell on the tram.

Your time has come

On the ten-minute walk from his home at 19 Belgrave Square to the tram stop at Monkstown, Bell had his usual police escort.[26] As he boarded the tram, he might have noticed a young man with a bicycle waiting nearby. Tom Keogh, a member of the squad, followed the tram and, going as fast as he could, overtook it before it arrived at the Aylesbury Road stop, where a five-member shooting party awaited his signal. Breathless, he pointed to Bell's tramcar.

Had Bell looked up from his paper, he would have seen five respectable-looking young men getting on at the stop.[27] Michael McDonnell and Liam Tobin sat together near the front. Vinny Byrne went upstairs. Joe Guilfoyle and Joe Dolan remained on the lower deck at the back. 'I have often wondered since if he had any suspicions when he saw a group of men board the tram,' Joe Dolan said later. 'He probably thought we were young men on our way to work.'[28] Dolan, a member of the intelligence unit, remembered Bell looking quite relaxed and happy.

McDonnell and Tobin were sitting opposite Bell. As the tram approached the Simmonscourt Road, McDonnell leaned over and asked him, 'Are you Mr Bell?'[29] Before Bell had finished his reply, McDonnell and Tobin had already grabbed him. Frederick Holmes, a young soldier wounded in the war, described the change in atmosphere: 'there was a moment of terrible suspense and anxiety in the tram. People looked at each other in utter bewilderment; nobody said a word.'[30]

Joe Guilfoyle stopped the tram at the corner of Simmonscourt Road.[31] With McDonnell and Tobin dragging him, and Dolan pushing from behind, Bell put his hands on either side of the door of the car to prevent their exit.[32] While breaking Bell's grip on the door, McDonnell said, 'Your time has come', and they hustled him off the tram.[33]

Bell had a frightened look on his face. 'Tobin's gun blazed. So did McDonnell's.' Alan Bell lay prone in front of the railings of the Royal Dublin

Society. Meanwhile, Vinny Byrne had cut the trolley rope when he heard the commotion on the lower deck. Joe Dolan had jumped off the tram to cover it in case anyone was brave enough to interfere. There were about 60 people on board, most of whom were going to work in the city, though there could have been military or police officers among them.

The assassination team escaped down Simmonscourt Road into Donnybrook.[34] In hindsight, squad members believed that they made one mistake that morning. 'The place selected for the elimination of Bell was not very populous,' recalled Jimmy Slattery, 'with the result that we had a long distance to run before we could mingle with people and lose ourselves.'

Bell's death was practically instantaneous. Major Arthur Bell, a cousin, identified the body. The post-mortem showed that one bullet had penetrated the skull, a second had entered the groin and a third had caused a superficial wound on the back of the left wrist. Bell had a loaded revolver in one of his pockets. In another were personally inscribed visiting cards for the United Service Club, a private members' club favoured by members of the British Army.

The coroner was exasperated after a week of murders. 'One wonders what we are coming to in this age,' he said, 'when murders like this occur day after day.'[35]

Reaction

Lady Taylor, the wife of Sir John Taylor, broke the news to Mrs Bell at her home. Lord French sent a telegram: 'Please accept my deep and heartfelt sympathy with you. Your gallant and distinguished husband has crowned a life of devoted and valuable services to Ireland by a noble death in fighting the cause of his country.' Macpherson also telegrammed: 'His outstanding courage, unfailing devotion to duty, and his unswerving loyalty had endeared him to us all, and the Irish Government has lost a faithful servant'.

Bell's shooting made the front page of the *New York Times*: 'Masked Men Kill Aged Official in Street as Passengers Look on in Horror'.[36] *The Times* in London described the shooting as 'a cold blooded atrocity which had seldom been exceeded in the annals of crime'.[37] The left-leaning *Daily Herald* was less sympathetic, reporting the story under the headline 'Notorious Irish Magistrate Killed'.[38] It was the second headline after coverage of the declining health of William O'Brien.

In Ireland the *Irish Times*, recalling his loyal service in the worst days of the Land League and his role in defeating that conspiracy of crime, wrote that the murder of Mr Bell 'was an even darker portent than were, in their day, the murders in the Phoenix Park'. Nationalist media ascribed the death of Alan Bell to the failure of government policy in Ireland. On the day after the shooting, the editorial in the *Freeman's Journal* opened with a description of the 'callous futility' of the government's decision to allow William O'Brien to die on hunger strike.

A £10,000 reward was offered for evidence leading to the arrest of the killers,[39] but no one was ever charged with the shooting. No one on the tram could identify the shooters, despite the fact that the assassination team had not even bothered to wear a disguise. After Bell was grabbed, Patrick Kearns, the conductor of tramcar No. 83, 'got weak, sat down and saw no more'. Some passengers with close connections to Dublin Castle were branded as cowards for not coming forward with evidence.

If Bell had lived, he would have been disappointed with the outcome of the big military raid, which again failed to capture any senior political or military leaders. Neither Richard Mulcahy, Liam Tobin nor Batt O'Connor were at home during the raids.[40] In a particularly embarrassing result—symbolic of an ongoing intelligence failure—a brother of Tobin's was arrested in another case of mistaken identity.[41] The *Freeman's Journal* commented: 'It is quite clear from what is happening that the authorities have been acting either blindly or upon wholly unreliable information'.[42]

Meanwhile, the counter-state administration continued as if nothing had happened. On the day of the shooting, Diarmuid O'Hegarty had sent a letter to Michael Collins confirming the decisions made at the Cabinet meeting the night before. Authorisation was given to pay for a 'Supply of 20,000 flags and 54,000 gummed stamps for the use of Dublin Constituencies in [the] Loan campaign'. Collins was authorised to interview a committee of the Artane Clothing Factory in Cork regarding a loan application, and 'if funds were required to keeping the business going for the present, he may advance up to £1000 for the purpose'.

15. Winter is coming

The shooting of Alan Bell marked what might be called the end of the beginning of the War of Independence. Within weeks there was a clear-out of the Dublin Castle administration. James Macpherson was appointed Minister for Pensions in London and was replaced as chief secretary by Sir Hamer Greenwood, a Canadian-born minister in Lloyd George's government. There was also a change in military command. General Nevil Macready was appointed commander-in-chief of the military forces in Ireland. His combined military and police experience—he had been appointed commissioner of the London Metropolitan Police in August 1918—was seen as an advantage by Lloyd George.

The counter-state administration enjoyed a period of *relative* calm in the immediate aftermath of Bell's death. This did not mean that Michael Collins could sit back and watch the Loan proceeds roll into the banks in Dublin. He had to harangue and cajole the less energetic Loan workers to get the job done.

Not known for his patience, Collins spilled out his frustration in a letter to Harry Boland on 19 April: 'This enterprise will certainly break my heart if anything ever will. I never imagined there was so much cowardice, dishonesty, hedging, insincerity, and meanness in the world, as my experience in connection with this work has revealed.'[1] By the end of the month, however, Collins was in a better mood. Writing to Seán Nunan, registrar of the American Loan, he told him that the fund-raising was about to end in Ireland and that 'the result is hopeful enough'.[2]

Two months later, on 29 June 1920, Michael Collins moved a motion in the Dáil, seconded by Terence MacSwiney, 'That the present issue of the Loan be definitely and finally closed as from close of business on Saturday, 17th July'. In his Department of Finance report to the same meeting, Collins wrote that the Loan accounts 'are perfectly safe as the non-success of the Bank Inquiry will assure you all.'[3] The only loss attributed to the inquiry was £100 less interest earned. 'We need not regret that now,' wrote Collins. 'Details verbally.'

A confident air swept through the counter-state movement. 'The alternative government of Dáil Éireann blossomed in the summer of 1920,' wrote Arthur Mitchell, '[but] its growth was rapid and the season short.'[4]

The first battle in the intelligence war may have been won, but within a week of Bell's shooting Black and Tans were deployed on the streets of Dublin for the first time.[5] The Auxiliaries, a counter-insurgency police unit made up of former British Army officers, arrived in July.

Better-trained undercover agents arriving in Ireland presented a much more formidable challenge to GHQ Intelligence and the squad. British military intelligence was expanded and reorganised to include a plain-clothes unit, with a mandate to gather both military and political intelligence.[6]

Police intelligence was reorganised under Ormonde Winter, the new deputy chief of police and director of intelligence. 'The Irishman, without any insult being intended,' wrote Winter, 'somewhat resembles a dog, and understands firm treatment, but, like the dog, he cannot understand being cajoled with a piece of sugar in one hand whilst he receives a beating from a stick in the other.'[7] It took a number of months for Winter to build up his resources and to introduce his Raid Bureau, a new tactic in the expanding war.

In the ten months from August 1920 to the truce in July of the following year, 6,311 raids and searches were carried out in the Dublin district alone. Ormonde Winter's Raid Bureau was able to gather a substantial amount of information because 'the Irish had an irresistible habit of keeping documents'.[8]

'Of all sources of information,' according to Winter, 'undoubtedly the most valuable was that derived from the examination of captured documents.'[9] He described a 'snowball' effect 'leading to fresh searches, new arrests and the obtaining of more intimate knowledge of the plans, resources and methods of the rebel organisation'. He claimed to have seized £30,000 through 'scrutiny of captured cheque books'.

Daithi O'Donoghue had personal experience of the efficiency of the new Raid Bureau. In early 1921, walking towards the Munster & Leinster Bank on Dame Street on a Saturday morning, he saw a large crowd gathered outside the building.[10] Inside, Auxiliaries were bullying and threatening the elderly manager, who was refusing to divulge details of the republican bank accounts. Only after the Auxiliaries took out their guns and threatened the manager did he hand over the keys to the strongrooms. The Auxiliaries had brought a team of expert accountants, who made a thorough search of the ledgers. They knew what they were looking for. A cheque-book seized in a raid on one of the IRA offices provided enough clues to locate specific accounts.

Unbeknownst to Daithi, who was waiting for the raid to end, the accountants were actually examining joint accounts in his name and the name of another person. There was a balance of £8,700 in a current account and £10,000 in a deposit account. Continuing their forensic examination, the accountants discovered that the funds had been transferred from an account in the name of Michael Collins and Daithi O'Donoghue. The Auxiliaries seized over £20,000 in the raid. Two staff members, Mr Kiernan and Mr Croke, were removed to Dublin Castle. They were released after a short time, but not until they had 'suffered' for refusing to disclose information.

Michael Collins was forced to change his system of distributing funds from the Department of Finance to the various government departments. Messengers like Seán McGrath, 'the Walking Bank', carrying large sums of money on their person had been giving him concern. In May 1921 he informed Diarmuid O'Hegarty that, in order to save time and trouble and to avoid 'possible danger', a cheque would be drawn in favour of the head of each department for weekly payments and similarly for the monthly payments.[11]

Nevertheless, the British forces failed to seize funds in a sufficient quantity to have a material effect on the operation of the Dáil government. On 28 January 1922, after the signing of the treaty, Daithi O'Donoghue met with Alfred Cope, the assistant under-secretary for Ireland. Cope handed Daithi a payment order for £22,250 for funds confiscated by the Crown, including accrued interest.[12] In the audited Loan accounts, Donal O'Connor had described the amount as 'Seized by the English'.[13] At the same meeting, Loan registers that had been taken in a raid in Upper Fitzwilliam Street were also handed back.

16. Fate

Sinn Féin Bank

David Kelly, the Sinn Féin Bank manager, continued the court case against the chief commissioner of the DMP and the military commander in Ireland after the shooting of Alan Bell. He was seeking the recovery of documents and funds seized in the raid on 27 February. On 23 March, three days before the shooting of Alan Bell, the case had been adjourned for a month to re-solve a legal technicality.[1] Major-General Boyd, who had authorised the raid as the competent military authority in Dublin, replaced the chief com-missioner and the military commander as defendant.

In May the court granted an application for discovery, and in June the seized funds and documents were returned to David Kelly. The Sinn Féin Bank reopened for business at 6 Harcourt Street.[2] This was a remarkable outcome after the disclosures during the bank inquiry and the boarding up of its offices at both 3 and 6 Harcourt Street. The dogs in the street knew the connection between the bank and the republican movement. If Alan Bell had lived, he might not have been able to prevent the court ruling in favour of the bank, but it is highly probable that he would have had it shut down before then, using evidence gathered before and during the inquiry, or in follow-up investigations, if they had been allowed to happen.

Like the other arms of the republican movement, the bank enjoyed a period of relative calm through the summer and autumn, but by winter 1920 the British forces in Ireland, including the Black and Tans, the Auxil-iaries and the military and police intelligence services, were on the offensive.

On the morning of Bloody Sunday, 21 November 1920, a mixed force of military and auxiliaries raided 6 Harcourt Street. False reports went out that Joe Clarke, the caretaker and a member of Dublin Corporation, had been arrested.

By the end of the day, 30 people were dead or fatally wounded in

Dublin. In the morning the squad killed twelve British intelligence agents in simultaneous attacks in multiple locations across the city. Two auxiliaries were also shot in a fire fight. In the afternoon British forces shot fourteen civilians at a Gaelic football game in Croke Park, including Michael Hogan, a Tipperary footballer. That evening, IRA Brigadier Dick McKee and Vice-Brigadier Peadar Clancy, the two senior officers in the Dublin Brigade, were arrested and shot by the British, allegedly while trying to escape. 'Amritzar Repeated in Dublin' was the op-ed headline in the *Freeman's Journal* on Monday morning.

Three days later David Kelly was arrested at 132 Pearse Street, where he lived with his sister.[3] Over 50 arrests were made across the city that night. Released the following day, Kelly opened the bank and carried on business as usual.[4]

Raiding expeditions by the military and Auxiliaries continued with increased intensity.[5] On the night of 28 November No. 6 Harcourt Street was targeted again. Mrs Clarke answered the door. The military were looking for her husband, who, as usual, was not at home. The raiding party entered the Sinn Féin Bank, took down signs from the window, disarranged the furniture and scattered documents about the floor. An attempt to force the safe failed. Around the same time as the raid, seventeen Auxiliaries were killed in an ambush in Kilmichael, Co. Cork.

The raiding party returned the following day. Two explosions were heard on Harcourt Street between 12.30 and 1 o'clock, forcing people to leave their homes. The military had blown open the safe at the second attempt. David Kelly, who was held up at the point of a revolver, and Mrs Clarke and her three children were moved to the street before the explosions. Books and documents were seized and £500 taken in the raid.

A photo showing Mrs Clarke standing in one of the smashed-up rooms was published in the *Irish Independent*, but her ordeal was not over. On the following night, shortly after 2am, the fire brigade received a call to 6 Harcourt Street,[6] where a fire had broken out in the lower part of the building. Two incendiary bombs had been thrown from a passing vehicle. That same night the offices of the *Freeman's Journal* were set on fire.

The war continued with increased ferocity through the winter, with attacks, counter-attacks, arrests and brutal reprisals by the British throughout the country. The Sinn Féin Bank continued to trade through it all. Then, on Wednesday 16 March 1921, the *Irish Independent* reported: 'Uneasiness is felt by his friends regarding the whereabouts of Mr David Kelly, manager of the Sinn Féin Bank'.

Two days earlier, at 8.15 in the evening, two military tenders and an armoured car had passed Kelly's house at 132 Pearse Street. On hearing the vehicles, Kelly ran out to warn an IRA unit at No. 144, but the shooting had already commenced. Kelly was 'riddled with bullets'[7] and was dead on admission to hospital. That was another bloody day in Dublin. Six IRA Volunteers had been hanged that morning. The fire fight on Pearse Street claimed seven more lives—two civilians, three IRA Volunteers and two Auxiliaries.

Not unexpectedly, the Sinn Féin Bank went into terminal decline after the death of David Kelly. Five months later, and one month after the truce, Michael Collins informed the Dáil that the bank was in an 'unstable position'.[8] Collins, who had found time to review the accounts himself, expressed his concern for the small depositors who had their life savings in the bank.

On 19 October the management committee, under a new chairman, Patrick Gleeson, passed a winding-up resolution. William O'Brien Hishon, an accountant and auditor at 9 Lower O'Connell Street, was appointed liquidator. He was handed a challenging task because the bank's books were 'in a state of chaos'. Not only had 'faked and bogus entries' been used to disguise transactions but also many of the account books had been returned by the British in a sack.[9] He attempted to prepare the accounts from pages, dockets and scraps of paper 'with notes in shorthand, Irish signs, and other marks' bearing no reference to individual accounts.[10] The only person who would have been in a position to unravel them was David Kelly.

On 28 February 1922 Michael Collins informed the Dáil that the government still had £1,660 in a current account in the Sinn Féin Bank. Unhappy with the progress being made by O'Brien Hishon, the Free State government appointed Donal O'Connor as liquidator in 1923. O'Connor claimed that the winding-up resolution passed in 1921 was invalid.[11] A lengthy court case lasting four years followed, and all the while the small depositors could not access their money.

Patrick Morgan, the dentist whom Alan Bell had identified as having a joint account with Patrick Gleeson in the Hibernian Bank, was called to appear in court. The records showed that almost £600 had been debited to accounts in Morgan's name in the Sinn Féin Bank. Morgan, a member of the management committee of the bank, had been a good friend to Dáil Éireann, allowing his private home to be used for Cabinet meetings.[12]

Morgan was represented in court by Corrigan & Corrigan, solicitors. He denied all knowledge of the accounts in question, stating that 'during the years 1918 to 1921 when these accounts were being operated upon, accounts were kept in fictitious names, especially accounts of persons who were on the run'.[13] He said that the 'late General Michael Collins' had already investigated these accounts and was satisfied that he was in no way indebted to the bank. No order was made against Morgan, who was allowed costs for his appearance.

The bank was eventually wound up under a court order in 1927, but that was not the end of the matter for the depositors, who still had not seen their money. Four years later, they received just 50% of the full amount due to them. The liabilities of the bank exceeded its assets. On 9 August 1933, however, Dáil Éireann voted for the full recoupment of depositor funds.[14]

Although the Sinn Féin Bank did not succeed in its original mandate to promote industrial development in Ireland, it played a front-line role in the money battle during the War of Independence. It facilitated the running of the Dáil government departments, including the overseas envoy offices, and played a crucial role in laundering the proceeds of the Loan.

The Irish State acknowledged the important role played by the bank when it agreed to recoup to the deposit holders the full amount due to them. The Minister for Finance stated that 'during the years in which an attempt was made to overthrow the Irish Republic and suppress the Sinn Féin organisation this bank received considerable and undesirable attention from the British forces in this country so that ultimately the bank was compelled to wind up'.[15]

The failure of the British authorities to close the bank was a strategic mistake. Credit must go to David Kelly, who fought every obstacle placed in front of the bank and used the media to good effect to defend its technical legal independence from the republican movement. During its final year of operation, he ran the bank out of three different locations on Harcourt Street—Nos 3, 6 and 7—as the need required.[16] Raids and arrests did not intimidate him. 'One time when the bank was raided and closed by the

British authorities,' recalled James Kavanagh, 'Davy Kelly put a table and chair on the top step in front of the hall door and carried on, or pretended to carry on as usual in defiance of the British authorities'.[17]

New Ireland Assurance

In addition to their duties in GHQ Intelligence, Liam Tobin and Frank Thornton were members of the management committee of New Ireland Assurance. At its annual general meeting in May 1920, two months after the shooting of Alan Bell, it was Thornton who proposed the motion for the adoption of the accounts after a second successful year of operation.

In June the New Ireland management, buoyed by the positive results, the confidence pervading in the summer of 1920 and the perceived lower security threat from raids and arrests, published a series of advertisements in the *Cork Examiner*.[18] These included the address of the new head office at 56 Lower O'Connell Street and the names of the entire management committee, in addition to Tobin and Thornton—Michael Staines, Dr Jim Ryan and Edmund (Eamon) Duggan, each identified in the advertisement as members of Dáil Éireann, and Michael O'Reilly, the general manager. Staines was separately identified as the treasurer of the business.

The only casualty during the summer was Joe O'Doherty, the Ulster inspector for New Ireland and Dáil member, who had spectacularly escaped arrest from his house the previous December.[19] He was arrested in Belfast in July and sent to Derry Jail on remand. Three courthouses in which he was due to be tried were burned down. After multiple remand hearings before Major Brett, he was eventually released without charge. 'I do not intend going on remanding the man indefinitely.' Dr Margaret O'Doherty, who had aided her husband's escape, would later be removed from her position as medical health officer for Derry Corporation for declining to make the 'Six-County allegiance declaration'.[20]

The business felt the full force of the Raid Bureau, however, during the winter of 1920–1. On 25 November Edward Staines, Michael's father, a former police officer, was arrested by Auxiliaries in his home.[21] The raiders were looking for Michael Staines, who had narrowly escaped arrest the previous February. On 30 November the Auxiliaries raided the old head office of New Ireland above the shop of Kapp and Peterson.[22] Dublin Castle may not have been aware of the change in head office or were suspicious of activity in the building.

On 6 December Staines was finally arrested by Captain William King, a British intelligence officer, who, accompanied by heavily armed Auxiliaries, raided the monthly meeting of Dublin Corporation at City Hall.[23] Councillor Joe Clarke, the caretaker of 6 Harcourt Street, was also arrested in the chamber. After many attempts, the British had finally got their hands on Clarke.

The New Ireland head office was raided in March 1921 by a party of soldiers, who carried out an 'exhaustive' search lasting two and a half hours.[24] No arrests were made, though some correspondence was seized. While the offices were being searched, a Lewis machine-gun commanded the street from one of the windows.

New Ireland's business nevertheless continued to prosper, despite the arrest of Staines, the raid on its head office and the constant threat to staff members. The third annual general meeting took place in May 1921, two months before the truce. Sales had risen by 500% during the previous year to over £37,000.[25] The business was experiencing rising claims, however, because of the death of members 'as prisoners or on active service'.[26]

Michael Staines was sent to Mountjoy prison, where he joined Arthur Griffith, Eoin MacNeill and Eamon Duggan, who had been arrested the same week. 'Griffith, MacNeill, Duggan and myself were *au fait* with every move that was made outside,' recalled Staines. 'We were kept informed by Collins through the medium of the underground post.'[27] His sister, May Staines, used the visits to her brother to smuggle two dozen 0.45 revolvers into the prison, carrying three or four at a time, to aid in the planned escape of other prisoners.[28]

Staines was released in June as part of the truce negotiations. During the truce, as a commandant of the IRA, he acted as liaison officer to the RIC in the west of Ireland to ensure observance of the truce and to carry out cessation arrangements.[29] Appointed the first commissioner of police in 1922, he struggled to integrate former members of the RIC and the Irish Republican Police. After a mutiny by new recruits in May, he resigned from the position later in the year.

Almost 100 years later, in September 2018, the newly appointed commissioner of police, Drew Harris, at a passing out ceremony at the Garda College invoked the words of Michael Staines, the first Garda commissioner and former IRA officer. He told the new recruits that 'the Civic Guard will succeed not by force of arms, or numbers, but on their moral authority as servants of the people'.[30] Harris was a former senior officer in the Police Service of Northern Ireland, the successor force to the Royal Ulster Constabulary and the RIC. His father had been killed by an IRA bomb in 1989.

Michael O'Reilly, who had discussed his plan to establish an Irish insurance business with Michael Collins in Frongoch, served as managing director of New Ireland into the 1950s. On the occasion of the 100th anniversary of the first official meeting of the company on 5 January 1918, his granddaughter and great-grandson were invited to the formal celebrations.[31]

The real founding meeting of the company, however, had been in June 1917, when five passionate, idealistic, brave and entrepreneurial young men had met in a flat over a shop in Wexford. That evening, Michael O'Reilly, in the words of Frank Thornton, 'experienced the delight of feeling that the project to which he had devoted so much time and thought was at last on the way to becoming a reality'.[32]

Today, New Ireland has sales of €1.3 billion, almost €17 billion in funds under management and over 800 employees. The Bank of Ireland acquired the business in 1997, but it continues to trade under the New Ireland brand.

National Land Bank

The National Land Bank finally opened its head office branch at 68 Leeson Street in April 1920, one month after the shooting of Alan Bell. The Dáil government invested £200,000 in the bank by June of that year.[33] The investment was made as 'guaranteed stock' paying interest of 2%.

Demand for loans was greater than expected. Collins was optimistic when he wrote to de Valera in February 1920. 'The Bank can absorb an enormous amount, as quite apart from its Land activities other enterprises are making applications which might with great advantage and success be granted.'[34] Lionel Smith-Gordon said that there were 'several hundred urgent cases pending, involving hundreds of thousands of pounds'.[35]

Collins wanted more of the American Loan injected as capital into the bank. The Department of Finance in a series of meetings with the bank's directors determined that a minimum of £50,000 would be required to open large branches (two were planned to open in January 1921) and £25,000 for six smaller branches.

In June Collins moved a motion in the Dáil providing £25,000 funding for the opening of the six branches. In July James O'Mara sent two bank drafts from America, for £10,471 and £15,706 respectively, to cover the cost. The drafts were carried to Ireland by Revd Maurice Brown, with instructions 'for immediate delivery to Mick and Arthur Griffith'.[36] On 14 August 1920, Collins wrote to Harry Boland confirming receipt of the drafts.

In September, during a private session held in Fleming's Hotel, Collins asked the Dáil to invest $500,000 (£125,000) more of the American Loan as capital in the bank.[37] Between October and December, six drafts totalling £106,776 were couriered to Ireland.[38] They were issued by the Kountze Brothers Bank, New York. The balance probably arrived in early 1921.

The business of the bank was initially conducted without frequent reference to Dáil Éireann. [39] The board met on a weekly basis to discuss the agenda prepared by Smith-Gordon and to make routine cash checks. Michael Collins had secret meetings with Smith-Gordon at his private home on Harcourt Terrace, a leafy residential road close to the city centre. Collins also had a house available to him on the road, which had been purchased by Mary Woods ostensibly on behalf of her nephew. Batt O'Connor had built a secret cupboard in the house for arms and ammunition, and big enough for a person to hide in.

In 1921 the bank encountered an obstacle for which Robert Barton, recently released from prison, required the intervention of Michael Collins.[40] The bank was being blocked from accessing the centralised cheque clearing system set up by the commercial banks. On one occasion, the bank could only settle a large cheque because an equally large lodgement had been made the same day by the Irish White Cross. Barton sought the assistance of Collins, as Minister for Finance, to bring pressure on the Irish Banks Standing Committee (ISBC) to admit the bank to the clearing system.[41] After many requests and repeated refusals, Collins resorted to other means to convince the committee. First, he needed to identify its members.

Collins struggled to get the information he required. One of his contacts reported that the 'composition and rules of the body are wrapped in mystery'. The contact had established, however, that Newman Thompson from the Bank of Ireland, the committee secretary, was the 'moving spirit and most troublesome person'.[42] Further investigation revealed the existence of a separate Dublin Banks Clearing Committee, whose members were the managers of the nine banks in Dublin and whose recommendations to the ISBC were 'practically certain to be accepted'.

On Monday 4 July Collins sent a memo to Daithi O'Donoghue, informing him that the committee was due to meet the following Friday.[43] Collins had received the information directly from one of the bank managers. 'It is most desirable that at this Meeting they should climb down and if it were possible to convince, say, the National and the Hibernian of the fact it would have a good effect.' O'Donoghue visited the bank managers before their meeting on Friday. 'The message I had to deliver was a serious one for those gentlemen', he wrote. 'I shall not enlarge on it.'[44] National Land Bank cheques were accepted in all banks the following Monday.

The message that O'Donoghue had given was certainly a serious one. Collins had sent a second memo to him on Tuesday: 'I think it could be made quite clear to the Committee that if they persist in the action they have taken, we can only regard them as being an enemy institution, and must hold Members of the Committee individually responsible ... the Members of the Committee place themselves—every one of them—in exactly the same position as ... Enemy Agents'.[45]

Dublin Castle became extremely suspicious of the bank and, like other arms of the counter-state, it became a target of Ormonde Winter and his Raid Bureau in late 1920.[46] On 3 November, two days after the execution of eighteen-year-old Kevin Barry, the first republican to be executed since 1916, the head office was searched as part of a series of raids throughout Dublin, though no documents or funds were seized.[47] It was a desperate week of shootings, raids and vicious reprisals throughout the country, especially in Kerry, where the town of Tralee was in a virtual state of siege.

Raids on the bank became more numerous and the books and documents were closely examined. Denis Cogan, an employee of the bank, said that the raids—conducted by the Auxiliaries, accompanied by accountants—became a 'constant irritation' that seriously interfered with the smooth running of the business.[48] Intimidation and threatening behaviour towards staff was common. During a raid on one branch, all the employees were taken out in a lorry and carried around the country as hostages to prevent an attack.[49]

Many of the head office staff, however, could stand up for themselves. The bank's directors may have been appointed to give an air of respectability to the institution but a number of the front office staff were senior IRA members. Michael Cowley, one of the first employees, was a member of the IRB and had fought in the GPO in 1916.[50] Another employee, Eamon Morkan, who had moved from the National Bank, was also a veteran of 1916 and had been adjutant of the south camp when interned in Frongoch. His sister, Pauline, had served bravely during Easter Week with Cumann na mBan.[51]

During one raid, according to Morkan, the Auxiliaries were searching for what they called 'illegal funds' and insisted on being given £20,000 'which they had traced to the possession of Michael Collins'.[52] When told of the raid, Collins was very upset and refused to accept Smith-Gordon's explanation as satisfactory. Morkan felt that the staff had done very well and had possibly avoided the seizure of a much larger sum. He said, however, that the loss of such a large amount of money was a blow 'certainly not lightly to be borne by Collins, who by his nature was intolerant of any slip-ups in such matters'. Morkan claimed that the bank issued a receipt for the money and that the funds were returned with interest after the truce.

Seán McCluskey, who had been hand-picked by Collins for the care-taker position, had moved his family from 76 Harcourt Street to 68 Leeson Street.[53] 'I remember a raid on this place by Black & Tans and a man in civilian clothes who was evidently an accountant,' he recalled. 'They examined books and documents of the Bank.' The raiders returned that evening. 'I remember at the time I was burning cheques in a back room when they again asked for Smith-Gordon, and, as he was not on the premises at the time, they asked me for his address. I said I did not know it.' On another occasion, McCluskey was returning to the office when he saw 'Tan' lorries pulled up outside the bank. He waited until the lorries had departed before entering the building. He had been fortunate. Mrs McCluskey told him that the raiders had been looking for him.

Large cash amounts received into the bank were taken to the IAWS head office by McCluskey. 'When cash lodgements in the Bank became very heavy,' he recalled, 'I had to take the money from Leeson Street and lodge it with a cashier of the Irish Agricultural Wholesale Society in Thomas Street.' He was entrusted with large sums of money. 'I remember on about six or seven visits … I was carrying on my person as large a sum as £14,000.'

There was another reason why Collins had chosen McCluskey for the caretaker role. Any letters delivered to the bank in McCluskey's name were to be forwarded to Collins. 'I remember on the eve of "Bloody Sunday" five letters were delivered to me from different parts of the country,' remarked McCluskey. 'I went to Croke Park … to deliver the letters to Collins as I expected to see him there. I was searched going through the barrier in Croke Park but the letters were not found as I had them well concealed.' Not meeting Collins at the game, he delivered the letters to Liam Devlin's public house the following day.

Despite the disruption caused by raids and searches, the bank survived through the most difficult phase of the War of Independence. By June 1921, one month before the truce, the bank had extended over £315,000 in loans to 40 co-operatives for the purchase of land. Smith-Gordon attributed the bank's survival to 'something in English psychology which inspires a respect for financial institutions'.[54] Robert Barton, after his release from prison, said that 'it was fairly well known in Dublin Castle that the Bank had a connection with the Dáil'.[55]

Edward Stephens, who had been instrumental in founding the bank and later became its legal adviser, believed that Dublin Castle not only was aware of the connection but also approved of the activities of the bank. 'If the Castle authorities were aware that these transactions were being carried out with Dáil money, they decided that it was being employed in a manner advantageous to the landlords, and decided not to interfere with the activities of the bank.'[56]

Michael Collins took the 'greatest interest' in the work of the bank, according to Barton.[57] Inevitably, there was some interference in lending decisions. Shortly after the treaty was signed, Collins was approached by some men asking for the grant of a loan to Jim O'Gorman to buy a public house in Cappawhite.[58] O'Gorman, who had served in France with the

Australian Army, was a member of the important 3rd Tipperary Brigade, whose views on the treaty would be closely watched nationally. Collins agreed to arrange the loan. This might have been an isolated incident. Edward Stephens said that many people applied for loans which they could not get from other banks. These were 'of course' refused, because the bank had a duty to its depositors to only issue well-secured loans.[59]

In August 1921 Robert Barton delivered a speech to the Dáil addressing what he called the 'smoke screen' that had been drawn over the bank.[60] He outlined the bank's history from the Dáil vote in June 1919 to its registration in December of that year, the opening of six branches and the decision to purchase a new head office on Dame Street, and the 'steady and continuous' progress being made. He paid tribute to the work done by Art O'Connor, who had deputised for him as Director of Agriculture while he was in prison. In a self-deprecating touch, he apologised for his absence, which he said had been a blessing in disguise for the Dáil. He told the assembled TDs that the future of the bank was dependent on the amount of capital it could raise from its branch network 'owing to the exhaustion of the funds allotted by the Dáil'. He urged the TDs present to support the transfer of capital from other banks, which were 'compelled to look to London for guidance in their financial and economic policy'.

Barton's speech was measured in tone until a question from the floor provoked him into an angry tirade concerning the lack of support given to the bank, and in particular to the new branches that had been opened.[61] 'The way the directors had been misled,' said Barton, 'by some important personages in the districts where they wanted branches of the bank established was nothing less than scandalous.'

Staff investigating locations for opening new branches had received promises of being 'snowed under by money'. Instead, one branch had only 25 current accounts after six months in business. The same people who wanted branches opened in their towns had not even transferred their own business. Barton contrasted this with his own behaviour. He told his fellow TDs that in Dublin 'he had to go round and do the tout [for business] himself'. Barton's invective echoed Michael Collins's criticism of ineffective Loan organisers.

Despite the lack of support received in some quarters, the bank was ideally positioned to thrive in post-treaty Ireland—State-owned, with a healthy balance sheet and ready to become the 'financial centre for Ireland' that had been envisaged by Collins and Barton. In its annual report, the Irish Agricultural Organisation Society (IAOS) said that the bank's ambition to establish itself as a national banking institution was successfully heading in the right direction.[62]

The deposit base increased substantially in early 1922 with the transfer of the Loan funds to the bank. On 23 February, at a meeting in the Mansion House attended by members of the Provisional Government (including Michael Collins) and the Loan trustees, Daithi O'Donoghue was instructed to call in all outstanding amounts held by private individuals and in other banks, and to lodge it all to one account in the Land Bank.

It also became the official bank of the Irish White Cross when it launched in March 1921.[63] Smith-Gordon had been appointed chairman of the agency, set up to distribute humanitarian funds raised by an influential American charity. The Irish White Cross was a 'who's who' of nationalism in Ireland and America. Michael Collins and Arthur Griffith were among the trustees of the fund. Strong management links existed between the Irish White Cross and the National Land Bank. In addition to Smith-Gordon, Erskine Childers was on the executive committee and James MacNeill was the honorary secretary.

The Civil War intervened, however, and the outlook for the bank became less certain. Robert Barton, a reluctant signatory to the treaty, eventually rejected it and aligned himself with the anti-treaty side. His opposition meant that Barton could have no role in the Provisional Government and ended his connection to the bank. It also marked the end of his great friendship with Collins. 'Our relations were completely severed after the Dáil debates,' recalled Barton. 'I never spoke to him again and never saw him.' And with the death of Michael Collins in August 1922 the bank had lost its two most energetic promoters.

In August 1923 the Free State government set up the Irish Land Commission and introduced a new land purchase scheme. The balance of the loans that had been extended to the co-operatives were refunded to the bank, which had now lost its original *raison d'être*. Management endeavoured to attract new customers and more commercial business, but it struggled to compete with the commercial banks.[64] It was given a limited amount of government business in 1924 and 1925, but otherwise Ernest Blythe, Minister for Finance, showed little interest in it.

In 1926, despite 'doing a good business', the bank's continued owner-ship by the State had come into question.[65] Ernest Blythe said, 'I have recog-nised for a very considerable time that the position of the Land Bank is anomalous. I have recognised that it is a State-owned bank which is not a State bank.'[66] A Banking Commission recommended that it be sold or wound up.[67] The Minister for Finance received an inquiry from the Bank of Ireland 'as to whether the Government would consider an offer'. In Oc-tober the National Land Bank was acquired by the Bank of Ireland for £203,000, the amount of the original capital invested, though £13,000 of the proceeds was used to cover compensation payments to staff and the State had injected substantially more than the initial capital into the bank.

The National Land Bank became the National City Bank in 1927. In 1968 Chase Manhattan acquired a 50% stake to develop an international bank in Ireland. The bank had maintained a good relationship with the Morgan Guaranty Trust Company of New York, with whom Michael Collins had worked in London. In 1979 the remaining 50% share of the bank was acquired by Chase Manhattan, marking the end of the company as an independent entity.

Patrick Moylett, an original champion of setting up a national bank, had envisioned its becoming the official bank to the government.[68] Instead, the Free State appointed the Bank of Ireland as its official bank. On 18 Jan-uary, when the Provisional Government was just four days old, Michael Collins approached the governors of the Bank of Ireland to secure financial support. The bank 'consented' to give one million pounds in financial credit to the young government.[69] A dramatic version of the meeting was told by Seán MacEoin, an IRA commander and future chief of staff and Minister for Defence. Tim Pat Coogan in his biography of Michael Collins related MacEoin's version of what happened:

> 'The directors at first demurred and Collins sprang up and began
> to pack his briefcase, saying to MacEoin, "Right so! General,
> when we get back to the office, make immediate arrangements
> to have the guard removed from this building." As they made for
> the door the puzzled MacEoin whispered, "What guard, Mick?"
> To which the reply was a sotto-voce growl, "Shut up you fucking

eejit, a large whiskey they'll be after us before we're well out the door." The pair hadn't even reached the door when there came an embarrassed cough and a "Mr Collins, can we discuss this matter a little further ...".[70]

MacEoin's account of the meeting, even if appearing overdramatic, provides an insight into the complex relationship between the Dáil government and the Bank of Ireland during the revolutionary period. Collins had Francis Brooke, a director of the bank, shot in July 1920, though the shooting may have had more to do with Brooke's position on a security committee set up by Lord French.

It appears that Collins had a good working relationship with Andrew Jameson, the Scottish-born director of the bank and owner of the whiskey business.[71] The latter was appointed to the Free State senate and played an important role during the Civil War period. Furthermore, loans from the bank kept Dublin Corporation afloat when local government funding from the British government was cut off in response to the corporation's declaration of allegiance to Dáil Éireann.

Given the precarious financial position of the new administration, there was really no option other than to appoint the Bank of Ireland as the official bank. Established in 1783, the bank had survived the Act of Union in 1800, and it seemed inevitable that it would survive through the transition to the Free State.

The Land Bank had performed a crucial function in the years 1919–21. Initially, it provided hope that a solution to the vexatious land problem was at hand and it was an important propaganda tool for the new Dáil government as it strove for credibility. Loans extended to co-operatives received wide press coverage. The timing of its establishment was also opportune as an alternative to the Sinn Féin Bank, which had become unstable following the arrest of Alderman Kelly in December 1919, the constant raids and the shooting of David Kelly in early 1921. The bank also provided an alternative to the commercial banks for safekeeping Loan funds in the name of trusted people. Michael Collins operated an account in the name of Cardinal Michael Logue.[72] Amounts of £20,000, and probably more, were held in these accounts.[73] Eamon Morkan felt the need to make it 'quite clear' that the practice of using disguised names in the accounts happened in 'isolated cases only'.

The Land Bank also worked in partnership with the Land Courts, which were set up to settle issues concerning trespass and the seizure of land. Two land commissioners had been appointed: Conor Maguire, who later became chief justice, and Kevin O'Sheil, who became a senior counsel. Maguire and O'Sheil were 'in constant peril not only of arrest but of physical injury or death'.[74] Warren Fisher, a senior British civil servant sent to Ireland, praised the Land Courts for preventing anarchy in disturbed rural areas.[75] The Land Bank worked 'harmoniously' with the Land Courts, according to Robert Barton, and their combined efforts 'probably averted an outbreak of violence which might have had very serious national consequences'.[76]

Daithi O'Donoghue described the bank's acquisition by the Bank of Ireland as a 'rather ignominious fate considering the work done and the hopes raised!'[77] The business ended up in the hands of the bank that had denied it access to the cheque clearing system until O'Donoghue conveyed the 'serious message'. Much work had indeed been done and many hopes had been raised. The first meeting to set up the bank had been held in the home of Edward Stephens on Leeson Street. Those present would have shared the same passion, enthusiasm and hopes as those who were at the first meeting of New Ireland Assurance over the shop in Wexford. And each of those present risked arrest and imprisonment to be part of the start-up business. The same passion was there when Robert Barton went around Dublin personally 'touting' for new business. Would the fate of the bank have been different if the energy of Robert Barton and Michael Collins had not been lost to it? Maybe it would have become the 'financial centre of Ireland' that both envisaged.

17. Financial civil war

Following the truce in July 1921, Dáil Éireann held its first public meeting in over two years on Tuesday 16 August. A marathon eight-day session commenced, adding to the already heavy workload on Michael Collins, who worked through the following weekend.[1] On the second day of the session, he presented the report of the Department of Finance. He told the Dáil that his department had 'operated throughout the period under review in a satisfactory manner' and that a 'complete audit of all Departmental Receipts and Expenditure is maintained at all times, and works well'.[2] The Dáil funds were secure. 'The arrangements made to meet the enemy attack on our funds have so far frustrated his designs'.[3]

On 7 January 1922, Dáil Éireann approved by a narrow majority the treaty between Great Britain and Ireland signed in London a month earlier. The Dáil had split into pro-treaty and anti-treaty factions, headed by Michael Collins and Éamon de Valera respectively. The treaty had established the 'Irish Free State', which had 'dominion' status within the British Empire, similar to Canada and Australia, and had jurisdiction in 26 of the 32 counties. It also required an oath of allegiance to the constitution of the Free State, and to be 'faithful to H.M. King George V, his heirs and successors by law'. Those opposed to the treaty considered it a betrayal of the Irish Republic declared in 1916.

One week later, as required under the terms of the treaty, the House of Commons of Southern Ireland met for the first time and approved the treaty by the unanimous vote of the 66 members present. No anti-treaty members of Dáil Éireann attended. The meeting constituted a 'Provisional Government' with Michael Collins as its chairman. The assembly never met again and Dáil Éireann continued as the *de facto* legislative body.

The new Provisional Government was in desperate need of finance, even after securing a line of credit from the Bank of Ireland. An important meeting took place on 23 February between members of the Provisional

Timeline

Date	Financial civil war
25 June 1919	Trust agreement signed by Bishop Fogarty, Éamon de Valera and James O'Mara.
26 August 1921	Stephen O'Mara replaced his brother James as trustee.
6 December 1921	Treaty between Great Britain and Ireland signed in London by Irish plenipotentiaries, including Michael Collins.
7 January 1922	Treaty passed in Dáil Éireann by a majority vote.
14 January 1922	Treaty passed by the House of Commons of Southern Ireland. The assembly never met again. Provisional Government established.
23 February 1922	Meeting between members of the Provisional Government, including Michael Collins, and the trustees of the Dáil funds (Bishop Fogarty, Éamon de Valera and Stephen O'Mara). Daithi O'Donoghue also present.
16 June 1922	Election to the Third Dáil.
28 June 1922	Civil War breaks out.
9 September 1922	First meeting of the Third Dáil.
13 September 1922	New trustees appointed. Bishop Fogarty continues in the role. Richard Mulcahy, Minister for Defence, and Dr Richard Hayes TD replace Éamon de Valera and Stephen O'Mara.
23 October 1922	Daithi O'Donoghue, while in Mountjoy prison, refuses to give instructions for the handover to the Free State of $10,000 cash in a parcel in the Munster & Leinster Bank.
15 November 1922	Writ issued against Éamon de Valera, Stephen O'Mara and Daithi O'Donoghue, declaring that the $10,000 constitutes part of the Dáil funds and to account for any Dáil funds in their possession.
21 December 1922	Free State granted an injunction restraining the three defendants from withdrawing or dealing with the $10,000. It had already been withdrawn on the instructions of Daithi O'Donoghue.
10 February 1923	Daithi O'Donoghue, while interned in Newbridge Camp, refuses to recognise the court, declaring himself a 'soldier of the Irish Republic, and … an official of the Government of the Irish Republic'.
24 May 1923	End of Civil War.
23 July 1924	In default of defence, Justice Murnaghan makes a declaration against Éamon de Valera and Daithi O'Donoghue that the $10,000 constituted part of the funds of Dáil Éireann and to account for any Dáil funds in their possession.
31 July 1924	Justice Murnaghan makes a similar declaration against Stephen O'Mara. He appeals to the Supreme Court.
17 December 1925	Supreme Court unanimously upholds Justice Murnaghan's decision.
7 February 1927	A court order appoints William Norman in the place of Éamon de Valera to concur with Bishop Fogarty and Stephen O'Mara in executing the release of the Dáil funds.

170

Government and the three trustees of the Dáil funds—Éamon de Valera, Stephen O'Mara (who had replaced his brother James) and Bishop Fogarty.[4] Daithi O'Donoghue was also at the meeting. Bishop Fogarty was the only one of the three trustees on the pro-treaty side. Without the agreement of de Valera and O'Mara, both treaty opponents, the new Provisional Government could not access funds held in the names of the trustees, although neither could de Valera and O'Mara without the support of Bishop Fogarty.

In preparation for the meeting, Donal O'Connor prepared the audited Dáil accounts for 1921. One entry signalled the growing political tensions. A charge of £1,341 was made in the accounts for money stolen from one of the Dáil offices on the night of 14 or 15 December.[5] Daithi O'Donoghue felt that someone 'in the know' had done the job. The money had been well hidden in the St Andrew Street office in a strongbox screwed down to a concealed shelf in a large, deep press. The theft occurred while the treaty was being debated in the Dáil. 'It left a very uncomfortable feeling,' recalled O'Donoghue, 'especially as there were even then evidences of an approaching split.'[6]

After reviewing the accounts, all agreed that there was no longer a need for Dáil funds to be held in individual names or controlled by trusted individuals. Donal O'Connor advised that the funds be consolidated into one Dáil Éireann account in the names of the official trustees to avoid 'possible complications'.[7] Daithi O'Donoghue was instructed to call in the outstanding balances and to lodge all the funds in the National Land Bank.[8] There was a lot of money at stake: the accounts showed that there was over £237,000 in 'Home' funds.[9]

The American funds presented a bigger headache for Michael Collins. There was over $2.1 million in America (£425,000) at the end of 1921.[10] The money was held in the name of Stephen O'Mara only. It was unanimously agreed at the meeting that title should be transferred to the trustees and that the funds should remain in America. There was no guarantee, however, that Stephen O'Mara would act on the decision, especially if the split over the treaty widened, which it did.

Negotiations to settle differences between the opposing sides proved futile. Pro-Treaty Sinn Féin and Anti-Treaty Sinn Féin candidates campaigned against each other in the general election in June 1922. Treaty supporters won by a significant majority and a bloody civil war erupted. Michael Collins was dead within two months and Daithi O'Donoghue, who opposed the treaty, was interned.

The Provisional Government needed funds to prosecute the civil war. In order to access the funds held in trust, the Dáil—boycotted by members opposed to the treaty—appointed new trustees. Bishop Fogarty continued in the role, but Éamon de Valera and Stephen O'Mara were removed. They were replaced by Richard Mulcahy, Minister for Defence, and Dr Richard Hayes TD. Richard Hayes was a medical doctor, a noted Francophile and a future director of the Abbey Theatre.

On 23 October the attorney general sent James O'Connor, a Dublin solicitor, to interview Daithi O'Donoghue in Mountjoy prison concerning $10,000 in cash that was held in safekeeping in the Munster & Leinster Bank on Dame Street.[11] Michael Collins had been given the dollars sometime before the civil war broke out. Wanting to keep it as a dollar reserve, he had handed the cash to O'Donoghue, who returned the equivalent in pounds out of the Dáil funds.[12] Because the dollars were not deposited into a bank account, they were kept in O'Donoghue's own name rather than in the name of the trustees. The bank would only release the money to the Provisional Government on written instructions from O'Donoghue, who at first seemed inclined to comply but then said that he could only do so in consultation with de Valera and O'Mara.[13]

The Provisional Government was also having trouble accessing the main Dáil funds. The National Land Bank would not release the money without the agreement of the three original trustees in whose names the accounts were opened. James O'Connor recommended that legal proceedings be initiated against Éamon de Valera and Stephen O'Mara, and Daithi O'Donoghue as secretary to the trustees, to determine the ownership of the $10,000 and the other Dáil funds.

The case of *Fogarty and others v. O'Donoghue and others* was set in motion. The plaintiffs sought a declaration that the $10,000 constituted part of the Dáil funds and so could be accessed by the new trustees, and they wanted the transfer of all other funds. The new trustees were joined as plaintiffs by Ernest Blythe, Minister for Finance; Liam Cosgrave, former Minister for Finance and now president of the Executive Council of the Free State; and John Collins as the personal representative of the late Michael Collins.

On 15 November a writ was served on Daithi O'Donoghue. Two weeks later a writ was served on Stephen O'Mara, who had also been arrested and interned. As Éamon de Valera could not be located, an order was given by the court that service of the writ could be effected by advertisements in national papers.[14]

The plaintiffs had an early victory. An injunction was granted restraining the three defendants from withdrawing the $10,000 in the Munster & Leinster Bank.[15] The plaintiffs were in for a surprise, however. On the following day, James O'Connor met the bank manager only to be told that the parcel containing the money 'had been already withdrawn to the order of Mr O'Donoghue'.[16] The manager refused to disclose the identity of the person who received the package. Somehow, O'Donoghue had arranged the withdrawal while still interned.

During the first hearing on the motion in December 1922, Philip O'Reilly, the solicitor acting on behalf of O'Donoghue, asked the court for an adjournment, as O'Donoghue had been transferred to the internment camp in Newbridge.[17] Solicitors for Stephen O'Mara also wanted to establish communication with their client, whom they believed to be in Mountjoy prison.

Three more adjournments were granted to Philip O'Reilly owing to delays in obtaining the required military permit to interview O'Donoghue. After the meeting eventually took place in January 1923, O'Reilly had to ask for another adjournment. He told the court that O'Donoghue had 'communicated certain facts' that needed to be put in an affidavit.[18] The judge, although losing patience, granted the adjournment to allow a commissioner for oaths to attend at the detention camp.[19]

The meeting took place on 10 February 1923. O'Donoghue handed O'Reilly prepared written instructions:[20]

'A Chara, I am obliged to you for the interest you have taken in the action against me in connection with the funds of Dáil Éireann, and I wish you to thank my friends who instructed you to look after my interests in this matter. I, however, as a soldier of the Irish Republic, and as an official of the Government of the Irish Republic, cannot recognise the purported jurisdiction of this court in which this case is listed. I am prepared to leave the issues between the plaintiffs and myself to a court of the Irish Republic. In the circumstance, you will kindly take no further steps on my behalf.'

On the following Monday, Justice Powell was not pleased when informed of O'Donoghue's statement. 'Was he now to understand that all those applications for adjournment had been made while Mr O'Donoghue did not intend to submit to the jurisdiction of the Court?'[21]

With Éamon de Valera still nowhere to be found and O'Donoghue refusing to recognise the court, only Stephen O'Mara continued a defence against the action, probably because a similar battle was being enacted in the courts in New York for the proceeds of the American Loan, which were in his sole name.

By this time the Free State forces had gained the upper hand in the civil war and controlled most of the country. The civil war finally ended in May 1923, though O'Donoghue and many thousands of others were kept in internment. In August, while still interned, O'Donoghue went forward for election to Dáil Éireann, the first election since the civil war had ended. He ran as a Republican Party candidate under the leadership of Éamon de Valera. The pro-treaty party, Cumann na nGaedheal, won a majority of the seats. O'Donoghue polled just 330 first-preference votes in the Dublin North constituency and was eliminated after the fifth count. Richard Mulcahy topped the poll with over 22,000 first preferences (40%).

In October O'Donoghue joined a mass hunger strike organised by republican prisoners.[22] And then he did the spectacular. On Saturday 20 October 1923, at 3 o'clock, while being transferred from Mountjoy Hospital to St Bricin's Hospital, O'Donoghue escaped from a Red Cross ambulance with Seán McBride and Michael Price.[23] Seán McBride was the son of Maud Gonne and John McBride, who had been executed in 1916. 'On arrival at a quiet street,' according to a military report released to the press, 'the three prisoners, who had said that they were unable to walk, jumped out of the ambulance, attacked the doctor, removed his uniform, and escaped.'[24] McBride and Price, although on the run, issued an immediate counter-statement that they had not requested an ambulance and denied that a doctor was even present.[25]

Meanwhile, the wheels of financial justice were turning slowly. In July

1924 Justice Murnaghan made a declaration against O'Donoghue and de Valera, in default of a defence, declaring that the $10,000 constituted part of the funds of Dáil Éireann and for them to account for any other funds in their possession.[26] After a similar declaration was made against Stephen O'Mara, he made an appeal to the Supreme Court on the grounds that the Free State did not have the authority to appoint the new trustees.

Almost one and a half years later, on 17 December 1925, the Supreme Court unanimously upheld Justice Murnaghan's decision,[27] although it disagreed with one part of the original judgement. It allowed O'Mara's costs to be met out of the funds. Justice Fitzgibbon believed that O'Mara was not 'acting unreasonably' in refusing to transfer the funds, as there was 'sufficient doubt' in relation to the appointment of the new trustees.[28]

The Free State government, however, was still not able to access the money, even after the decisions handed down by the High Court and the Supreme Court. Although O'Mara was prepared to abide by the ruling, de Valera 'refused or neglected' to cooperate with the decision, despite copies of Justice Murnaghan's decision and the Supreme Court order being personally served on him in December 1926.[29] Finally, in February 1927, the court made an order appointing William Norman in de Valera's place to concur with Bishop Fogarty and Stephen O'Mara in executing the discharge of the moneys.[30]

The Free State had already passed legislation for the repayment of the Loan in 1924, under the Loans and Funds Act signed into law on 18 February of that year.[31] A special team of staff was organised in the Department of Finance to prepare an 'authentic' Register of Subscribers. Payment was to be made using Post Office Savings Certificates on 1 June 1927. Subscribers to the Loan received a 40% return on their investment, in line with the terms of the original prospectus. The 40% return consisted of the 5% interest rate paid for seven years and the repayment of the principal at 105%.[32]

18. Conclusion

Enabling the first step

'If it had not been for the generosity and the faith of the people who subscribed to the Loan, there would be no Free State to-day'—Ernest Blyth, Minister for Finance, December 1923.

The raising of the First Dáil Loan was an exceptional achievement for an alternative government setting up a counter-state in open defiance of the established and hostile British administration. The official amount raised, published in October 1920, was £371,849, almost 50% above the funding target of £250,000.[1] The final total was even higher. With the receipt of outstanding payments and funds sent from London, Michael Collins was able to inform the Dáil in August of the following year that the Loan had reached £400,000.[2]

When the legislation was passed to repay the Loan in 1924, Ernest Blyth, Minister for Finance at the time, spoke of the State's moral obligation. 'Many people at great sacrifice subscribed substantial sums, for people of their means, in order to enable the struggle that was getting under way.'

There was also good politics in the decision to make the repayment. As Francis M. Carroll pointed out in his seminal work on the American Loan, repayment by the Free State 'demonstrated the good faith of its intentions regarding the External Loan' during the protracted legal battle in America for control of the funds there.[3]

The subscribers to the Loan had backed the prospect of self-government on a distant, even unrealistic, promise of future repayment. 'Few, if any, of the subscribers expected to see their money again,' wrote Béaslaí; '… it must have come as a pleasant surprise to many of them to find the Free State Government, in fulfilment of the pledge given by Michael Collins during the debate on the Treaty, honouring those bonds.'[4]

The Free State established after the treaty negotiations was not the republic that many subscribers to the Loan had hoped to achieve. If the Free State was a 'stepping stone' to that goal, then it was the subscribers to the First Dáil Loan who had enabled that first step to be taken. 'If it had not been for the generosity and the faith of the people who subscribed to the Loan,' Ernest Blyth said, 'there would be no Free State to-day.'[5] The Loan paid for the day-to-day activity of the underground government departments, the overseas envoys and the first steps in the constructive programme, besides providing the 'sinews of war' for the Ministry of Defence. The success of the Loan was not achieved without a price, however: Loan organisers, workers and subscribers were harassed, arrested and imprisoned.

Raising the American Loan was also an impressive accomplishment, though the organisers there did not face the same oppressive measures as in Ireland. The American Loan raised over $5.2 million (£1.2 million) by the end of 1921.[6] Regulatory and other issues had delayed commencement of fund-raising until January 1920, and the actual amount received in Ireland by 24 June 1920, three months after the shooting of Alan Bell, was only $200,000.[7] The most valuable contribution of the American funds to the counter-state was the provision of capital for the National Land Bank.

Plans had been made for a second loan in both Ireland and America. Although the truce had been signed, new loans of £500,000 in Ireland and approximately $20 million (£5.5 million) in America were approved by the Dáil in August 1921. It was planned to start the new fund-raising drive in mid-October of that year. The Loan was launched in America on 15 October and raised $622,720 (£140,000) before being stopped when the treaty was signed in December.[8] In total, between the two loans, over $5.8 million, or about £1.2 million, was raised in America.[9]

Reasons for success

'Considering the desperate conditions obtaining at the time, the results were wonderful'—Daithi O'Donoghue.

Leadership and teamwork, combined with planning, efficient organisation and attention to detail, underpinned the success of the Dáil Loan. Arthur

Griffith attributed much of the achievement to Michael Collins, who, he said, 'had accomplished one of the most extraordinary feats in the country's history … in spite of the most determined opposition of England'.[10] Béaslaí praised Collins's 'vigorous control' in the face of 'some doubt, when the Loan was started, whether it would be possible to raise so large a sum'.[11]

Michael Collins was a hands-on leader, working long days on all aspects of the Loan. Daithi O'Donoghue commended Collins for his 'organising ability and tireless energy'.[12] He was not the easiest person for whom to work, and, as is often the case, was liked by those who worked most closely with him and disliked by those with whom he had only infrequent contact. He was as quick to reward as to admonish. Seán McCluskey, the caretaker in 76 Harcourt Street, found Collins 'a very gruff but big-hearted individual' who, when there was a big price on his head, 'didn't forget to give me a nice present at Christmas'. The four provincial Loan organisers were paid a bonus of £25.

An innovative marketing campaign enhanced the sense of national solidarity towards the Loan. This togetherness—us against them—was reinforced by the oppressive policy of Dublin Castle, including the arrest and imprisonment of TDs, which in turn inspired others to support the Loan, often at great personal risk. 'Not alone were the TDs and those helping them in great personal danger,' recalled Daithi O'Donoghue, 'but even subscribers, should their applications be found in raids … Nevertheless, the response was magnificent and something of which to be proud.'[13] Each act of leadership and defiance in promoting the Loan resulted in a continuous news flow cycle.

It was the work performed by those on the ground, however, that ultimately determined the success of the Loan. Meetings had to be organised, prospectus and Loan material delivered, posters hung, walls painted, money collected and receipts provided. Although provincial and constituency suborganisers were paid, the majority helped raise the money out of patriotism.

Seán Wall helped raise over £30,000 in East Limerick, making it the best-performing constituency in the country.[14] He had his own unique way of soliciting subscriptions when canvassing door to door. 'Giving his visit the appearance of an ordinary social call he would in due course entertain the household to a (rebel) song or two, … having softened the heart and awakened possible dormant patriotism, the assault on the pocket began as by an afterthought—and he rarely departed empty-handed.'[15] Wall was also a first-class organiser and chairman of Limerick County Council. The success in East Limerick was also helped by parish pump politics. The Dáil promised to fund the Limerick Technical School, which was in danger of closing.[16]

Where the money went

The total outlay of the Dáil government in 1919 and 1920 was £374,026, equivalent to $25.5 million today. Spending on economic development activity, including funding the National Land Bank, accounted for a surprising 70% of total expenditure in that period. The Loan, of course, was also used to fund the setting up of the legislative, executive and judicial arms of the fledgling state, but, again surprisingly, only 6% of Dáil expenditure in its first two years went on the Department of Defence, though other funds may also have been used to purchase arms. Expenditure on military activity, however, ratcheted up substantially in 1921. In the six months before the truce in July of that year, the Department of Defence accounted for 35% of government spending, and, despite the signing of the truce, for 48% of expenditure in the second six months of the year.

The Loan prospectus, newspaper interviews and political speeches made it clear that the primary purpose of the Dáil Loan was to enhance economic activity; to enable better utilisation of the industrial and other resources of the country; to create a new source of financial capital for business development; and to open international trade routes independent of the British government by establishing a trade consul network and setting up an Irish merchant marine. To that end, £200,000 ($13.7m) was invested in the National Land Bank and a further £25,000 ($1.7m) was given as a loan to open new branches. The national government also extended loans of £19,330 ($1.3m) at a 4% interest rate to fishery co-ops for business development, including boat-buying and setting up a fish-curing business.[17] And the combined cost of the Department of Trade, the overseas trade consul network and the 'Commission of Inquiry into the Resources and Industries of Ireland' totalled £12,107 ($830,000). A further £11,593

($790,000) was spent on the latter activities in 1921.

Excluding the funds disbursed on economic development activity, Dáil government expenditure in 1919 and 1920 totalled £117,589 ($8m). At first glance this may appear to be a relatively small amount expended on the legislative, executive and judicial functions of the state, but it reflected a number of factors and conditions at the time.

The counter-state government was not financing a full national civil service. Only the Local Government Department and, to a certain extent, the Department of Home Affairs, which was responsible for the Republican Courts and for policing, exercised any meaningful government activity on the ground. By the time of the treaty, the Local Government Department had 79 staff.[18] In contrast, the civil service in the Dublin Castle administration numbered over 25,000.[19] Furthermore, the Dáil government did not have to fund a standing army—the Volunteers were mostly part-time and largely unpaid. Only £21,210 ($1.5m) was expended on the Department of Defence in 1919 and 1920. As the conflict escalated, however, military expenditure rose substantially. In 1921 total expenditure on defence rose to £137,403 ($9.4m).

Another reason for the relatively small spending on the state apparatus in the first two years of the Dáil government was a shortage of funds until the final quarter of 1919; only £10,160 of the Loan had been received by October of that year. Up till then, the government had to rely almost exclusively on contributions to the Self-Determination Fund (SDF), a national funding campaign primarily set up to attract money that had been contributed to the anti-conscription fund, which was being handed back to subscribers. The SDF received contributions of £42,054 ($2.9m) by October 1919.[20] After the Loan was launched, subscriptions to the fund declined, though some money (not Loan-related) received from America would continue to go into it. The SDF accounted for less than 10% of government receipts to the end of December 1920.

Many of the ambitious spending plans of the Dáil were also negatively affected by the oppressive measures adopted by Dublin Castle, beginning in September 1919 with the prohibition of Dáil Éireann and followed by raids and mass arrests, the nationwide prohibition of Sinn Féin, the first intelligence battle and the bank inquiry. During this period Ernest Blythe, Director of Trade, was arrested, though he was released shortly after. Robert

Barton, Director of Agriculture, was not so fortunate. Arrested in January 1920, he was not released until shortly before the truce in 1921. The Commission of Inquiry into the Resources and Industries of Ireland, which had operated openly in 1919, was forced underground in early 1920.

The arrival of the Black and Tans and the Auxiliaries, combined with a re-energised British intelligence service, including Ormonde Winter's Raid Bureau, intensified pressure on the government departments. The audited accounts for the Loan and the Self-Determination Fund for the eight months to December 1920 recorded an 'amount seized' of £18,732 ($1.2m). Michael Collins was more expressive in his Department of Finance report when describing the money seized—'Stolen by the English'.[21]

At the Department of Labour, Countess Markievicz reacted to the increasing number of resignations from the RIC by setting up a 'Police Employment Bureau' to find alternative employment for members of the force who had resigned, and probably to encourage others to do so.[22] On 17 September 1920 the Dáil voted £350 towards the expenses of the bureau. The Cabinet also authorised advertisements to be placed in newspapers promoting the body. These were to be 'well displayed and to be inserted in two issues', and an employee of the department was authorised to spend a month in England to make 'enquiries as to possibility of placing ex-RIC men in employment [there]'. The department also set up Labour Arbitration Tribunals and a sum of £500 was voted for their operation in September 1920, of which £95 had been spent by the end of the year. Expenditure on the Department of Labour rose to £6,795 ($465,000) in 1921, from just £977 in the previous two years.

Activity in the Department of Local Government ramped up significantly in the latter part of 1920, despite being under constant threat of raids, as more local authorities declared loyalty to Dáil Éireann. On 17 September the Dáil voted £5,000 'to cover the cost of supervision of Public Bodies'.[23] On 18 December the appointment of two local government inspectors was approved on an annual salary of £400, 'inclusive of hotel expenses but … exclusive of locomotion expenses'.[24] Rory O'Connor, a civil engineer with Dublin Corporation, took a leave of absence to work for the department. O'Connor, who was also Director of Engineering for the IRA, was given a monthly salary of £45.[25] Four staff members of the department received a pay rise on 20 December, probably as the burden of work increased. Expenditure on the department rose from £1,696 in 1919 and 1920 to £17,930 ($1.2m) in 1921.

In December 1920 the Cabinet provisionally agreed to make £100,000 ($6.8m) available to the Department of Local Government for loans to 'hard-hit councils'. Dublin Castle had withdrawn funding from local authorities that had declared allegiance to the Dáil. The first loans were issued in the second half of 1921 and totalled £16,800, though this was a small amount compared to the requirements of the local authorities. Dublin Corporation alone had a deficit of £200,000 ($13.7m) in September 1920.[26] A motion put to the Dáil in June of that year to invest up to £300,000 in Corporation stock was 'negatived without a division.'[27] Dublin Corporation was only rescued by negotiating an extended overdraft from the Bank of Ireland (possibly with some coercion, though it was also in the bank's interest to keep the Corporation solvent), which also invested £200,000 in Corporation stock carrying a rate of 3.25%.

Other departments also experienced a substantial increase in expenditure as 1920 closed. The Department of Home Affairs received just under £2,000 for the courts service in the eight months to December 1920, but the Cabinet ratified the appointment of four members of the judiciary at a salary of £750 in September of that year.[28] Expenditure on the department rose to £16,426 in 1921 ($1.1m), from £2,705 in the previous two years. The Department of Foreign Affairs, which had been reasonably well funded by the Dáil, saw its expenditure more than double in 1921 to £30,123 ($2m) compared to the prior two years. Paris, Rome and London absorbed most of the funding, with expenditure also in Berlin, Madrid and South Africa. In November 1920 the Cabinet approved the establishment of a 'Propaganda Bureau' in Paris at an estimated annual cost of £1,000.[29] A payment of £250 was made to an unknown 'Special Agent 13'.

Some of the other more unusual spending items funded by the Loan included: £4,000 ($275,000) given to the Limerick Technical School, which was under threat of closure; £2,500 ($170,000) in support of the motor permit strike; £1,130 ($77,000) to purchase 76 Harcourt Street, the home of the Department of Finance until it was raided on 11 November 1919; a loan of £1,000 ($68,000) given to the Artane Clothing Factory in Cork 'to keep the business going for the present';[30] £300 ($20,000) used to purchase a portrait of Mr Kuno Meyer, a German national and renowned

Celtic scholar, for presentation to the Municipal Art Gallery;[31] and 500 francs to acquire the publisher's rights to a book written by a Mr Goblet.[32]

Ernest Blythe, Director of the Department of Trade and Commerce, displayed big ambition in 1920. On 17 September the Dáil voted £400 to his department to cover the expenses of setting up a 'National Economic Council'.[33] It was at the Dáil meeting on 29 June, however, that the most ambitious project was approved. Blythe was given the authority to establish an 'import and export company' and to invest up to £150,000 ($10m) in the enterprise. And earlier in the year, on 20 February, the Cabinet had approved the sourcing of a warehouse in the docks at an annual rent of £180 and the erection of a store on the site at a cost of £1,000.

After his release from prison, Blythe opened an office in Fleet Street. 'We went through the formality of registering what was called the Irish and Overseas Shipping and Trading Co., Ltd as a limited company. We got a huge brass plate and put it up on the office door.'[34] He perused trade newspapers to source international goods manufacturers and offered to act as a sales agent for them in Ireland. 'By this means we got a good deal of commercial correspondence into the office and a large pile of samples of all sorts of things which, as a rule, we never tried to sell, though on one occasion we did sell some French soap.'

But the Irish and Overseas Shipping and Trading Company, and the warehouse in the docks, also had a more clandestine function. The directors of the company were Frank Maher, who had been an agent in Ireland for the Nobel explosives business of the Imperial Chemical Company, and Patrick Moylett, a well-known and outspoken Sinn Féin businessman.[35] Moylett said that the warehouse handled goods coming into the country, but that for him goods 'had a double meaning'. A number of keys were made for the warehouse and six were given to Cathal Brugha, Minister for Defence.

In addition, Moylett and Maher operated two funds in the Irish and Overseas Shipping and Trading Company. According to Moylett, 'Gearoid O'Sullivan, who was adjutant general of the army at the time, told me that one of the funds with which we were buying guns was the IRB fund, and the other was the Loan Fund.' They operated two bank accounts and reported to Michael Collins, Cathal Brugha *and* Ernest Blythe. It appears that Blythe was unaware of the clandestine nature of the business. 'About 1942 or 1943 Blythe told me that he never knew we operated under anyone but himself.'

Funding and expenditure overview

Dáil government receipts: 1919 and 1920				
	To 31.10.19	To 30.04.20	To 30.12.20	Total
Loan and SDF Subscriptions (1)	6 months	6 months	8 months	20 months
Loan: Ireland and America	10,160	203,479	347,844	561,483
SDF: Ireland and America	42,054	2,945	11,842	56,841
	52,214	206,424	359,686	618,324

(1) NAI DE 2/7, 015,177,182 (excludes refunds and interest)

Dáil government spending: 1919 and 1920				
	To 31.10.19	To 30.04.20	To 30.12.20	Total
Loan and SDF (1)	6 months	6 months	8 months	20 months
Loan	23,406	42,683	279,176	345,265
SDF	6,672	8.765	13,324	28,761
	30,078	51,448	292,500	374,026

(1) NAI DE 2/7, 015,177,182

Michael Collins prepared his first 'Statement of Accounts' for the Dáil for the period to 31 October 1919, covering the first nine months of the national government.[36] Government receipts in the period totalled £52,214, equivalent to $3.5 million today, of which £10,160 (19%) came from the recently launched Loan and the balance of £42,054 from the Self-Determination Fund (SDF).

Total expenditure for this first period of the Dáil was £30,078 ($2m). Although only £10,160 was received in Loan subscriptions, spending using Loan funds was £23,406. This apparent anomaly is explained by the fact that Michael Collins charged spending on permanent items ('acts of a Governmental nature') and external items (foreign affairs, consular services) to the Loan. Ministerial payments, printing, stationery etc. were charged to the SDF. Collins prepared the accounts showing a 'balance overdrawn' of £13,275 on the Loan funds.

A second set of accounts was prepared for the six-month period to 30 April 1920.[37] Total government receipts for the period increased by almost 300% to £206,424 ($14m). This included £144,598 from the Loan in Ireland and £58,880 from the American Loan. The latter was a single draft sent from America, payable to Bishop Fogarty, and represented the only American Loan funds to reach Ireland before June 1920.[38] It is probable that the £58,880 was used to fund the initial £200,000 invested in the Land Bank and did not cover other governmental expenditure.

Total spending for the period was £51,449 ($3.5m). The Dáil government ran a surplus of £154,976 ($10.5m) and had a cash balance of £229,372 ($15.7m) on 30 April 1920.

Audited accounts were prepared for the *eight-month* period from 1 May to 31 December 1920.[39] The extended period facilitated the move to a calendar year end. Total government receipts for the period were £359,686 ($24.7m). Subscriptions to the Loan in Ireland accounted for £220,278 or 61% of the total; funds sent from America were £127,566 (36%); and the SDF accounted for the balance of £11,842 (3%). Again, it is probable that the American money was used to fund the Land Bank.

The accounts included only the money sent to Ireland from America, not the full amount of the Loan raised there. By 30 October, $4,694,377 dollars (equivalent to £1.1m at the time; or approximately $75m today) had been raised for the American Loan.[40]

The majority of the government expenditure of £292,500 ($20m) in the period went towards the initial investment in the Land Bank and three loans totalling £35,309—£25,000 to the bank to open six branches, £4,159 to the bank for additional set-up costs, and a further £6,150 for fishery co-op loans.

Terence MacSwiney's forgotten role

'… the greatest factor in making the Loan a success'—Michael Collins.

Terence MacSwiney is remembered for his prophetic words on being elected lord mayor of Cork in March 1920: 'it is not those who can inflict the most but those that can suffer the most who will conquer'.[41] Less than seven months later, on 25 October 1920, Terence MacSwiney TD, playwright and author, died after refusing food for 74 days.

His long hunger strike, covered widely by the international press, played a major part in making Ireland a global political issue. Virginia Woolf said that MacSwiney's story was enthralling because it was daily retold with all the detail of a great novel,[42] and Marcel Proust followed his hunger strike with interest. While writing *In search of lost time*, Proust dismissed a visitor eager to discuss the latest instalment of the work. 'Don't speak to me about Le Côté de Guermantes', Proust interrupted, 'but about the Lord Mayor of Cork, that will be very interesting.'[43]

MacSwiney's importance to the success of the Dáil Loan has been overshadowed by his ultimate sacrifice for his country. His significance was not only that he risked arrest and imprisonment when speaking in support of the Loan and soliciting subscriptions. Neither was it the amount of money raised in his Mid-Cork constituency. Although over £7,200 was raised in what Collins called the 'remote and mountainous' region, 40% more than the median in Munster, this represented only 2% of the funds raised nationally.

What differentiated MacSwiney was the speed and efficiency that he brought to organising the funding and the example that he set for the rest of the country. 'I am of the opinion the prompt response in mid-Cork was the greatest factor in making the Loan a success,' wrote Collins to MacSwiney; '... it had the effect, not only of urging neighbouring constituencies to a sense of their duty, but all the constituencies all over Ireland.'[44] Collins added that 'Mid-Cork ... made a headline at the time when it was badly needed'.

Daithi O'Donoghue—revolutionary gatekeeper

'The people gave a lot of money—by revolutionary standards. Keeping it safely was Daithi's job'—Máire Comerford.[45]

'Daithi O'Donnchadha was one of the best Irishmen of his generation. He never desired the spotlight or publicity but was entirely unselfish. He was always, under any circumstances, even the direst, in the best of humour'—Robert Brennan, Irish diplomat.[46]

Dressed in a formal business suit and wearing a bowler hat, Daithi O'Donoghue was little suspected by the British authorities until Alan Bell discovered his name and address on a bank docket. How much was this a contributing factor in Michael Collins's decision to authorise the shooting of Bell? It is clear that Collins could not have protected the Loan funds and run the day-to-day financial activities of the counter-state government without O'Donoghue.

It was O'Donoghue who opened the bank accounts, made the payments and moved the money. He also put systems and processes in place to record, control and safeguard those funds. 'I can personally vouch for the fact that a receipt was issued for every application and amount received at Headquarters.' He maintained a coded system of accounts that were unintelligible to anyone but himself and George McGrath, whom Collins had appointed accountant-general in charge of the accounts of all the government departments.

In relation to the Loan receipts, O'Donoghue was careful to add that 'it didn't necessarily follow that every applicant received his official receipt because some may have been lost in transit or may have been destroyed by the couriers or by local officers when raids threatened'. He himself knew the risks, often carrying thousands of pounds and incriminating documents through the streets of Dublin. Threats, raids and searches did not faze him. After 76 Harcourt Street was raided, he and his wife Lucy worked at home late into the night with blankets fixed across the window blinds.

He narrowly escaped arrest a number of times, and possible death when collecting Loan proceeds from the mayor of Limerick. On 7 March 1921, he was at the home of George Clancy on Loan business[47] and left the house with an attaché case full of Loan money. All of a sudden 'military pandemonium' broke out in the city. O'Donoghue had to run—and hide and crawl—before he could get back to his hotel. On the train to Dublin the next morning, he read of the murder of George Clancy the night before by the Auxiliaries, and of the killings of Michael O'Callaghan, the former lord mayor of Limerick, and Volunteer Joe O'Donoghue. 'The train was searched for Daithi but he was safe enough in his first-class carriage, smoking a cigar and reading his paper with apparent unconcern.'[48]

O'Donoghue and Collins had a close working relationship and mutual respect. It was to O'Donoghue that Collins turned to give the 'serious message' to the members of the Banks Standing Committee. Collins arranged the payment of a £25 bonus to O'Donoghue in recognition of his work on the Loan. At the height of the War of Independence, Collins wanted to raise O'Donoghue's salary to £500, more than doubling his existing wage and putting him on a par with a government minister.[49] In his witness statement to the Bureau of Military History, O'Donoghue showed immense respect for Collins, despite being on opposite sides in the Civil War.

After escaping from internment in 1923, O'Donoghue went to Manchester to work as the manager of *Eire*, an Irish magazine edited by Patrick J. Little.[50] He returned to Ireland in 1925 and was appointed to the board of New Ireland Assurance.[51] O'Donoghue, however, was a public servant at heart and, despite his opposition to the treaty, the Free State government reinstated him in the civil service in 1928[52]—a true indication of the esteem in which he was held.

O'Donoghue resigned from the board of New Ireland Assurance. At the annual general meeting in March 1929, the chairman 'expressed regret at the loss the directors and the company sustained by the resignation of Mr Daithi O'Donoghue from the Board'.[53] He continued to work in the civil service until his retirement in 1944, at which time he was an accountant in the Office of Public Works.[54]

On 6 August 1957 Daithi O'Donoghue died at the Mount Carmel Hospital, Rathgar. He was 78 years old.[55] An Taoiseach Éamon de Valera was present at the funeral in Glasnevin Cemetery. Other attendees included Dr James Ryan, Minister for Finance and one of the founders of New Ireland Assurance; Dr Michael Hayes, then a senator, who had been one of the new trustees appointed to the Dáil Funds by the Free State to whom O'Donoghue refused to release the $10,000; Frank Thornton, former intelligence officer and co-founder of New Ireland; Seán MacEntee, Minister for Health and former Minister for Finance; and Aindreas O'Caoimh, the attorney general.

First intelligence battle: victory

The shooting of Alan Bell marked the end of the first intelligence battle. Victory had gone to GHQ Intelligence and the squad. The initial phase of the battle had been a campaign of intimidation against G Division members to stop detectives from working on 'political crime'. This quickly developed into a campaign of assassination of its most stubborn members. A demoralised force was unprepared for the lethal tactics deployed against it. And it was not just the G Division that was ill equipped for the new type of warfare; an inexperienced intelligence unit and squad were learning on the job.

It was only in late 1919, however, that the first intelligence battle began in earnest.[56] The experience gained during the shootings of Detectives Smith, Hoey, Wharton and Barton was timely. Counter-state forces faced infiltration by undercover agents, a revitalised G Division under Redmond and mass arrests under the counter-insurgency powers given to the military. This was accompanied by a concerted effort to suppress the promotion of the Dáil Loan and to go after the funds raised.

The shootings of Redmond and Bell in the New Year, and of the three undercover agents, were carried out in an increasingly professional manner. Equally important in the victory was the role of the national government's own counter-intelligence operations, run through people like James McNamara, Ned Broy and Lily Mernin. Despite multiple raids carried out by the police and military, information passed on by these agents within the British administration ensured that few senior political, military or intelligence leaders were captured.

The victory was cemented in April by the release of those who had been arrested in the mass raids, mainly local IRA commanders, after a mass hunger strike and a national workers' strike in support of the prisoners, and in May by the repeal of the counter-insurgency powers granted to the military in January.[57] Chance also played a part in the victory: Assistant Commissioner Redmond and Byrnes narrowly missed capturing Collins at Batt O'Connor's house.

The first battle had been won, but there were still sixteen months to go in the war. Within a week of Bell's death Black and Tans were deployed on the streets of Dublin[58] and the Auxiliaries arrived in Ireland in July. Better-resourced and better-trained police and military intelligence officers and undercover agents presented a more formidable challenge, but GHQ Intelligence and the squad had matured into professional units. The squad had become a full-time paid unit in March and had expanded to the twelve members who became known as the 'Twelve Apostles'. These men 'had a complete mastery of the situation,' wrote Ned Broy, '... and were sufficiently case-hardened to meet the new situation ...'.[59]

Understanding the shooting of Alan Bell

In 1984 Eunan O'Halpin, Professor of Contemporary Irish History at Trinity College Dublin, writing on the shooting of Bell, said that the usual explanation given was that he was investigating the secret bank accounts.[60] Challenging this view in a ground-breaking work on British Intelligence in Ireland during the period, he wrote that 'In fact the evidence suggests that he was doing rather more: he led secret enquiries into the attempt on Lord French and the killing of Redmond, and appears to have been an unofficial head of intelligence for the administration'.[61]

Professor O'Halpin based his assumption on information in Bell's report and notebook—in particular, written on the inside cover of the notebook in Bell's handwriting, 'The Director of Intelligence, Scotland House, London, SW1'. He also references examples of Bell's investigative activities: getting in touch with a person in a prominent position in the Dublin dockyard, being on the track of an escapee from Mountjoy prison and receiving an offer of information on the Ashtown ambush. Elsewhere he says that 'It appears also that some covert agents were put to work under the direction of Alan Bell'. He refers to Bell's report to Lord French, in which he reported that 'in the course of their moving about my men have picked up a good deal of useful information which leads to raids'.[62]

In 2002 Dr Michael Hopkinson, at the time in the Department of History at Stirling University in Scotland, echoed Professor O'Halpin's view: 'Bell has generally been depicted at this time as leading an investigation into the location of Sinn Féin bank accounts but it is clear from his personal papers that he was involved in detective work relating to the French and Redmond shootings'.[63] Elsewhere he referred to Bell's participation in a 'small, secret committee ... forced to consider the consequences of ... the virtual extermination of the Intelligence system', and that 'While the committee was still sitting, Bell was shot dead by Collins' men'.[64]

Both Professor O'Halpin and Dr Hopkinson imply the primacy of Bell's non-financial activities in Michael Collins's decision to authorise his shooting. The evidence, however, suggests that Bell's shooting related solely to his financial investigations rather than to any role he had in the investigation into the Ashtown ambush or the shooting of Assistant Commissioner Redmond, or any intelligence role, or his membership of

Lord French's secret committee.

Firstly, Bell's official inquiry into the Ashtown ambush had failed by the time of his assassination. Unlike Assistant Commissioner Redmond, who had very nearly captured Michael Collins in the aborted raid on Batt O'Connor's house and paid the price, Alan Bell never got anywhere close to Collins. His inquiry and investigation were never a threat to Collins, GHQ Intelligence or the squad.

On 30 December Alan Bell had secured a room at the Children's Court and launched an official inquiry (commonly referred to as a Star Chamber inquiry) into the attack on Lord French at Ashtown under Section I of the Crimes Act 1887. By the time of his shooting on 26 March, however, the investigation had failed. It effectively ended on 19 March following a failed identity parade in the Bridewell police station.[65] There is no evidence that any members of GHQ Intelligence or the squad were questioned or arrested in relation to the ambush.

Secondly, Bell appears to have had only a minor unofficial role, next to the official police and military investigations, in the case of the Redmond shooting. He began investigating a separate line of enquiry from a lead provided by Saunderson, Lord French's private secretary.[66] Bell was aware that General Boyd had information that he hoped would lead to the identification of the assassins,[67] but Bell did not have the information. It was Colonel Edgeworth-Johnstone, commissioner of the DMP, and Major Hill-Dillon of Military Intelligence who interviewed suspects, not Bell.

As in the inquiry into the attempt on Lord French, no member of GHQ Intelligence or the squad was arrested or picked up for questioning concerning the Redmond investigation. In fact, the shooting of Assistant Commissioner Redmond had severely curtailed Bell's investigative powers. Through Redmond, Bell had been able to make inquiries that he 'should not care to entrust to the G Division'.[68] He wrote to Lord French that 'The murder of Mr Redmond has been a great set back to us'.[69]

Thirdly, although Bell was engaged in other investigative work, it was at a very early stage. Bell used his inquiry into the Ashtown ambush to carve out a broader investigative role for himself. He told Lord French that the inquiry raised matters 'which are useful in other directions'.[70] He continued an investigation into Frank Leopold, despite the DMP's conclusion that Leopold was not involved in the attack on Lord French and had been ruled out as a suspect in the Redmond case. Bell believed that there were 'one or two points in the matter which require further inquiry', because his men had information that Leopold attended Sinn Féin meetings when on leave in Dublin.[71] While Bell may have believed that the Dublin dockyards would be a 'happy hunting ground' and was 'on the track' of a Sinn Féin escapee from Mountjoy, none of these leads ever looked like getting close to Michael Collins or to members of the intelligence unit or the squad.[72]

Fourthly, there is little evidence that Bell's intelligence work was of any substance. Bell was not running his own agents. Frequent references to 'my men' in his notes relates to DMP constables on the beat in Dublin.[73] And although he was building a network of informants, such as his contact in the Dublin dockyards, there is a difference between having an informer (a person on the inside) and handling trained intelligence officers infiltrating an organisation from the outside.[74] None of the informants appear to have generated material information.

Bell did appear to act as a special adviser to Lord French and as his conduit to the intelligence agencies, a role that can be characterised as 'un-official head of intelligence for the administration', as Professor O'Halpin put it.[75] He had been in contact with the G Division through Redmond (until his death) and with military intelligence through General Boyd and Major Hill-Dillon, and he had been developing a relationship with Basil Thomson, Director of Intelligence in London.

Nevertheless, Bell appears not to have come to the attention of GHQ Intelligence prior to the bank inquiry. 'Though Collins maintained an efficient intelligence service,' David Neligan pointed out, 'it had blind spots like all such proceedings. It knew nothing of Mr Bell and his activities.'[76] Michael Knightly, an *Irish Independent* journalist, was asked to get a photograph of Alan Bell only after the bank inquiry had commenced.[77]

On 27 February 1920, four weeks before Alan Bell was shot, a raid was conducted on the office of Donal O'Connor, who was the auditor of Dáil Éireann and involved in almost every financial transaction of significance connected to the counter-state. On the same day the Sinn Féin Bank, which was facilitating the day-to-day financial transactions of the government departments, was also raided. These raids alone represented a material threat to the operation of the counter-state government and the work of Collins's Department of Finance.

On 2 March, 24 days before he was shot, Bell issued subpoenas to ten branch managers of the Munster & Leinster Bank and the Hibernian Bank. The specific branches targeted held Dáil Loan accounts or facilitated the cashing of Sinn Féin Bank cheques. It is probable that Collins was aware of the content of the summonses served on the bank managers. One of those served was J.F. Dawson, manager of the Munster & Leinster Bank on Dame Street, who helped Collins to dispose of money taken in a raid on a mail van on Westland Row in August 1920.[78] He also worked with Michael Staines during the Belfast Boycott campaign.[79]

The subpoenas required the bank managers to attend a bank inquiry set up under the Crimes Act and to produce documents relating to 'any dealings and transactions' between their bank and Sinn Féin and Dáil Éireann. The establishment of the bank inquiry represented another material threat to the operation of the counter-state government. As David Neligan put it, 'Collins was not the man to allow this war-chest which had been so painfully gathered to be taken from under his nose'.[80]

On 8 March, eighteen days before the shooting, Alan Bell deposed three of the bank managers. He asked each in turn whether they had an account in the name of Michael Collins. Though none of the three confirmed the existence of any such account, the line of questioning would have marked Bell as a target. Two of the three bank managers deposed that day, Henry Campbell and Christopher Tierney, had nationalist tendencies and both of their branches were closely connected to the Dáil funds.[81] It is likely that Collins was informed of the line of questioning, but even if he was unaware of the questions being asked in the inquiry Bell was still a target, as Collins could not take the risk that the bank managers would disclose, even inadvertently, material information.

On 11 March, fifteen days before the shooting, the deposition of James Charles Davidson revealed that Bell had information that would have sealed his fate if Collins knew. His questions showed that he knew about money held in accounts in the names of Patrick Gleeson and Patrick Morgan, and about specific transactions relating to those accounts; about the activities of Art O'Brien, the Dáil envoy in London, and that the London office was financed by the Dáil through bank drafts; about the financing of the Dáil envoys in Paris; and that Daithi O'Donoghue was involved in making international bank payments. Bell also had Daithi's home address, exposing him to internment or to being followed to reveal even more information on the financial activity of the underground government. Bell had also specifically requested information on a cheque payable to Richard Mulcahy, chief of staff.

Michael Collins may not have known what Bell revealed in the deposition that day. It is unclear where the sympathies of James Charles Davidson lay, but the banking circle in Dublin was small and the Hibernian Bank had a nationalist bias. There was also a shorthand typist in the room who may have been working for Collins. Information from the inquiry, despite its being held in private, started to leak out to the press. Through legal and banking sources, and contacts in the Police Courts, journalists likely knew more about the proceedings than was being printed. If so, this information was being passed to Collins. 'Nearly all my colleagues on the editorial staffs were sympathetic,' recounted Michael Knightly, a friendly journalist in the *Irish Independent*, 'and helped the movement in no small way.'[82] Collins, of course, had other sources of information, including J.F. Dawson in the Munster & Leinster Bank.

On 18 March, eight days before Bell was shot, Chief Secretary Macpherson said in the House of Commons that the bank inquiry was being held as a result of seizures made in the Sinn Féin Bank.[83] Michael Collins must have considered that the National Land Bank could be targeted next. The seizure of documents from the offices of Donal O'Connor concerned him. Donal O'Connor had helped set up Natland Limited, the dummy corporation used to launder the Dáil's investment in the Land Bank.

The launch of the inquiry presented a new and undetermined threat to the Dáil funds. Merely calling the inquiry put Alan Bell in the firing line. Collins would have known about Bell's history and his determination to get a result, even if that involved extra-legal means to get a conviction, as in the case of the Craughwell prisoners during the Land War.[84]

'I am a builder, not a destroyer,' Michael Collins once told Ned Broy. 'I get rid of people only when they hinder my work.'[85] And Bell's activity *was* interfering with his work. Becoming more cautious, he delayed dealing with a $200,000 bank draft that James O'Mara had sent from America 'owing to a certain Banking Inquiry that was going on here'.

Contemporary accounts of the shooting of Alan Bell also link the assassination only to his pursuit of Dáil funds.

- Piaras Béaslaí wrote: 'The funds entrusted by the people of Ireland to Dáil Éireann were in grave danger of being stolen by the English ... Mr Bell was taken off the car at Merrion by a party of armed men and shot dead.'[86]

- David Neligan wrote: 'Collins had Sinn Féin funds and proceeds of the Dáil Loan—the "sinews of war"—banked in various banks ... It was to these accounts and to the worming out of such secret nest-eggs that Bell set himself ... his death was urgently necessary merely as a defence measure and a warning to others.'[87]

- Patrick Caldwell, GHQ Intelligence, who was present at Crowe Street when plans for Bell's execution were discussed, said: 'Alan Bell was a British financial expert engaged in examining the various Banks' Accounts in this country with a view to locating or identifying Dáil Monies. A decision was arrived at that this man should be eliminated.' [88]

- Joe Dolan, GHQ Intelligence, who was on the tram when Bell was shot, wrote: 'Alan Bell was a Resident Magistrate who came from the North of Ireland to Dublin to locate the Dáil Funds, which were in the bank, and it was decided that he should be executed.'[89]

- Vinny Byrne, squad member, knew exactly why Bell was shot: 'His job was to examine the banking accounts in order to find out where the Volunteer money was. As this was a danger to the movement, orders were given to the squad that he was to be got out of the way.'[90]

- Jimmy Slattery, squad member, recalled that they 'were informed that a British financial agent by the name of Alan Bell was over here on behalf of the British Government, trying to locate Republican and Dáil funds, and that in our own interests he should be disposed of'.[91]

Paddy O'Daly was the only squad member to say that he did not know why Alan Bell was shot. It seems questionable that he would not have known the reason, or even surmised it, from media coverage of the bank inquiry or from discussion among fellow squad members. Paddy O'Daly's witness statement tends to be agenda-driven, even claiming that Michael McDonnell was not a member of the squad.[92] In stating that he was not aware of the reason for Bell's assassination he may have been trying to reinforce his point that the squad 'were soldiers carrying out orders and we did not ask any questions'.[93]

Appendix

Amount raised

The official total raised in the First Dáil Loan in Ireland was £371,849, the equivalent of $25 million today, almost 50% above the target of £250,000.[1]

The final number was even higher. By the end of 1920, the total had reached £374,921, but that excluded '£1,000 or £1,250' in London which had not yet been transferred and balance payments of about £10,000 relating to a few thousand applications, of which there was 'little doubt that the bulk of this sum will be received during the next few months'.[2]

Over £17,000 in gold had been received and this was 'increasing gradually from week to week'.[3] The value of the gold that was eventually transferred to the vaults of the Bank of Ireland was £25,071, comprising gold coin of £24,957 and 'some bags containing gold bars and foreign coins' valued at £114.[4]

In August 1921 Michael Collins told the Dáil that the Loan had reached £400,000.[5]

In 1927 the Free State made a provision for only £378,900 for the expected total liability for repayment of the Loan. The loss of records or incomplete records may account for the difference.[6]

Michael Collins prepared a detailed geographical breakdown of the Loan proceeds as at 14 September 1920, when £370,165 had been raised. Munster was the best-performing province, generating 46% of the Loan proceeds, followed by Leinster (24%), Connacht (16%) and Ulster (11%).[7] In Britain and France £11,647 had been raised, representing 3% of the total proceeds.[8] Cumann na mBan raised over £800.

The national average collected in the constituencies was £4,019. The best-performing constituencies were all in Munster: Limerick East (£31,875), Limerick West (£17,385), Clare East (£13,609) and Cork City (£12,067). In Leinster the top performing constituency was 'Leix and Os-

Geographical breakdown of the Loan proceeds

Loan subscriptions	Province total £	%	Constituency average £
Munster	171,177	46.0	7,442
Leinster	87,445	24.0	3,238
Connacht	57,797	16.0	4,446
Ulster	41,298	11.0	1,588
Britain and France	11,647	3.0	NA
Cumann na mBan	801	0.2	NA
Total*	370,165		4,019

* Average is based on the funds excluding Britain and France and Cumann na mBan

sory' (£10,030). An average of just £2,000 was raised in the Dublin constituencies.

The constituency average in Ulster was £1,588. The top constituencies were Monaghan South (£5,705) and Cavan East (£4,215). Not surprisingly, subscriptions were lowest in the unionist-controlled areas. Less than £500 was raised in five constituencies in the province.

In Connacht, Mayo South (£7,057) was the stand-out constituency. Outside Ulster, the only constituencies to raise under £1,000 were those where the Irish Parliamentary Party performed well in the 1918 election: Waterford City (£636) and Wicklow East (£819).

Subscribers

Between 140,000 and 150,000 people subscribed to the Loan in Ireland. 'I fancy the number of subscribers will be about 150,000', Michael Collins wrote in his Department of Finance report to the Dáil, prepared on 19 January 1921.[9] Ernest Blythe, Minister for Finance, said in the Dáil on 22 June 1928 that 'the total number of subscribers is estimated to be approximately 140,000, but, owing to the circumstances in which the Loan was raised, only 120,000 names are recorded in the primary register, which was compiled at the time the Loan was raised or almost immediately afterwards'.

By analysing statements made in the Dáil by Blythe, it can be shown that the majority of subscriptions, at least over 70%, were for £1.[10] There is some circumstantial evidence supporting this number. A list of subscribers from Ballyvourney in Cork, sent by Michael Collins to Terence MacSwiney in July 1920, included the names of nine persons, each of whom had subscribed £1.[11] The average subscription amount was £2.71, though there were, of course, much larger amounts subscribed as well.[12]

Loan subscribers represented a broad cross-section of mainly nationalist supporters, from those who clubbed together to meet the minimum subscription amount to successful businessmen who subscribed £50. 'Those who could not subscribe £1 at once,' Collins told a meeting in Dunmanway in August 1919, 'could with 19 others pay in 1s. a week, which would purchase a certificate each week.'[13] Six employees of Kapp & Peterson, the pipe manufacturers on O'Connell Street, collected fifteen shillings each— over £4—to subscribe to the Loan. Unfortunately, the Loan worker, a certain Howard Hudson, fled with the money.[14]

Michael Collins also targeted high-net-worth individuals to raise subscriptions for the Loan. He arranged for 50,000 personalised letters to be printed and distributed to prominent republican supporters. At the Dunmanway meeting, attended by 30 constituents, Collins raised £400, representing an average subscription amount of £13.30. Gearoid O'Sullivan, adjutant-general of the IRA, and a J.B. O'Driscoll, who could not attend the meeting, sent telegrams subscribing £50 each to the loan.

Tadhg Kennedy, an accountant with Kerry County Council and a brigade intelligence officer, described how he and another senior IRA member raised funds from nationalist businessmen:[15]

> '[We] called on the principal men in Tralee, such as Messrs Jeremiah H. Slattery, owner of the big bacon factory; Maurice Kelliher, one of the big millers and merchants and an IRB man in his young days; John Griffin, merchant, another old IRB man, John Bally, principal grocer and publican and other such monied people. We collected a large amount of money from these people ...'

The mother of Martin Finn, a company commandant in the Dublin Brigade, contributed 25 gold sovereigns to the Loan.[16] Batt O'Connor received £650 from a 'North of Ireland man and a Presbyterian' on whose house he had been doing some repairs. The man's grandfather had been a United Irishman and 'had suffered for his faith'.[17]

Not all subscriptions were given willingly. Ormonde Winter, British director of intelligence, wrote that people were 'forced to contribute to the Irish Republican loan in order to secure immunity'. After reviewing a list of the Loan subscribers captured in a raid, Winter wrote that 'it was surprising to see the price that had been paid for immunity; and I may say that on the list I discovered the names of several of my personal friends'.[18] The RIC inspector in Kerry said that there was a fear among people that they would be intimidated into subscribing.[19] In December 1919 the inspector in Mayo reported that subscriptions 'were coming out by fear and intimidation rather than from love and devotion'.[20]

It is unclear how widespread was the use of intimidation to solicit subscriptions, but certainly it was a feature in Cork. Francis Healy, a member of the IRA, described how a levy for the Loan was fixed according to the valuation of each landholding.[21] One man, a member of the 'ascendancy class' who refused to recognise Dáil Éireann, would not hand over £25 levied on him to the 'Dáil collectors'. 'In order to enforce the decision,' said Healy, 'we would not permit any ordinary farming functions ... marketing of cattle, threshing of the harvest, etc., and, finally, it was decided to enforce the order by arranging a cattle drive.' In the end, the levy was paid over 'very reluctantly' and, because the identity of the collectors was 'disclosed to the enemy', raids for wanted men followed.

Money was raised across the globe. In Argentina, Larry Ginnell, who had moved from Ireland to Chicago, and then to Argentina in July 1921, and Eamon Bulfin, the Argentine-born Irish republican who had fought in 1916, raised £1,600.[22] According to Béaslaí, subscriptions were received from 'every country in Europe, and from places as far away as China, Bombay, and Australia', including a £1,000 draft sent from South Africa and subscriptions from British army officers stationed on the Rhine.[23]

Repayment

The Loans and Funds Act was passed on 18 February 1924.[24] Payment was to be made using Post Office Savings Certificates on 1 June 1927. Subscribers to the Loan received a 40% return, being 5% interest for seven years and the repayment of the principal at 105%.[25] Staff in the Department of Finance prepared an 'authentic' Register of Subscribers.

Applications for repayment had to be submitted by 31 March 1925 and notices were placed in the national daily newspapers and in 43 provincial weeklies. Subscribers were required to submit official receipts and completed repayment applications. Considerable delay arose in the processing of these applications, however, though largely outside the control of the Department of Finance.

The absence of receipts or incomplete central records created difficulties in substantiating valid claims. This was not a surprising development. Although a receipt had been issued for every application received at headquarters, some were lost in transit or destroyed by couriers and local Loan organisers when threatened with raids and searches.[26] Head office Loan registers had been seized by the British. In addition, repayment applications were received from people who had subscribed to the anti-conscription fund and other fund-raising schemes, which had no right of repayment. Ongoing Civil War tensions frustrated the process. Some anti-treaty republicans who had been involved in Loan collection refused assistance in the identification of valid claims.[27]

The volume of work required to substantiate the claims was enormous. Only 20,000 applications, out of an expected 140,000, had been received 'with sufficient particulars to enable their claims to be substantiated' by the official closing date.[28] The time-limit fixed for receiving applications had to be waived. In March 1927 the Minister for Finance was authorised to add people to the register in cases where there was no central record of their subscription but they had sufficient evidence to show that they had subscribed to the Loan. During the last three months of 1927 alone, over 35,000 communications were received by the Department of Finance. By 1928 repayment had been *authorised* for £342,000 relating to 70,615 applications, representing 90% of the expected total liability of £378,900 and 50% of the expected applications.[29]

By May 1930, however, only £292,221 (77%) had actually been paid out.[30] The process was proving extremely difficult. Staff in the Department of Finance were dealing with small amounts, mostly £1 subscriptions. They had to be careful and suspicious. 'Very often there were applications from people who are not entitled to receive any money,' reported the Minister for Finance. He cited the case of 'a man in County Wexford [who] claimed the return of not alone his own subscription but the subscriptions of the entire parish'. The final date for receipt of applications was 30 April 1931.[31]

Organisation

A sixteen-member Finance Committee met on 18 July and 12 August 1919 to finalise the systems for the issue of the Loan and the collection of sub-scriptions.[32] It was decided that each member of the Dáil was to organise his own constituency. Each TD was to establish a 'central committee' in the constituency, made up of the most prominent supporters of Sinn Féin.[33] The central committee was tasked with forming a 'collecting and advertising committee' in every parish, or half-parish where necessary, throughout the constituency. Special arrangements were made for TDs in prison, or who were in America or Paris, or where the Sinn Féin candidate had been withdrawn or defeated in the election.

In early October 1919 Michael Collins recognised that the initial structure put in place was insufficient. 'As matters proceeded it became increasing plain that if the Loan was to be a success many additional Organisers had to be taken on.'[34] An organiser was required for most constituencies, but the local Sinn Féin organisation was not willing to pay for an organiser working full-time on the Loan. The Department of Finance took over the costs of the provincial directors employed by Sinn Féin and used them instead as provincial Loan organisers. The costs of Sinn Féin constituency organisers, where they existed, were also taken over.

By 30 April 1920 the cost of the Loan was £10,244.[35] The largest cost was payments to Loan organisers of £4,861 (47% of the total), followed by printing (18%), advertising (17%), 'Preliminary Expenses' (15%) and travel expenses for TDs (3%). The four provincial organisers cost 'about £30 weekly' and the 43 sub-organisers 'about £172 weekly'.[36] Payments were also made to men who had been arrested.

The majority of the printing had to be done in Dublin: 'over three million handbills and leaflets were sent from Dublin, and about 400,000 copies of the prospectus'. The prospectus was the most expensive item, as it had to be printed on 'good paper, and in Irish and English'. Not much has changed!

Newspaper advertising cost £980 (of the total advertising cost of £1,714); this was originally budgeted to be £2,170, but many of the papers did not publish the advertisement. The promotional film cost £600.

'Preliminary expenses' related to the £25 paid to each constituency to cover local Loan-related expenses, including the 'distribution of leaflets, circulars and such activities'.[37] Michael Collins decided to fund this from headquarters 'to avoid endless trouble and arguing as to where they would obtain the money from, and probably eventually, in certain places at any rate, it would be deducted from the Loan itself'.[38]

Loan organisation costs totalled £12,484 in 1919 and 1920.[39] In the Dáil on 26 August 1921 Collins said that the cost of the Loan was 'something like 2%', though this implies a cost of just c. £8,000 (at £400,000 raised) or £7,437 (at £371,849 raised). Collins said that the cost would not have been 'so high as that, but it was necessary to send organisers into many parts of the country'.

Courier network

Couriers distributed the Loan prospectus, promotional material and receipts from Dublin to the rest of the country—400,000 copies of the prospectus, three million promotional leaflets and 50,000 personalised letters were printed and distributed.[40]

Couriers carried Loan subscriptions (cheques, notes, coin, gold) back to Dublin when local bank managers would not, or could not, accept funds connected to Dáil Éireann or Sinn Féin. Subscriptions made by cheque by business people and farmers caused a problem when the banks declined to accept cheques made payable to the Minister for Finance.[41] When bank managers did cooperate, cash collected from subscribers was converted to a draft. The bank sent the draft to one of its branches in Dublin, where it was collected by Daithi O'Donoghue, Seán McGrath or one of the other Finance Department staff.[42]

As the repressive measures became 'more drastic', the problem of transmitting money from the remote parts of the country districts became more pressing.[43] Dublin Castle went after this network with 'determination and savagery'.[44] Couriers were searched sometimes three or four times a day, often at bayonet point, and those caught were jailed.

Piaras Béaslaí said that no money was ever seized from couriers.[45] This was not surprising, even with the suppressive tactics employed by Dublin Castle. Even modern law enforcement agencies struggle to locate money laundered using cash couriers. In a report published in 2015, the Financial Action Task Force said that the physical transportation of cash is one of the oldest forms of money-laundering and is still widespread today. Measures employed in the detection of illegal cash movements include the use of cash declaration forms at borders, detection dogs, X-rays and sophisticated data analytics.

The Finance Department had its own courier network within Dublin. Bob Conlon, the official messenger, knew the Dublin streets as only a born Dubliner can, according to Daithi O'Donoghue.[46] On one occasion Bob was taken by the military in a raid. 'I saw him later the same day seated on a military lorry.' Civilians were carried as hostages on lorries to prevent attacks. Seán McGrath helped O'Donoghue to carry funds and messages to the government departments, and O'Donoghue nicknamed him 'the Walking Bank' (*Banc ar siubhal*).[47]

The head office of New Ireland Assurance was an important drop-off station for money and gold. One of the most enthusiastic workers was Maura O'Kelly. According to Frank Thornton, 'Not alone did she fit in dealing with the Dáil Loan, but also was always ready to receive parcels of arms (and) ammunition and have them sent to their proper destination'.[48]

Dick Tynan, whose name Daithi O'Donoghue used to set up a bank account to hide the Loan proceeds, allowed his butcher's shop at 5 Wexford Street to function as a drop-off and pick-up point for Loan money and literature.[49] Margaret MacGarry, who hosted Dáil Cabinet meetings in her home, collected Loan subscriptions from people coming up from the country.[50] James Kirwan's public house at 49 Parnell Street, one of the three 'joints' used as regular meeting places, was also a clearing-house for messages and Loan proceeds.[51]

The Volunteers provided the backbone of the courier network. 'The system of communications for this and other such work, e.g. Army, was amazing', according to Daithi O'Donoghue. He gave credit for this to his boss: 'thanks to the organising ability and tireless energy of Micheál Ó Coileáin'.[52]

One Volunteer regularly made a 160km round trip from Portlaoise to Dublin by bicycle to hand over personally to Michael Collins much of the £13,000 raised in his local area. Couriers often had to destroy Loan material if they felt that a raid was threatened. Even Michael Collins had to act quickly on occasions. One night in early 1920 he was staying in Julia O'Donovan's home with Gearóid O'Sullivan, adjutant-general of the IRA. They were working on Dáil Loan paperwork late into the evening when they were startled around midnight by a loud knock on the door. Thinking that it was a raid, they bundled their papers into the fire. This time, however, it was a false alarm—only Tom Cullen with seized Dublin Castle papers that needed immediate attention.[53]

The courier network extended to London, which was the hub for sending money and communications onward to Brussels, Berlin, Paris, Rome, Milan, Madrid and Barcelona. The primary route for correspondence between Dublin and London was through the port of Liverpool. In London, Sam Maguire, a Protestant from West Cork, met the couriers from the various government departments each morning at Euston Station.[54] Maguire, a Post Office employee, reported daily to the London office of Art O'Brien, the Dáil envoy. That office was the main link for anyone who came to London on political business.

Towards the end of 1920, the communication route via Liverpool became dangerous and several of the contacts had been arrested.[55] It was the task of Sam Maguire and George Fitzgerald, who frequently travelled to London on intelligence operations, to establish a new, safer alternative between London and Dublin. A new route was established using Irish sorters on the mail train between London and Crewe, and also working between Crewe and Dublin. Maguire informed Michael Collins of the new arrangement. The route was efficient and was never discovered. Correspondence put on the mail train in London's Euston Station at 6.30pm would arrive in Dublin at 7am in the morning, and when necessary a reply would be received back that evening.

Safekeeping the gold

'This reads like a boy's story-book' was how Daithi O'Donoghue described the methods used to safeguard the gold from seizure.[56] The gold was securely sealed in small tobacco tins, each flat tin containing either £250 or £500 in gold. Once the small tobacco tins had been made up, O'Donoghue brought them to Corrigan's Undertakers on Camden Street. Peter Corrigan buried the gold at the back of the premises 'at dead of night'.[57] Only Peter, his brother William, Michael Collins and O'Donoghue knew where the gold was buried. 'Upwards of £25,500 was disposed of in this way,' according to O'Donoghue, 'a fact which ought to indicate the generosity and courage of Mr Corrigan in taking on such a tremendous job.'

In October 1921, after the signing of the truce but before the treaty had been negotiated, O'Donoghue brought the boxes of gold under armed escort to Batt O'Connor's house on Brendan Road. First, however, the gold was counted and audited by Donal O'Connor and two family members working in his accountancy practice. It was put into four large wooden butter boxes and a baby's coffin, which were securely bound, sealed and signed off by Donal O'Connor. Each box had a tag on the inside showing the amount of gold it contained.

O'Donoghue had been very reluctant to move the gold from its hiding place and protested the decision to Collins. 'I was rather perturbed about removing the gold from the place where it had been so safely hidden for over a year,' he recalled, 'but M. Ó Coileáin said in reply to my protest "There will be more gold coming in from the second Dáil Loan and you can put that in Corrigans".'

Batt O'Connor felt a heavy responsibility with so much gold under his protection in his house. 'I worked all night alone burying the boxes beneath the concrete floor of my house in Brendan Road.' Working with only a hammer and chisel under a timber floor, he broke through the cement foundation to create a 2ft-wide cavity. After dragging the boxes and the baby's coffin, each weighing over 100kg, into the gap in the foundation, he made good the concrete again. It took seven hours of back-breaking work to complete the task. The hiding place was known only to O'Connor and his wife; even Collins did not know the exact location. The house was raided a number of times and the appearance of the floor never aroused suspicion.

· The gold was left undisturbed until September 1922, one month after the death of Michael Collins. At the request of George McGrath, the gold was transferred to the vaults of the Bank of Ireland. Fourteen bank clerks counted the gold in McGrath's presence after close of business. According to Batt O'Connor, the count matched the tag in each box 'to a half sovereign'. The Bank of Ireland gave George McGrath a receipt for £25,071, comprising the gold coin value of £24,957 and 'some bags containing gold bars and foreign coins' valued at £114.[58]

The gold bars may have come from Cork and have been carried in a baby's coffin sitting on the floor of the touring car used by Michael Collins on the day he was shot. According to Barry Keane, a Cork historian, citing an unsigned and undated typescript from the Desmond Fitzgerald papers, 'the coffin sat on the floor of the touring car and was placed in a secret vault in Dublin shortly after his death'.[59] Daithi O'Donoghue wrote that 'some small bars of gold were received' from Cork.[60]

Notes

Prologue

[1] *Irish Independent*, 22 January 1919, p. 3.
[2] See Macardle 1968, 236.
[3] Mitchell 1995, 49.
[4] Major William Hamilton Davey, a Protestant nationalist, in the *Freeman's Journal*, 28 June 1919, p. 6.
[5] Mitchell 1995, 49.
[6] Barry 1949, 180.
[7] Mitchell 1995, 49.
[8] By October 1919 the fund had raised £42,054. By this stage the Dáil Loan had raised only £10,160 (Statement of Accounts for period ended 31 October 1919, DE 2/7, 183). An RIC report said that Sinn Féin received £17,000 of the returned Anti-Conscription Fund (RIC reports, May–August 1919, TNA, Dublin Castle papers, CO 904/109; see Evans 2012).
[9] The plan was to issue a £1,000,000 loan with a first tranche of £500,000 (Éamon de Valera, Dáil Éireann Debates, Vol. F No. 6, www.oireachtas.ie, 10 April 1919). It appears that the RIC knew that the Dáil was planning to issue a £500,000 bond as early as January 1919. See Evans 2012, 32; RIC Reports, January–April 1919, TNA, Dublin Castle papers, CO 904/108.
[10] *Irish Independent*, 18 August 1919, p. 4.
[11] Joseph V. Lawless, BMH WS 1043; he was the brother of Eibhlin Lawless, secretary and typist for Michael Collins and Diarmuid O'Hegarty.
[12] Besides the £10,000 voted for one year for the consular service, £10,000 for the development of Irish fisheries and £5,000 to finance the commission, other amounts were allocated to a preliminary investigation into the establishment of a national civil service, the setting up of a Ministry for Forestry and saving the Irish language (*Irish Independent*, 22 August 1919, p. 5).
[13] *Irish Times*, 19 July 1919.
[14] Over £6.7 million was subscribed through the Bank of Ireland alone, according to the *Financial Times*, of which over £4 million was new money. That excluded money sent directly to the government in London from Ireland.
[15] *Irish Examiner*, 5 July 1919.
[16] *Irish Times*, 12 July 1919.
[17] The film shows Michael Collins and Diarmuid O'Hegarty taking subscriptions from 30 prominent republicans. It was intended for use principally in America. 'I am informed that they have been of very great service there. They were also shown a good deal at home. The cost of this item was £600' (Michael Collins, Department of Finance Report,

DE 2/7, 090, National Archives). Some cinemas may have been forced to show the film at gunpoint: '… it was planned for a few volunteers in fast cars to visit certain cinemas, rush the operator's box, and, at gun-point, force the operator to take off the film he was showing, and put on the Loan film' (MacDonagh 1976). See https://ifiplayer.ie/historical-material-republican-loans/.

[18] Evans 2012, 59–60.

[19] Daithi O'Donoghue (BMH WS 548) said that the founding of the National Land Bank was Robert Barton's idea. Piaras Béaslaí (1922, 345) said that it was Collins 'of course' who was the principal promoter of the bank. Patrick Moylett (BMH WS 767), an influential businessman and member of the Sinn Féin executive, claimed that the bank was his idea. Michael Collins said of Moylett: 'I fancy him to be a man who thinks nobody can tell him anything' (Hopkinson 2002, Kindle location 4145; citing Collins to Art O'Brien, 15 December 1920, DE/251).

[20] In a public speech Barton said that if anything happened to Tom Fleming, his election agent, and Patrick Etchingham, both of whom had been arrested, reprisals would be taken against Lord French and Frank Brooke, a director of the Bank of Ireland and a close associate of French (Robert Barton, BMH WS 979).

[21] Robert Barton, BMH WS 979.

[22] See O'Connor 2004, 93.

[23] Dáil Éireann, 17 June 1919.

[24] The office was known as the 'Republican Hut' (Robert Barton, BMH WS 979).

[25] *Ibid.*

[26] O'Connor 2004, 60.

[27] *Ibid.*

[28] Barton, BMH WS 979.

[29] *Ibid.*

[30] Over 316,000 tenants had purchased their farm holdings under various Land Acts, in particular the 1903 and 1909 Acts. Owner–occupancy of holdings had risen to almost 65% by 1916, from just 3% in 1870 (Ferriter 2005).

[31] *Irish Times*, 30 December 1916.

[32] Edward Stephens, BMH WS 616.

[33] Dáil Éireann, 18 June 1919.

[34] Barton, BMH WS 979.

[35] Frank Thornton, BMH WS 510.

[36] See 'Extract from the history of the New Ireland Assurance Company' via Frank Thornton, BMH WS 510.

[37] Liam Tobin, BMH WS 1753.

[38] 'The story of Richard Coleman who gave his life for Ireland's freedom' (www.swords-dublin.com/richard-coleman.com).

[39] See 'Extract from the history of the New Ireland Assurance Company' via Frank Thornton, BMH WS 510.

[40] 'The story of Richard Coleman'.

[41] *Freeman's Journal*, 20 July 1908; 'Sinn Féin Co-operative People's Bank Limited, Prospectus and Rules' (1908).

[42] *Freeman's Journal*, 21 June 1910.

[43] Professor C.H. Oldham, 'The public finances of Ireland', paper read to the Statistical and Social Enquiry Society of Ireland, 23 January 1920.

[44] McGowan 1990.

[45] *Nationality*, 25 January 1919 (via McGee 2015).

[46] Lionel Smith Gordon, *The place of banking in the national programme* (Dublin, 1921), 6–7 (via McGee 2015).

[47] Allen 2003.

[48] Yeates 2012, Kindle location 1466.

[49] The founding management committee comprised Alderman Tom Kelly, William Shackleton, James Deakin, Richard P. O'Carroll, Donal O'Connor, M.J. Lord and Thomas Cuffe ('Sinn Féin Co-operative People's Bank Limited, Prospectus and Rules').

[50] Yeates 2000.

[51] 'The 1913 Lockout and Lucan', *Lucan Newsletter* (http://www.lucannewsletter.ie/history/lockout.html).

[52] Memorial website to Richard O'Carroll, created by his great-granddaughter, Sinéad Browne (www.richardocarroll1916.wordpress.com/).

[53] James Kavanagh, BMH WS 889.

[54] *Ibid.*

[55] 'Alderman Tom Kelly was regarded by all parties in the City as a very respectable, worthy citizen … even his most vigorous political opponents always had the highest respect and regard for Alderman Tom Kelly … his character for honesty was so highly respected …' (Seán T. O'Kelly, President of Ireland, BMH WS 1765).

[56] *Irish Independent*, 16 June 1920.

[57] *Freeman's Journal*, 20 May 1920.

[58] James Kavanagh, BMH WS 889.

[59] Michael McDonnell, BMH WS 225.

[60] *Ibid.*

[61] Patrick McCrea, BMH WS 413.

[62] James Slattery, BMH WS 445.

[63] *Ibid.*

[64] *Ibid.*: 'he said we had made a right mess of the job'.

[65] *Ibid.*

[66] Michael Collins, Department of Finance Report, NAI DE 2/7, p. 159.

[67] *Ibid.*, p. 158.

[68] *Freeman's Journal*, 22 August 1919.

[69] Michael Collins, Department of Finance Report, NAI DE 2/7, p. 159.

[70] According to Francis Carroll (2002), the FOIF sent $115,000 to the Dáil in autumn 1919. In his report to the Dáil on 19 August, Collins noted the receipt of $25,000 (£5,552) from America (NAI DE 2/7,158). On the following day, Collins told the Dáil that 'the amount received from America was not shown separately in the Financial Statement, but it was given in the General Report'.

[71] Walter Long predicted that 'the Sinn Féin MPs would troop off to Westminster as soon as they discovered they could not draw their salaries' (Fanning 2013).

[72] 'Upon this loan the whole constructive policy of Dáil Éireann depends', Report of the Honorary Secretaries of Sinn Féin on 21 August 1919 (*Freeman's Journal*, 22 August 1919, p. 5).

[73] A letter to the editor of the *Irish Independent* from the Chief Secretary's Office in reply to a query about the legality of publishing the prospectus gives 6 September as the date of receipt of the request: 'Chief Secretary's Office, Dublin Castle, 11th Sept., 1919. Sir,— In reply to the inquiry contained in your letter of the 6th inst. and enclosure, I am directed by the Lord Lieutenant to inform you that his Excellency is advised that the

publication of the prospectus enclosed is illegal, and that if published your company must take the consequences.—I am, Sir, your obedient servant, J.J. Taylor'; 'Dáil Éireann Loan Prospectus', *Irish Examiner*, 22 September 1919.

74 Michael Collins, Department of Finance Report, DE 2/7, 159.

75 *Ibid.*

Chapter 1

1 *Irish Examiner*, 17 September 1919: 'Irish Republican Loan' and 'Meeting in Macroom'.

2 'Chief Secretary's Office, Dublin Castle, 11th Sept., 1919. Sir,—In reply to the inquiry contained in your letter of the 6th inst. and enclosure, I am directed by the Lord Lieutenant to inform you that his Excellency is advised that the publication of the prospectus enclosed is illegal, and that if published your company must take the consequences.—I am, Sir, your obedient servant, J.J. Taylor'; 'Dáil Éireann Loan Prospectus', *Irish Examiner*, 22 September 1919.

3 Lord Stamfordham on behalf of King George V to Bonar Law, 11 September 1919; Bonar Law Papers, 98/2/8 (via Foy 2006).

4 *Freeman's Journal*, 11 September 1919, p. 3.

5 Mitchell 1995, 61.

6 Dáil Éireann debate, Wednesday 20 August 1919.

7 Quoted in the *Irish Independent*, 21 April 1919.

8 *Leitrim Observer*, 25 October 1919.

9 *Irish Examiner*, 17 September 1919.

10 *Sunday Independent*, 14 September 1919.

11 *Sligo Champion*, 27 September 1919.

12 *Irish Independent*, 21 January 1919; *Freeman's Journal*, 13 September 1919.

13 See Fanning 2013 on why 'policy-making on Ireland, as on everything else, was paralysed in Lloyd George's absence'.

14 *Irish Times* editorial, 15 September 1919.

15 *Sunday Independent*, 14 September 1919.

16 *Irish Independent*, 13 September 1919.

17 Fisher's Supplementary Report, 15 May 1920, F/31/1/33 (via Hopkinson 2002, Kindle location 1476).

18 Fanning 2013, citing TNA CAB 23/15/65–8.

19 *Freeman's Journal*, 13 September 1919.

20 *Irish Times* editorial, 15 September 1919.

21 *Irish Independent*, 13 September 1919.

22 *Freeman's Journal*, 11 September 1919. The proclaimed districts were Dublin (city and county), Tipperary (N.R. and S.R), Limerick (city and county), Clare and Cork (city and county).

23 House of Commons debate, 26 June 1888, Hansard Vol. 327.

24 Michael Collins to Éamon de Valera, 13 September 1919: Béaslaí 1922, 356.

25 Report of the Inspector General of the RIC, September 1919, NLI CO 904/110.

26 Eithne E. Lawless, BMH WS 414.

27 *Irish Independent*, 13 September 1919.

28 Eamon Broy, BMH WS 1280.

[29] Eithne E. Lawless, BMH WS 414.

[30] James Kavanagh, BMH WS 889.

[31] *Irish Independent*, 13 September 1919.

[32] *Ibid.*

[33] *Ibid.*

[34] James Kavanagh, BMH WS 889.

[35] *Irish Independent*, 13 September 1919.

[36] *Freeman's Journal*, 11 October 1919.

[37] *Irish Independent*, 13 September 1919.

[38] *Irish Examiner*, 13 September 1919.

[39] *Irish Independent*, 13 September 1919.

[40] *Ibid.*

[41] *Sunday Independent*, 14 September 1919.

[42] *Irish Independent*, 15 September 1919.

[43] James J. Slattery, BMH WS 445.

[44] *Ibid.*

[45] *Ibid.*

[46] *Ibid.*

[47] *Irish Independent*, 13 September 1919.

[48] *Irish Independent*, 18 September 1919.

[49] *Irish Examiner*, 22 January 1919.

[50] 'Recollections of the Irish War' by Darrell Figgis; via *Dantonien Journal* (http://danton.us/recollections-of-the-irish-war).

[51] *Irish Independent*, 23 September 1919; *Freeman's Journal*, 22 September 1919.

[52] *Connacht Tribune*, 20 September 1919.

[53] *Derry Journal*, 24 September 1919.

[54] *Ibid.*

[55] *Irish Independent*, 23 September 1919.

[56] *Irish Examiner*, 25 September 1919.

[57] *Irish Independent*, 23 September 1919.

[58] *Freeman's Journal*, 23 September 1919.

[59] *Ibid.*

[60] *Ulster Herald*, 27 September 1919.

[61] *Freeman's Journal*, 27 September 1919.

[62] *Irish Independent*, 8 October 1919.

[63] Béaslaí 1922, 346.

[64] *Ibid.*

[65] *Irish Independent*, 15 September 1919.

[66] *Irish Independent*, 23 September 1919.

[67] *The Times*, 27 September 1919; *Freeman's Journal*, 27 September 1919.

[68] Collins to de Valera, 6 October 1919 (Béaslaí 1922, 355).

[69] Letter from Collins to de Valera, 10 February 1920 (Béaslaí 1922, 414–16).

[70] Department of Finance Report to 30 April 1920, NAI DE 2/7, 090.

[71] *Ibid.*; in a letter to de Valera on 10 February 1920 Collins says 2,000,000 (Béaslaí 1922, 414–16).

[72] Department of Finance Report, NAI DE 2/7, 090.

Chapter 2

[1] House of Commons, 22 October 1919, Hansard Vol. 20.

[2] *Irish Independent*, 18 October 1919.

[3] *Sligo Champion*, 25 October 1919.

[4] *Ibid.*

[5] *Irish Times*, 20 September 1919.

[6] *Wicklow News-Letter*, 27 September 1919.

[7] *Irish Examiner*, 22 September 1919.

[8] *Freeman's Journal*, 22 November 1919.

[9] *Irish Times*, 13 October 1919.

[10] *Connacht Tribune*, 18 October 1919.

[11] *Irish Times*, 13 October 1919.

[12] Collins to de Valera, 6 October 1919 (Béaslaí 1922, 355).

[13] *Ibid.*

[14] Mitchell 1995, 62.

[15] Michael McCoy, BMH WS 1610.

[16] Béaslaí 1922, 344–5.

[17] *Irish Independent*, 11 October 1919.

[18] Letter from Matthew Doyle to Terence MacSwiney, 30 September 1919 (CCCA, Papers found on Patrick O'Donoghue, U104/4/3) (Evans 2012).

[19] Reports on Sinn Féin meeting in Macroom for organising Dáil Éireann Loan, 6 October 1919 (CCCA, Reports by Royal Irish Constabulary Officers, U104/1/4) (Evans 2012).

[20] *Irish Independent*, 7 October 1919.

[21] Reports on Sinn Féin meeting in Macroom for organising Dáil Éireann Loan, 6 October 1919 (CCCA, Reports by Royal Irish Constabulary Officers, U104/1/4) (Evans 2012).

[22] *Irish Examiner*, 28 October 1919.

[23] *Irish Examiner*, 17 October 1919.

[24] *Irish Examiner*, 15 October 1919.

[25] *Evening Herald*, 9 October 1919, p. 1.

[26] *Freeman's Journal*, 9 October 1919, p. 3.

[27] *Irish Independent*, 10 October 1919.

[28] *Ibid.*

[29] 'The mystery of what happened to Most Rev. Dr Fogarty's cheque for the Sinn Féin Loan is commented on by Mr Floyd Gibbons, the correspondent of the "Chicago Tribune" (Paris Edition). He says the Bishop of Killaloe sent on his subscription accompanied by a letter, which did not reach its destination. On hearing this his Lordship cancelled the cheque and sent a duplicate and a duplicate of the letter by hand', *Irish Independent*, 10 October 1919.

[30] *Irish Independent*, 11 October 1919, p. 8.

[31] Michael Collins circular to Loan committees, 27 September 1919 (CCCA, Papers found on Daniel Corkery, U104/3/12) (Evans 2012).

[32] *Freeman's Journal*, 11 October 1919.

[33] Seán Prendergast, BMH WS 755 (section 2).

[34] *Irish Examiner*, 14 October 1919.

[35] *The Kerryman*, 18 October 1919, p. 2.

[36] *Ibid.*

[37] *Irish Times*, 14 October 1919.

[38] Report of the Inspector General of the RIC, November 1919, NLI CO 904/110.

[39] Central Statistics Office, 'Life in 1916 Ireland: Stories from statistics': number of private cars and motorcycles under current licence in 1915.

[40] Report of the Inspector General of the RIC, November 1919, NLI CO 904/110.

[41] Cabinet meeting, 5 December 1919, NAI DE 2/7, 152.

[42] Collins to de Valera, 10 February 1920 (Béaslaí 1922, 415).

[43] *Freeman's Journal*, 15 October 1919. Dr Ryan, a 27-year-old doctor and a new TD, had been the medical officer in the GPO in 1916 and was interned in Frongoch—a lifetime of experience already gained at a young age. But this was just the beginning of a tremendous political career. He would later serve two terms as Minister for Health and became Minister for Finance in 1957, a position he held until 1965, when he was appointed to the Senate. He retired from politics in 1969 and died, aged 78, in 1970.

[44] *Derry Journal*, 17 October 1919; *Irish Examiner*, 16 October 1919.

[45] *Freeman's Journal*, 17 October 1919.

[46] *Irish Independent*, 17 October 1919.

[47] *Freeman's Journal*, 17 October 1919.

[48] Report of the Inspector General of the RIC, October 1919, NLI CO 904/110.

[49] *Irish Independent*, 16 October 1919.

[50] *Irish Independent*, 18 October 1919.

[51] *Irish Independent*, 17 October 1919.

[52] Eithne E. Lawless, BMH WS 414.

[53] *Ibid.*

[54] Béaslaí 1922, 342.

[55] Mitchell 1995, 53.

[56] O'Connor 2004, 94. Eithne Lawless said that W.T. Cosgrave carried on the negotiations for acquiring the house.

[57] O'Connor 2004, 94.

[58] Mitchell 1995, 53.

[59] Daithi O'Donoghue, BMH WS 548.

[60] O'Connor 2004, 94.

[61] Eithne Lawless, BMH WS 414.

[62] Daithi O'Donoghue, BMH WS 548; Seán McCluskey, BMH WS 512.

[63] O'Connor 2004, 94.

[64] Eithne Lawless, BMH WS 414.

[65] Laurence Nugent, BMH WS 907.

[66] Béaslaí 1922, 358.

[67] Peter Browne, BMH WS 1110.

[68] Michael O'Leary, BMH WS 1167.

[69] Frank Thornton, BMH WS 510.

[70] *Irish Independent*, 2 November 1919.

[71] *Freeman's Journal*, 3 November 1919.

[72] Report of the Inspector General of the RIC, October 1919, NLI CO 904/110.

[73] Collins to de Valera, 24 October 1919 (Béaslaí 1922, 358).

[74] *Freeman's Journal*, 21 November 1919.

[75] Frank Donnelly, BMH WS 941.

76 *Connaught Telegraph*, 29 November 1919.

77 *Irish Examiner*, 18 November 1919.

78 *Ibid.*

79 *Evening Herald*, 11 October 1919, p. 1; *Irish Times*, 18 October 1919.

80 Macpherson in the House of Commons, 30 October 1919, Hansard Vol. 120; *Irish Independent*, 31 October 1919.

81 *Irish Independent*, 25 October 1919, p. 4.

82 Mitchell 1995, 86.

83 *Sligo Champion*, 13 September 1919.

84 Robert Barton, BMH WS 979.

85 Mitchell 1995, 81; *Freeman's Journal*, 20 September 1919.

86 'Obituary, Mr John O'Neill', *Irish Times*, 2 December 1941.

87 Paddy O'Daly, BMH WS 387.

88 Dwyer 2005, Kindle location 792.

89 *Evening Herald*, 11 November 1919, p. 2.

90 Daithi O'Donoghue, BMH WS 548.

91 *Ibid.*

92 *Ibid.*

93 *Ibid.*

94 Ernest Blythe, BMH WS 939.

95 Seán McCluskey, BMH WS 512.

96 *Ibid.*

97 Eithne Lawless, BMH WS 414.

98 Head office staff arrested were Paddy Sheehan, Dan O'Donovan, Fintan Murphy and Michael Lynch. Three TDs were also arrested—John O'Mahony, Frank Lawless and Seán Hayes. Daithi O'Donoghue, BMH WS 548.

99 *Freeman's Journal*, 13 November 1919.

100 Seán McCluskey, BMH WS 512.

101 Daithi O'Donoghue, BMH WS 548.

102 Daithi O'Donoghue, BMH WS 548. See also Clare 2011, 245.

103 Daithi O'Donoghue, BMH WS 548. Béaslaí (1922, 406) says that the address was 6 Mespil Road. See also Seán McCluskey, BMH WS 512, and Eithne Lawless, BMH WS 414.

104 O'Connor 2004, 133.

105 Eithne Lawless, BMH WS 414.

106 Béaslaí 1922, 351; Frank Thornton, BMH WS 510.

107 Daithi O'Donoghue, BMH WS 548; Eilis Bean Ui Chonaill (Ní Riain), BMH WS 568.

108 Seán McCluskey, BMH WS 512.

109 Eilis Ui Chonaill (Ní Riain), BMH WS 568.

110 Daithi O'Donoghue, BMH WS 548.

111 Béaslaí 1922, 351.

Chapter 3

1 Daithi O'Donoghue, BMH WS 548.

2 Frank X. Thunder, BMH WS 466.

[3] Daithi O'Donoghue, BMH WS 548.

[4] *Irish Times*, 29 October 2009.

[5] Daithi O'Donoghue, BMH WS 548.

[6] *Ibid*.

[7] Patricia Lavelle, *James O'Mara: the story of an original Sinn Féiner* (Dublin, 2011 edn). Originally sourced from Joe Humphreys, *Irish Times*, 23 May 2013.

[8] Daithi O'Donoghue, BMH WS 548.

[9] *Ibid*.

[10] James Kavanagh, BMH WS 889.

[11] *Ibid*.

[12] Patrick Moylett, BMH WS 767.

[13] *Freeman's Journal*, 27 January 1920.

[14] See www.irishpapermoney.com.

[15] *Ibid*.

[16] Seán T. O'Kelly, BMH WS 1765.

[17] Daithi O'Donoghue, BMH WS 548.

[18] The manager of the Dorset Street branch received a summons to attend the bank inquiry, though he was not called, and cheque no. 1805, mentioned during the bank inquiry, was lodged into an account in Dorset Street. The manager of the O'Connell Street (Sackville Street) branch was called to attend the bank inquiry, during which it was revealed that cheque no. 2080 was lodged into an account in his branch. The manager of the Thomas Street branch received a summons to attend the bank inquiry but was not called.

[19] Hart 2006, 196.

[20] Liam T. Cosgrave, BMH WS 268.

[21] *Freeman's Journal*, 5 January 1920.

[22] *Irish Independent*, 31 December 1919.

[23] Donal Ó Drisceoil and Diarmuid Ó Drisceoil, *Beamish & Crawford: the history of an Irish brewery* (Cork, 2015).

[24] George Fitzgerald, BMH WS 684.

[25] Michael Staines, BMH WS 944.

[26] Daithi O'Donoghue, BMH WS 548.

[27] See http://www.irishpapermoney.com.

[28] Eamon Morkan, BMH WS 411.

[29] Mr Justice Cahir Davitt, BMH WS 993.

[30] Daithi O'Donoghue, BMH WS 548.

[31] Dan MacCarthy, BMH WS 722.

[32] Julia O'Donovan, BMH WS 475.

[33] Béaslaí 1922, 351–2.

[34] Daithi O'Donoghue, BMH WS 548.

[35] In Tournier v. National Provincial and Union Bank of England, the court established limitations to the contractual duty of privacy owed by bankers to their clients (Gallant 2005, 22).

[36] Vera McDonnell, BMH WS 1050.

[37] Daithi O'Donoghue, BMH WS 548.

[38] Hart 2006, 195.

[39] Mrs Elizabeth MacGinley (née Brennan), BMH WS 860.

[40] Mitchell 1995, 87.

[41] Letter of 14 August 1920: 'please see that a draft is not drawn on one of the Belfast Banks, or any Bank having its head office in that city, or elsewhere than in Dublin or Cork', UCD Archives, De Valera papers, P150/1125; cited in McGee 2015, 470.

[42] Lavelle 2011, 186.

[43] *Ibid.*

[44] *Ibid.*

[45] Mrs Kitty O'Doherty, BMH WS 355.

[46] Mrs Nora Connolly O'Brien, BMH WS 286.

[47] Dan MacCarthy, BMH WS 722.

[48] *Ibid.*; Art ÓBríain Papers, NLI MS 8446 /26 1921–22; *Bank of London & South America Limited: a short history* (London, 1957).

[49] Introduction to the Art Ó Briain Papers, NLI.

[50] Art Ó Briain Papers, NLI MS 8446 /26 1921–22; the name on the account is Gerald Fitzpatrick Dutton. One letter signed 'G.F. Dutton' appears to be in C.B. Dutton's hand.

[51] Introduction to the Art Ó Briain Papers, NLI; Mrs Elizabeth MacGinley (née Brennan), BMH WS 860; Miss Mary MacGeehin, BMH WS 902.

[52] Introduction to the Art Ó Briain Papers, NLI.

[53] *Ibid.*

[54] Supplement to the *London Gazette*, 7 January 1918.

[55] Dan MacCarthy, BMH WS 722.

Chapter 4

[1] Report of the Operations of the Department of Finance to 24 June 1920, NAI DE 2/7, 088. Daithi O'Donoghue wrote that the amount invested was £203,018, which agrees with the Dáil Éireann debate on 23 August 1921: 'Under the Land Acquisition Scheme a sum of £203,000 was transferred by the Minister of Finance to the bank'. According to Daithi, the £18 was subscribed by a 'privileged individual', but it is more likely to have come from the directors. Edward M. Stephens (BMH WS 616) said that the capital consisted of very small amounts subscribed by signatories (i.e. directors) and of money provided by Dáil Éireann. Denis Cogan (BMH WS 1556) also said that the promoters subscribed for one £1 share.

[2] Daithi O'Donoghue, BMH WS 548.

[3] Mr Justice Cahir Davitt, BMH WS 993.

[4] Daithi O'Donoghue, BMH WS 548.

[5] *Ibid.*

[6] Edward M. Stephens, BMH WS 616.

[7] *Evening Independent* (St Petersburg, Florida), 14 January 1924, second section, p. 1.

[8] 'Report of Lionel Smith-Gordon on co-operative societies in Switzerland and Italy': Edward M. Stephens, BMH WS 616.

[9] Robert Barton, BMH WS 979.

[10] Patrick Moylett, BMH WS 767.

[11] *Ibid.*

[12] Hopkinson 2002, referencing Collins to Art O'Brien, 15 December 1920, DE/251.

[13] Edward M. Stephens, BMH WS 616.

[14] By April 1920, £4,150 was still unspent: Statement of Expenditure up to and including

30 April 1920, NAI DE 2/7, 181.
[15] Robert Barton, BMH WS 979.
[16] *Ibid.*, Appendix.
[17] 'Report of Lionel Smith-Gordon on co-operative societies in Switzerland and Italy': Edward M. Stephens, BMH WS 616.

Chapter 5

[1] *Irish Times*, 8 March 1920.
[2] *Irish Times*, 6 March 1920.
[3] Eilis Ui Chonaill (Ní Riain), BMH WS 568.
[4] O'Connor 2004, 87; Daithi O'Donoghue wrote that 'A large quantity of gold was also received in exchange for paper currency'.
[5] Mrs Mary Flannery Woods, BMH WS 624.
[6] Oliver St John Gogarty, BMH WS 700.
[7] Patrick J. Little, BMH WS 1769.
[8] Joseph Kinsella, BMH WS 476.
[9] Frank Thornton, BMH WS 510.
[10] Eilis Ui Chonaill (Ní Riain), BMH WS 568.
[11] *Ibid.*
[12] Martin Finn, BMH WS 921.
[13] Maeve MacGarry, BMH WS 826.
[14] *Ibid.*
[15] Daithi O'Donoghue, BMH WS 548.

Chapter 6

[1] *Freeman's Journal*, 27 November 1919.
[2] Foy 2006, Kindle location 584; Valiulis 1992, 41, P7/D/96.
[3] Valiulis 1992, 41, P7/D/96.
[4] *Freeman's Journal*, 27 November 1919, p. 5.
[5] *Ibid.*
[6] French to Bonar Law, 13 September 1919, Bonar Law Papers, 98/2/11; Foy 2006, Kindle location 578.
[7] *Irish Independent*, 27 November 1919, p. 10.
[8] Michael McDonnell, BMH WS 225.
[9] *Irish Times* editorial, 20 December 1919.
[10] *Irish Times* editorial, 22 December 1919.
[11] *Irish Independent* editorial, 20 December 1919.
[12] Prime Minister's Statement, 22 December 1919, Hansard Vol. 123.
[13] Report of the committee of inquiry into the detective organisation of the Irish police forces, dated 7 December 1919: IWM, French Papers, 75/46/12 (O'Halpin 1984).
[14] Lord French to Macpherson, 10 December 1919, Macpherson Papers (Foy 2006, Kindle location 653).
[15] Lord French, 3 January 1920, French Papers (Foy 2006, Kindle location 648).

[16] Saunderson to Long, 19 December 1919, WRO, Long Papers, 947/348 (O'Halpin 1984).

[17] Townshend 2013, 103; Lloyd George to Bonar Law, 30 December 1919, HLRO, Lloyd George Papers, F/31/1/16.

[18] Report of the committee of inquiry into the detective organisation of the Irish police forces, dated 7 December 1919: IWM, French Papers, 75/46/12 (O'Halpin 1984.).

[19] *Ibid.*

[20] Foy 2006, citing 'A Record of the Rebellion in Ireland in 1920–1921 and the Part Played by the Army in dealing with it (Intelligence)': TNA, PRO WO 141/93.

[21] Kautt 2014, 26.

[22] *Ibid.*, 30.

[23] Townshend 2013, 135.

[24] French to Macpherson, 5 January 1920: IWM JDPF 8/2; Townshend 2013, 35.

[25] Foy 2006, Kindle location 844.

[26] Neligan 1999, 50.

[27] *Freeman's Journal*, 2 December 1919, pp 5 and 9.

Chapter 7

[1] *Irish Times*, 3 January 1920, p. 7; *Irish Examiner*, 3 January 1920.

[2] *Irish Examiner*, 3 January 1920.

[3] The business, trading today on Nassau Street, is the oldest continuously operating pipe-maker in the world (Peterson of Dublin, www.peterson.ie).

[4] *Irish Examiner*, 3 January 1920; *Irish Independent*, 3 January 1920.

[5] O'Connor 2004, 71.

[6] *Evening Herald*, 2 January 1920, p. 1.

[7] Mrs Batt O'Connor, BMH WS 330. The house had been a hive of republican activity. Mrs O'Connor had watched Thomas Ashe leave the house on the day of his arrest. 'I shall always remember him as I saw him then. He was a beautiful man with his tall noble figure and lovely wavy hair.' In her self-described 'old age', it gave Mrs O'Connor solace to remember that she had had 'the privilege of cooking, washing for and putting up all those great men who sacrificed themselves for Ireland and I would be very happy to do it all over again'.

[8] *Irish Examiner*, 3 January 1920.

[9] *Freeman's Journal*, 5 January 1920, p. 1. (The paper had been suppressed but continued to publish under the banner of the '*Evening Telegraph*, Early Morning Edition'.)

[10] *Irish Independent*, 5 January 1920.

[11] *Ibid.*

[12] *Evening Telegraph*, 8 January 1920, p. 1.

[13] *Irish Independent*, 8 January 1920.

[14] *Freeman's Journal*, 8 January 1920, p. 1.

[15] *Evening Herald*, 6 January 1920.

[16] *Irish Independent*, 8 January 1920; *Freeman's Journal*, 8 January 1920, p. 1.

[17] *Freeman's Journal*, 14 May 1920, p. 6; *Freeman's Journal*, advertisement, 3 January 1923.

[18] Frank Thornton, BMH WS 510.

[19] *Irish Independent*, 8 January 1920.

20 *Evening Herald*, 6 January 1920.

21 *Irish Times*, 13 December 1919; *Leitrim Observer*, advertisement, 5 April 1919; *Irish Times*, 15 December 1919.

22 Béaslaí 1922; *Freeman's Journal*, 23 January 1920, p. 1.

23 *Belfast Newsletter*, 22 January 1920, p. 5.

24 *Freeman's Journal*, 23 January 1920, p. 1.

25 *Irish Independent*, 23 January 1920, p. 5.

26 Kautt 2014, 31.

27 *Ibid.*, 28.

28 Hart 2002, 45.

29 The intelligence branch of the Dublin District 'was under the control of Colonel Hill-Dillon, Chief Intelligence Officer': Frank Thornton, BMH WS 615. The undercover agent was Fergus Bryan Molloy.

30 'I beg to report that I have on this date called upon the two Metropolitan Police Magistrates at Dublin Police Courts and they have arranged to let me have the use of the Children's Court which is a small room … for the purposes of an Inquiry under Sect I of the Crimes Act': letter dated 30 December 1919, Alan Bell, Dublin Castle Papers, NLI CO 904/188.

Chapter 8

1 *Irish Times*, 27 August 1879, p. 5 (Evans 2012).

2 'Charlotte Bronte and her association with Banagher and some notes on the Bell family', compiled by Michael Byrne, https://www.offalyhistory.com/wp-content/uploads/2014/11/Charlotte-Bronte-and-her-association-with-Banagher.pdf.

3 *Irish Times*, 27 August 1879, p. 5 (Evans 2012).

4 *Belfast Newsletter*, 30 March 1920, p. 7.

5 Lt. Colonel Blacker, a leading anti-Home Ruler and member of the Ulster Volunteer Force, in the *Belfast Newsletter*, 30 March 1920, p. 7.

6 Evans 2012, referencing a synopsis of reports from the resident magistrates on the state of Ireland, 1919, Dublin Castle Papers, NLI CO 904/227.

7 Josephine MacNeill, BMH WS 303.

8 Charles Dalton, BMH WS 434.

9 *Freeman's Journal*, 2 January 1915, p. 6.

10 Neligan 1999.

11 Finnegan 2012.

12 *Ibid.*

13 *Ibid.*

14 *Ibid.*

15 *Sligo Champion*, 19 July 1884, p. 2.

16 Finnegan 2012.

17 *Freeman's Journal*, 11 August 1882, p. 5; *Belfast Newsletter*, 10 August 1882, p. 5.

18 '[H]e has refused to me the 10 or 12 minutes that I should have craved to refer to a villainous and barefaced forgery which appeared in *The Times* of this morning, obviously for the purpose of influencing the Division, and for no other purpose':

Parnell, House of Commons, Adjourned Debate, 18 April 1887 (Hansard).

[19] *Belfast Newsletter*, 8 November 1888, p. 5.

[20] *Irish Examiner*, 8 November 1888, p. 3.

[21] *Irish Examiner*, 10 April 1889, p. 4.

[22] *Freeman's Journal*, 12 November 1898.

[23] 'Mayo representative strikes out, September, 1900', *Mayo News*, 17 December 1960, p. 6.

[24] *Connaught Telegraph*, 21 December 1901, p. 1.

Chapter 9

[1] Eoin Ryan, *An Irish banking revolution* (Dublin, 1995).

[2] *Ibid.*

[3] Patrick Moylett, BMH WS 767.

[4] Robert Barton, BMH WS 979.

[5] Edward Stephens, BMH WS 616.

[6] *Ibid.*; Denis Cogan, BMH WS 1556.

[7] Edward Stephens, BMH WS 616; Denis Cogan, BMH WS 1556.

[8] Denis Cogan, BMH WS 1556.

[9] *Ibid.*

[10] Robert Barton, BMH WS 979.

[11] Yeates (2012, chapter 3) provides an in-depth review of the municipal elections in Dublin.

[12] Yeates 2012.

[13] *Freeman's Journal*, 31 January 1920, p. 5.

[14] Yeates 2012.

[15] *Freeman's Journal*, 31 January 1920, p. 5.

[16] Patrick C. O'Mahony, BMH WS 745.

[17] 'Waterford and the 1918 General Election', an explanatory publication by Waterford City and County Council (http://www.waterfordcouncil.ie/media/archives/ Waterford%201918%20Election%20Schools%20Pack.pdf).

[18] *Irish Independent*, 16 January 1920, p. 5.

[19] Mitchell 1995.

[20] The circular amended paragraph 4 of the Loan Prospectus. The time for receipt of the final two Loan instalments of 25% each was extended to 1 March (from 1 December) and 1 May (from 1 February). Additionally, a new term allowed applications to be received up to 1 May on payment of 75% upfront. 'No later date can be fixed,' wrote Michael Collins (Circular, Department of Finance, 17 January 1920).

[21] Inspector General, October Report, 14 November 1919, NLI CO 904/111.

[22] Béaslaí 1922, 413.

[23] *Ibid.*

[24] *Ibid.*

[25] *Ibid.*, 414–46.

[26] Surgeon Joseph P. McGinley, M.Ch., Brigade Medical Officer, BMH WS 1473.

[27] Patrick J. Ramsbottom, BMH WS 1046.

[28] Costello 1995, 112.

[29] MacSwiney and Collins had a 'cordial and productive relationship', according to Francis Costello. His sombre, intellectually inclined and romantic personality ruled out a close friendship. MacSwiney possessed a 'keen capacity for hard work and an adherence to sound financial practices' (Costello 1995, 110).

[30] Costello 1995, 112.

[31] Circular, Department of Finance, 17 January 1920.

[32] *Freeman's Journal*, 19 January 1920, p. 2.

[33] *Freeman's Journal*, 20 January 1920, p. 1.

[34] *Ibid.*

[35] *The Anglo-Celt*, 31 January 1920, p. 5.

[36] *Ibid.*

[37] *Irish Independent*, 21 January 1920, p. 6; *Irish Examiner*, 20 January 1920, p. 3.

[38] *Irish Examiner*, 6 December 1919, p. 5.

[39] *Irish Times*, 25 November 1919.

[40] House of Commons, Dáil Éireann Inquiry, 4 December 1919, Hansard Vol. 122.

[41] Mitchell 1995; Kevin O'Sheil, BMH WS 1770.

[42] Kevin O'Sheil, BMH WS 1770.

[43] *Evening Echo*, 21 January 1920, pp 4–5.

[44] *Irish Examiner*, 23 January 1920, p. 6.

[45] Mitchell 1995, 83.

Chapter 10

[1] Bell to French, Dublin Castle Papers, NLI CO 904/188/1.

[2] Alan Bell Notes, Dublin Castle Papers, NLI CO 904/188.

[3] Bell to French, Dublin Castle Papers, NLI CO 904/188/1.

[4] *Irish Independent*, 23 January 1920, p. 5.

[5] Neligan 1999, 64.

[6] Béaslaí 1922, 408.

[7] Paddy O'Daly, BMH WS 387; Béaslaí 1922, 405.

[8] James J. Slattery, BMH WS 445.

[9] Thomson to French and Macpherson, 19 December 1919: Macpherson Papers, MS Eng. Hist. C. 940 (Foy 2006).

[10] Béaslaí 1922, 405.

[11] Paddy O'Daly, BMH WS 387.

[12] Foy 2006.

[13] Sir Basil Thomson, *The scene changes* (London, 1939), 389 (Foy 2006).

[14] Neligan 1999, 65.

[15] Béaslaí 1922, 406–7; Dwyer 2005.

[16] Frank O'Connor, *The Big Fellow* (London and New York, 1937), Kindle location 1248.

[17] *Ibid.*, Kindle location 1268.

[18] Béaslaí 1922; David Neligan, BMH WS 380.

[19] Béaslaí 1922, 405. Neligan uses a slightly different wording: 'If we don't get him he'll get us' (David Neligan, BMH WS 380).

[20] *Belfast Newsletter*, 22 January 1920.

[21] Frank Thornton, BMH WS 615.

[22] Patrick O'Daly, BMH WS 387.

23 Vincent Byrne, BMH WS 423.
24 Paddy O'Daly, BMH WS 387.

Chapter 11

1 *Le Journal* (Paris), 23 January 1920, cited in Macardle 1968, 308.
2 Fanning 2013, Kindle location 4276; NLI MS 2269/73–4.
3 *Kerry Weekly Reporter*, 21 February 1920, p. 6.
4 *Irish Independent*, 3 February 1920, p. 5.
5 *Irish Independent*, 2 February 1920, p. 4.
6 *Ibid.*, p. 5.
7 Hart 2002, 19.
8 *Ibid.*, 19–20.
9 *Ibid.*, 20.
10 Robert Barton, BMH WS 979.
11 Béaslaí 1922, 417.
12 *Ibid.*
13 James J. Slattery, BMH WS 445.
14 Robert Barton, BMH WS 979.
15 *Ibid.*
16 *Freeman's Journal*, 14 and 19 February 1920.
17 *Irish Independent*, 4 March 1920.
18 Neligan 1999, 64. Neligan says that the meeting took place in November 1919, but Redmond only arrived on 20 December 1919. Neligan, however, made other dating errors in this period.
19 According to Béaslaí (1922, 407), 'MacNamara also reported that 'Redmond had lectured his detectives on their alleged inability to locate Collins, and declared that "a man only just across from London had been able to see him"—apparently referring to Jameson'.
20 Béaslaí 1922, 406; Frank Thornton, BMH WS 615.
21 Frank Thornton, BMH WS 615; Béaslaí 1922, 408.
22 Frank Thornton, BMH WS 615.
23 Long to the Cabinet on 31 May 1920, as recorded by Thomas Jones, *Whitehall Diary, vol. 3: Ireland 1918–1925* (ed. Keith Middlemas) (London, 1971), 19 (Foy 2006).
24 Richard Walsh TD, BMH WS 400.
25 Foy 2006, Kindle location 1556.
26 Foy 2006, Kindle location 1586.
27 Michael Murphy, BMH WS 1547. Murphy provides details of Quinlisk's activity during his final days in Cork.
28 Richard Walsh TD, BMH WS 400.
29 *Ibid.*
30 Yeates 2012, Kindle location 2207. According to Coogan (2016), 'Molloy was a precious contact, for he worked alongside Colonel Stephen Hill-Dillon, who was the chief intelligence office [*sic*] at Parkgate Street barracks in Dublin—where Lily Mernin, Ireland's Mata Hari, also worked as a secretary for the unsuspecting Hill-Dillon'. According to T. Ryle Dwyer (2005), Molloy 'was working for Colonel

Hill-Dillon, the chief intelligence officer of the British army at Park Gate Street …'.

[31] Frank Thornton, BMH WS 615.

[32] James Slattery, BMH WS 445.

[33] 'The murder of Mr Redmond has been a great set back to us as through him I was able to make inquiries which I should not care to entrust to the "G" Division': Bell to French, Alan Bell, Dublin Castle Papers, NLI CO 904/188/1.

[34] Charles Mulholland, military secretary to Lord French, in a letter to Bell on 19 January gives him the title of 'Assistant Commissioner'. In an earlier letter, on 29 December, he referred to Bell as 'Chief Commissioner'. Bell had neither of these roles, though the use of the titles, even mistakenly, indicates his status in the eyes of French's subordinates. Bell signed letters and memos as 'RM', and those addressed to him almost always refer to him as RM (apart from the Mulholland letters).

[35] Neligan 1999, 65.

[36] Alan Bell, Dublin Castle Papers, NLI CO 904/188/1.

[37] Bell was not running his own agents. Frequent references to 'my men' in his notes relate to DMP constables on the beat in Dublin; 'my men have picked up a deal of useful information which leads to raids. I inform General Boyd of anything which I think may be of use to him'. Bell to French, Alan Bell, Dublin Castle Papers, NLI CO 904/188/1.

[38] Bell wrote to Lord French, 'We have had no assistance yet from Scotland Yard in the direction of which Your Excellency is aware'. Basil Thomson worked from Scotland House, not Scotland Yard, though it is probable that Bell was referring to him. Thomson's address was on the cover of Bell's notes. Alan Bell, Dublin Castle Papers, NLI CO 904/188/1.

[39] Alan Bell, Dublin Castle Papers, NLI CO 904/188/1.

[40] *Ibid.*

[41] *Ibid.*

[42] 'In the same case one of General Boyd's officers has got some information which he hopes may lead to the identification of the man who actually committed the murder': Bell to French, Alan Bell, Dublin Castle Papers, NLI CO 904/188/1.

[43] Bell to French, Alan Bell, Dublin Castle Papers, NLI CO 904/188/1.

[44] *Ibid.*

[45] Alan Bell Notes, entry for 15 February, page marked 31, Dublin Castle Papers, NLI CO 904/188.

[46] *Ibid.*

[47] Bell to French, Alan Bell, Dublin Castle Papers, NLI CO 904/188/1.

[48] Béaslaí 1922, 414–16.

[49] *Sligo Champion*, 7 February 1920, p. 4.

[50] *Irish Examiner*, 12 February 1920, p. 4.

[51] *The Anglo-Celt*, 28 February 1920, p. 7; *Evening Echo*, 12 February 1920, p. 3.

[52] Mackay 1996, 119.

[53] In his letter to de Valera, Collins wrote that North Fermanagh and East Down had raised £3,000 and £4,000 respectively. Applications received at head office from these areas by 4 March were just £40 and £1,185.

[54] Report of Inspector Alan Bell, 5 December 1889 (National Archives, Crime Branch Special, Midland Division, 1887–94): Keyes 2011, Kindle location 3826. Piaras Béaslaí and David Neligan make reference to Bell's having investigated Land League funds: 'A gentleman named Alan Bell, who had conducted a similar investigation in the

Parnellite days' (Béaslaí 1922, 442); 'It is thought that he carried out similar enquiries into Parnell's funds' (Neligan 1999, 77).

55 Keyes 2011, Kindle location 3572.

56 The financial strategy came into operation only after the failure of French's other plans. Bell made no reference to a financial investigation in his report to Lord French in late February. The first financial entry in Bell's notes is a reference to a communication between the American Express Bank in Paris and a bank in Dublin concerning the Republican Loan. Bell's notes also reference Seán T. O'Kelly and Charles Gavan Duffy, the two Dáil envoys in Paris.

Chapter 12

1 *Irish Times*, 27 February 1927, p. 5.

2 New York Times, 25 February 1920, p. 17.

3 *Irish Times*, 27 February 1927, p. 5.

4 A sale of rare books and manuscripts nearly 100 years later was underpinned by his collection of Celtic and Anglo-Irish literature: Fonsie Mealy Auctioneers, Rare Book and Manuscript Sale, 4 December 2018.

5 *Irish Times*, 27 February 1927, p. 5.

6 'Michael Collins did not go into any camp. He was staying in Rathdown Road. Donal O'Connor, a chartered accountant in Westmoreland Street, allowed him to go into his office, so that he would have an objective. Collins went up and down to the office without being paid': Kitty O'Doherty, BMH WS 355.

7 *Evening Herald*, 27 February 1920, p. 1.

8 *Ibid.*

9 *Ibid.*

10 *Freeman's Journal*, 16 June 1920, p. 5.

11 *Irish Independent*, 28 February 1920.

12 Deposit receipts worth £7,204 had been taken from the safe and € 1,040 in cash and gold. The total monetary loss was £8,370. *Sunday Independent*, 29 February 1920, p. 1; *Freeman's Journal*, 16 June 1920.

13 *Sunday Independent*, 29 February 1920, p. 1.

14 *Freeman's Journal*, 13 March 1920.

15 *Irish Examiner*, 17 March 1920.

16 *Freeman's Journal*, 4 March 1920.

17 *Irish Examiner*, 4 March 1920, p. 5; *Freeman's Journal*, 4 March 1920, p. 4; *Irish Times*, 5 March 1920, p. 5.

18 *Irish Times*, 5 March 1920, p. 5; *Freeman's Journal*, 4 March 1920.

19 *Irish Independent*, 4 March 1920.

20 *Irish Times*, 5 March 1920, p. 5.

Chapter 13

1 The summons was similar to that issued to James Charles Davidson in Bell's Notes (page marked 268). The serving of the summons on Campbell (page marked 280)

and the time and date of his appearance (page marked 278) are separately noted. Bell's Notes, NLI CO 904/177.

2 Hibernian Bank: Henry Joseph Campbell (College Green), Thomas Francis Read (Camden Street), Christopher Tierney (Sackville Street), Mr O'Rourke (Dorset Street) and D. Carbury (Thomas Street); Munster & Leinster Bank: J.F. Dawson (Dame Street and Lower Baggot Street), Mr Stokes (Sackville Street), Mr Fuge (Rathgar), Mr Coakley (Phibsborough) and Mr Julian (Lower Baggot Street); Bell's Notes (pages marked 278 and 280) and Depositions, NLI CO 904/177.

3 Neither Bell's notes nor the documents seized refer to any transactions on 31 October and Bell did not mention the date during the inquiry.

4 *Irish Independent*, 6 March 1920, p. 6; *Freeman's Journal*, 6 March 1920, p. 3; *Irish Times*, 6 March 1920, p. 4.

5 The quote is from a letter from Collins to James O'Mara, 20 April 1920, NAI DE 5/57/14 (cited in Hart 2006, 196).

6 Although it is difficult to decipher Bell's handwriting, there appears to be a reference to the Land Bank in his Notes, page marked 371, NLI CO 904/177.

7 Bell's Notes, page marked 277, NLI CO 904/177.

8 *Irish Times*, 8 March 1920, p. 6.

9 *Ibid.*

10 *Freeman's Journal*, 8 March 1920, p. 5.

11 *Irish Independent*, 8 March 1920, p. 3.

12 *Ibid.*

13 *Freeman's Journal*, 10 March 1920, p. 5.

14 *Irish Times*, 19 March 1919, p. 4.

15 *The Times*, 9 March 1920.

16 *Irish Independent*, 12 March 1920, p. 3.

17 Deposition of Henry Joseph Campbell, NLI CO 904/177.

18 *Freeman's Journal*, 10 March 1920, p. 5.

19 *Ibid.*

20 'We understand that some of the banks will take a very firm attitude in this matter', *Freeman's Journal*, 10 March 1920, p. 5; 'It is understood that the staff of this particular bank received instructions on Wednesday to adopt a "stiff attitude" with regard to the matter', *Irish Independent*, 12 March 1920, p. 3. The latter relates to staff of the Munster & Leinster Bank, but it is evident from his deposition that Henry Campbell received a similar instruction.

21 *Freeman's Journal*, 9 March 1920, p. 5.

22 *Irish Times*, 9 March 1920; *Freeman's Journal*, 9 March 1920, p. 3.

23 Deposition of Christopher Tierney, NLI CO 904/177; *Freeman's Journal*, 9 March 1920, p. 5.

24 Keyes 2011, Kindle location 4006.

25 See Tierney deposition and Bell's Notes (pages marked 277 and 364), NLI CO 904/177.

26 Seán O'Sullivan, BMH WS 426.

27 Bell's Notes, page marked 364, NLI CO 904/177.

28 Deposition of Thomas Francis Read, NLI CO 904/177; Bell's Notes, NLI CO 904/177.

29 In his Witness Statement, Gleeson claims that he was 'Vice-Chairman of the Land Bank in 6 Harcourt Street for a few years until it was smashed up'. He must have

meant the Sinn Féin Bank. The Land Bank was on Leeson Street and later on St Stephen's Green, and there is no record of his involvement in the National Land Bank. Patrick Gleeson, BMH WS 354.

30 Ernest Blythe, BMH WS 939.

31 Bell's notes referenced this and other transactions. Bell's Notes, pages marked 364 and 371, NLI CO 904/177.

32 *Freeman's Journal*, 9 March 1920, p. 2.

33 *Irish Bulletin*, 9 March 1920.

34 *Irish Bulletin*, 10 March 1920.

35 *Irish Independent*, 9 March 1920, p. 5.

36 Deposition of James Charles Davidson, NLI CO 904/177.

37 *Irish Independent*, 12 March 1920, p. 3.

38 Deposition of James Charles Davidson, NLI CO 904/177 (Evans 2012, 123).

39 Bell's Notes refer to 'Art O'Brien London Office', page marked 370, NLI CO 904/177. Another reference is made to 'handed to "Paris" (?Art O'Brien) same day' (page marked 367). There is another reference to '£1,000 for Paris. & passed to Paris' (page marked 369).

40 Bell's Notes (page marked 367) refer to '24 May 1919 £1,000 advanced by M & L Bank for Paris a/c'. Although not in Bell's Notes, a cheque for £4,000 was paid to the Munster & Leinster Bank on 15 April 1919 (Collins Files, Military Archives, MA_CP_06_03_01).

41 Bell's Notes (page marked 367) refer to 'Refunded to the M&L Bank 28 May by cheque. by M. Collins on S.F. Bank cheque (attached)'. Later notes (page marked 369) refer to '£1,000 for Paris' on 24 May 1919, was 'passed to Paris' and 'Refunded by M. Collins' on 28 May 1919.

42 Alan Bell, NLI CO 904/188/1.

43 *Ibid.*

44 Béaslaí 1922, 356–7.

45 Cheque no. 667, Davidson Deposition, NLI CO 904/177. There is a stub for cheque no. 667 for £1,000 payable to the Munster & Leinster Bank on 28 May 1919 in the Collins Papers (IE_MA_CP_06_03_01).

46 Michael Noyk, BMH WS 707.

47 *Ibid.*

48 *Ibid.*

49 *Freeman's Journal*, 10 March 1920, p. 5.

50 *Irish Independent*, 12 March 1920, p. 3.

51 Michael Knightly, BMH WS 834.

52 Letter from Diarmuid O'Hegarty to Michael Collins confirming the decisions 'involving the expenditure of money' made by the cabinet, NAI DE 2/7, 126.

Chapter 14

1 *Irish Independent*, 12 March 1920, p. 3.

2 *Ibid.*

3 *Freeman's Journal*, 24 March 1920, p. 5.

[4] *Ibid.*, p. 4.

[5] *Ibid.*

[6] *Ibid.*, p. 5.

[7] *Irish Examiner*, 24 March 1920, p. 4.

[8] *Ibid.*, p. 5.

[9] *Freeman's Journal*, 24 March 1920, p. 5.

[10] *Irish Independent*, 25 May 1920, p. 5.

[11] *Irish Examiner*, 26 March 1920, p. 5.

[12] During the official inquest, the officer in charge admitted that 51 rounds were fired, but he was certain that no one had been killed by the soldiers. The inquest jury found differently. In the shooting of Michael Cullen and Ellen Hendrick, it found that the bullets had been fired by the military, that the military were not justified in firing and that the military authorities exhibited gross negligence in sending out such a large body of men without providing for their proper control. *Irish Examiner*, 16 April 1920, p. 6.

[13] *Irish Independent*, 26 March 1920, p. 5.

[14] *Freeman's Journal*, 31 March 1920, p. 4.

[15] *Freeman's Journal*, 22 March 1919, p. 7, and 25 March 1919, p. 5.

[16] Yeates 2012, Kindle location 2267.

[17] Vincent Byrne, BMH WS 423.

[18] *Ibid.*

[19] *Ibid.*

[20] *Ibid.*

[21] According to David Neligan (BMH WS 380), the squad 'would not believe that Bell was daily escorted by RIC to the tram in Dalkey and met in College Green by "G" men'. According to Frank O'Connor (1937, Kindle location 148), 'The Intelligence officers even doubted Collins' story that Mr Bell was seen to his tram each morning at Monkstown and escorted from it at Nassau Street by detectives—that seemed too gross a piece of stupidity even for Dublin Castle'.

[22] Neligan 1999, 77.

[23] House of Commons, Murder of Mr Alan Bell, 30 March 1920, Hansard Vol. 127.

[24] *Freeman's Journal*, 13 March 1920, p. 5.

[25] Michael Knightly, BMH WS 834. Joe Dolan, a member of GHQ Intelligence, said, 'We had no possible means of identifying him until the "Irish Independent" published his photograph': Joe Dolan, BMH WS 663.

[26] Primary sources for the shooting of Alan Bell: Joseph Dolan, BMH WS 663; Vincent Byrne, BMH WS 423; James Slattery, BMH WS 445; *Irish Times*, 26 March 1919, p. 8; *Irish Examiner*, 27 March 1919, p. 7; *Freeman's Journal*, 29 March 1919, p. 2; *Sunday Press*, 23 July 1961 (Foy 2006, Kindle location 1649).

[27] *Irish Times*, 27 March 1919, p. 8.

[28] *Sunday Press*, 23 July 1961 (Foy 2006, Kindle location 1649).

[29] Joseph Dolan, BMH WS 663.

[30] *Irish Times*, 27 March 1920, p. 8.

[31] Joseph Dolan, BMH WS 663.

[32] *Irish Times*, 27 March 1920, p. 8.

[33] *Sunday Press*, 23 July 1961 (Foy 2006, Kindle location 1649).

[34] Joseph Dolan, BMH WS 663.

[35] *Freeman's Journal*, 29 March 1920, p. 2.

[36] *New York Times*, 27 March 1920, p. 20.
[37] *The Times*, 7 April 1920, p. 11.
[38] *Daily Herald*, 27 March 1920, p. 1.
[39] Ormonde Winter, A Report on the Intelligence Branch of the Chief of Police, Dublin Castle, from May 1920 to July 1921 (Hart 2002, 73).
[40] Yeates 2012, Kindle location 2267.
[41] The list of those arrested included David Tobin (probably Liam's father) and William Tobin; *Freeman's Journal*, 27 March 1920, p. 6. Yeates (2012, Kindle location 2277) said: 'At Liam Tobin's house in Munster Street, Phibsborough, a brother was dragged away as a result of mistaken identity, the second time this had happened'.
[42] *Freeman's Journal*, 27 March 1920, p. 4.

Chapter 15

[1] Béaslaí 1922, 358.
[2] Letter from Collins to Seán Nunan, 29 April 1920, Dáil Éireann Secretariat files, 1919–1922, DE 2/285 (Evans 2012, 69).
[3] NAI DE 2/7, 169.
[4] Mitchell 1995, 54.
[5] Yeates 2012, Kindle location 2145.
[6] Hart 2002, 35.
[7] A Report on the Intelligence Branch of the Chief of Police from May 1920 to July 1921, PRO WO 35/124 (Hart 2002, 94).
[8] Ormonde Winter, *Winter's tale: an autobiography* (London, 1955), 303–4.
[9] Hart 2002, 68–9.
[10] Daithi O'Donoghue, BMH BS 548.
[11] Letter from Collins to Diarmuid O'Hegarty on 13 May 1921, NAI DE 2/9, 125.
[12] Cash Summary as at 18 February 1922, DE 2/9, 023; Daithi O'Donoghue, BMH WS 548.
[13] The amount accrued in the accounts was £21,265; Trustees' Accounts, Totals to 31 December 1921, NAI DE 2/9, 022.

Chapter 16

[1] *Freeman's Journal*, 24 March and 20 May 1920.
[2] *Freeman's Journal*, 20 May and 16 June 1920.
[3] *Irish Independent*, 25 November 1920, p. 5.
[4] *Evening Herald*, 27 November 1920, p. 1.
[5] *Evening Herald*, 29 November 1920, p. 1.
[6] *Irish Independent*, 30 November 1920, p. 6.
[7] John Donnelly, BMH WS 626; *Freeman's Journal*, 15 March 1921.
[8] Michael Collins, Dáil Éireann Debate, 18 August 1921.
[9] *Irish Times*, 12 December 1923.
[10] *Freeman's Journal*, 17 January 1924.

[11] *Ibid.*

[12] Ernest Blythe, BMH WS 939.

[13] *Irish Times*, 30 June 1926.

[14] Committee on Finance, Vote 74, Dáil Éireann Debate, 9 August 1933.

[15] *Ibid.*

[16] *Irish Examiner*, 15 January 1920.

[17] James Kavanagh, BMH WS 889.

[18] *Irish Examiner*, 22 June 1920, p. 4.

[19] *Freeman's Journal*, 9 July and 31 July 1920; *Irish Independent*, 10 January 1921. Joe O'-Doherty retired from politics in 1937 to become a barrister and became an acknowledged expert on local government. He died in 1979, the third-last surviving member of the First Dáil.

[20] *Irish Independent*, 19 February 1923.

[21] *Freeman's Journal*, 26 November 1920, p. 3.

[22] *Irish Examiner*, 1 December 1920, p. 5.

[23] Michael Staines, BMH WS 944; Yeates 2012.

[24] *Freeman's Journal*, 1 March 1921, p. 6.

[25] *Freeman's Journal*, 6 May 1921.

[26] *Irish Independent*, 1 June 1922.

[27] Michael Staines, BMH WS 944.

[28] *Ibid.*

[29] *Freeman's Journal*, 14 July 1921, p. 5.

[30] *Irish Times*, 7 September 2018.

[31] *Irish Times*, 18 May 2018.

[32] Frank Thornton, BMH WS 510.

[33] 'Of the money in the hands of the Trustees as on 30th April the sum of £102,000 had been paid over and was held as guaranteed stock in the Bank. Since then £98,000 has been similarly disposed of, thus making the full sum of £200,000 paid. This money, under terms of Dáil decision bears interest at 2% per annum': Report of the Operations of the Department of Finance to 24 June 1920, DE 2/7, 088. See also Mitchell 1995, 87.

[34] Mitchell 1995, 87.

[35] *Ibid.*

[36] See NAI DE 2/7, 001–014, for copies of the drafts; Lavelle 2011, 185.

[37] Department of Finance, General Statement covering period from 5 August 1920 to 14 September 1920, NAI DE 2/7, 059. De Valera agreed to send $500,000 (Mitchell 1995, 87).

[38] Author's analysis of drafts sent from America. See NAI DE 2/7, 001–014. The balance to make up £125,000 was probably sent in early 1921. According to Mitchell (1995, 87), this money was received by the bank *apparently* in late 1920 and early 1921. See also Lavelle 2011, 185.

[39] Edward M. Stephens, BMH WS 616.

[40] Robert Barton, BMH WS 979.

[41] *Ibid.*

[42] Memo sent to Collins, Collins Papers, 4 July 1921, BMH, IE-MA-CP-06-03-06.

[43] Collins Papers, Memo (probably) to Daithi O'Donoghue, 4 July 1921, BMH, IE-MA-CP-06-03-06.

[44] Daithi O'Donoghue, BMH WS 548.

[45] Collins Papers, Memo to Daithi O'Donoghue, 5 July 1921, BMH, IE-MA-CP-06-03-06.
[46] Denis Cogan, BMH WS 1556.
[47] *Irish Independent*, 3 November 1920, p. 5.
[48] Denis Cogan, BMH WS 1556; Seán McCluskey, BMH WS 512.
[49] Minister for Finance, Dáil Éireann debate, 20 July 1926.
[50] Michael P. Cowley, BMH WS 553.
[51] Mrs Pauline Keating, BMH WS 432.
[52] Eamon Morkan, BMH WS 411.
[53] Seán McCluskey, BMH WS 512.
[54] Lionel Smith-Gordon, quoted in Mitchell 1995, 88 (Walsh 2015).
[55] Dáil Éireann debate, Department of Agriculture Report, 23 August 1921.
[56] Edward M. Stephens, BMH WS 616.
[57] Dáil Éireann debate, 23 August 1921.
[58] Eamon O'Dwyer, BMH WS 1474; Patrick H. O'Dwyer, BMH WS 1432.
[59] Edward M. Stephens, BMH WS 616.
[60] Dáil Éireann debate, 23 August 1921.
[61] Barton had been asked by Thomas O'Donoghue TD whether the Dáil had any official connection with the 'Irish People's Bank'. Barton replied brusquely that the 'Irish People's Bank had no connection whatever with the Dáil and anyone who was foolish enough to put money into it he considered fair game for the fellow who was running it'. The meeting of the Cabinet on 4 March 1920 had discussed the Irish People's Bank; 'it was thought that the Land Bank should obtain an explanation from M.L. Casey in regard to his connection with the Irish People's Bank', NAI DE 2/7, 129.
[62] Annual Report of the Irish Agricultural Organisation Society on 31 March 1921; Ryan 1995.
[63] *Irish Times*, 14 March 1921.
[64] Ryan 1995.
[65] Seanad Éireann debate, 16 June 1926.
[66] Statement of the Minister for Finance, cited in Seanad Éireann debate, 16 June 1926.
[67] Dáil Éireann debate, 20 July 1926.
[68] Patrick Moylett, BMH WS 767.
[69] *Irish Examiner*, 20 January 1922, p. 6.
[70] Story told to Tim Pat Coogan by a nephew of Michael Collins, as told to him by MacEoin (Coogan 1990, 379).
[71] See Yeates 2012 for background on the role of the Bank of Ireland and Andrew Jameson in funding Dublin Corporation.
[72] Eamon Morkan, BMH WS 411.
[73] 'I am not quite sure whether it was from this account that the large sum mentioned in the preceding paragraph [£20,000] was seized': Eamon Morkan, BMH WS 411.
[74] Joseph M. O'Byrne, BMH WS 1142.
[75] Fisher's Report in the Lloyd George Papers, F/31/1/32 (Foy 2006).
[76] Robert Barton, Dáil Éireann debate, Department of Agriculture Report, 23 August 1921.
[77] Daithi O'Donoghue, BMH WS 548.

Chapter 17

1. Letter from Collins to Diarmuid O'Hegarty on Friday 19 August 1921, requesting reports to be completed that day 'as I am working over the week-end'; NAI DE 2/9, 057.
2. Department of Finance, Statement of the position as at close of business on 30 June 1921, dated 15 August 1921, NAI DE 2/9, 059.
3. *Ibid.*
4. Carroll 2002, Appendix IV, Kindle locations 1544–1988. Daithi O'Donoghue (BMH WS 548) gave the date as 22 February 1922: 'At a meeting in the Mansion House on the 22nd February, 1922, of the Trustees with Collins and some other representatives of the Free State Party, I was directed to call in all outstanding balances held for the Trustees by individuals, as well as those in the various banks'.
5. Letter from Donal O'Connor, Chartered Accountant, NAI DE 2/9, 004.
6. Daithi O'Donoghue, BMH WS 548.
7. Letter from Donal O'Connor, Chartered Accountant, NAI DE 2/9, 004.
8. Daithi O'Donoghue, BMH WS 548.
9. The actual amount was £237,603: 'Trustees' Accounts, Totals to 31st Dec., 1921', NAI DE 2/9, 022.
10. The actual amount was $2,130,364: 'American Accounts for six months to 31st December, 1921', NAI DE 2/9, 020.
11. Carroll 2002, Kindle location 616, citing Hugh Kennedy to George McGrath, 16 October 1922, Kennedy Papers, UCDA P4/2121.
12. Affidavit from President Cosgrave, *Irish Independent*, 22 December 1922, p. 5.
13. Carroll 2002, Kindle location 616.
14. *Evening Herald*, 4 December 1922, p. 2.
15. *Irish Independent*, 22 December 1922, p. 5.
16. *Irish Independent*, 13 February 1923, p. 8.
17. *Freeman's Journal*, 16 January 1923, p. 6.
18. *Evening Herald*, 29 January 1923, p. 1.
19. *Ibid.*
20. *Irish Independent*, 13 February 1923, p. 8.
21. *Ibid.*
22. *Westmeath Independent*, 27 October 1923, p. 3.
23. *Ibid.*; *Irish Independent*, 23 October 1923, p. 8.
24. *Westmeath Independent*, 27 October 1923, p. 3.
25. *Freeman's Journal*, 24 October 1923, p. 6.
26. *Irish Independent*, 24 July 1924, p. 7.
27. *Evening Herald*, 12 November 1925, p. 2.
28. Carroll 2002, Kindle locations 1544–1988.
29. *Evening Herald*, 31 January 1927, p. 6.
30. *Irish Examiner*, 8 February 1927, p. 2.
31. The same act enabled the Minister for Finance to redeem the External Loan.
32. Subscribers received 28 shillings for every pound invested. The Loan certificates had been redeemable within twenty years of the international recognition of the Irish Republic at 105%.

Chapter 18

1. 'In the issue of October 9th, 1920, "Old Ireland" published the official report of the results of the First Dáil Loan, amounting to £371,849.1.0. signed by Michael Collins': P.J. Little, BMH WS 1769.

2. 'That Loan eventually realised £400,000, and the Loan in the United States just over 5,000,000 dollars': Michael Collins, Dáil Éireann debate, 26 August 1921.

3. Carroll 2002, Kindle location 678.

4. Béaslaí 1922, 350.

5. Dáil Éireann debate, 13 December 1923.

6. The actual amount was $5,233,315. This increased to $5,235,167 at the end of January 1922: USA Account, Total to 31 January 1922, NAI DE 2/9, 021.

7. Statement of Receipts and Expenditures for the period ending 31 October 1919, and the half-year ending 30 April 1920, and a note to 24 June 1920, NAI DE 2/7, 087. Michael Collins wrote that he included only the sum of $200,000, 'being the actual amount received here'.

8. Dáil Éireann debate, 13 December 1923. The amount at the end of January 1922 was $619,640: USA Account, Total to 31 January 1922, NAI DE 2/9, 021.

9. Dáil Éireann debate, 13 December 1923.

10. Dáil Éireann debate, 29 June 1920.

11. Béaslaí 1922, 346–7.

12. Daithi O'Donoghue, BMH WS 548.

13. *Ibid.*

14. The actual amount was £31,875: Net Amounts Received at Head Office as at 14 September 1920, NAI DE 2/9, 062.

15. John M. MacCarthy, BMH WS 883.

16. *Irish Independent*, 22 August 1919.

17. Recipients of the loans, made in advance of the setting up of the Land Bank, included the West Carbury Co-op Fishing Society (for the purchase of a boat) and the West Kerry Co-op Fishing Society (to establish a fish-curing station). Aware of the risks attaching to the loans, only given after a review by a Dáil appointee and only after receiving personal guarantees, Michael Collins 'was strongly of the opinion' that the interest on the loans should not be recorded as income but should instead be placed in a 'permanent reserve fund', as further security against a loss on the loans and to help the fishermen in case of a continuously bad season.

18. See Martin Maguire, *The civil service and the revolution in Ireland, 1912–38* (Manchester, 2008), 98, sourcing information from T.J. McArdle, BMH WS 501.

19. *Ibid.*: 'In July 1914 the Irish service was 25,192. In July 1921, at the Truce, it was still only 27,671', citing UCDAD, Hugh Kennedy Papers, P4/735, 'Saorstát Éireann return of staff in govt depts', March 1924.

20. By October 1919 the fund had raised £42,054. Only £2,945 was received in the six months to April 1920 and £11,842 in the eight months from April to December 1920. By the end of 1921 the SDF had reached £89,053, of which £35,709 was raised at 'Home' and £53,343 was raised 'Abroad', mainly America (Trustees' Accounts, Totals to 31 December 1921, NAI DE 2/9, 022).

21. NAI DE 2/7, 021, 016.

[22] NAI DE 2/7, 036, 041, 053, 065, 068.

[23] NAI DE 2/7, 053.

[24] NAI DE 2/7, 028.

[25] NAI DE 2/7, 052.

[26] See Yeates 2012 for an excellent analysis of the funding of Dublin Corporation during the War of Independence.

[27] Dáil Éireann debate, 2 June 1920.

[28] NAI D2/7, 064.

[29] NAI DE 2/7, 036.

[30] NAI D2/7, 123.

[31] The Cabinet also agreed to recoup £125 to the London office for the travel costs of Mrs Meyer and her daughter to America and the cost of their hotel stay in London: NAI DE 2/7, 043, 055.

[32] NAI DE 2/7, 055.

[33] NAI DE 2/7, 053.

[34] Ernest Blythe, BMH WS 939.

[35] Patrick Moylett, BMH WS 767.

[36] NAI DE 2/7, 182.

[37] NAI DE 2/7, 177.

[38] A copy of the draft can be found in the Dáil Éireann files, NAI DE 2/7, 002.

[39] NAI DE 2/7, 015. Michael Collins also prepared an interim statement of receipts and expenditures for the short period from 1 May to 24 June 1920, in preparation for a meeting of the Dáil the following week. He also prepared a statement of receipts and expenditures for the six months to 31 October 1920, with a note bringing them up to 31 December 1920 (NAI DE 2/7, 160, 167).

[40] The US dollar amount is translated to £1.1m using the rate used by Michael Collins in the accounts. See NAI DE 2/7, 025.

[41] Walsh 2015.

[42] *Ibid.*, Kindle location 3448.

[43] *Ibid.*, Kindle location 3439.

[44] Collins to MacSwiney, 21 July 1920, SPO/Dáil Éireann Files (Costello 1995, 13).

[45] Comerford 1969, 89.

[46] *Irish Press*, 7 August 1957, p. 10.

[47] Comerford 1969, 89.

[48] *Ibid.*

[49] Collins to de Valera, 12 April 1921, NAI DE 2/244.

[50] *Irish Independent*, 7 August 1957, p. 6.

[51] O'Donoghue is listed as one of the directors in a half-page advertisement in the *Irish Examiner*, 3 October 1925, p. 1; *Irish Examiner*, 17 September 1926, p. 8.

[52] 'Cases of unemployment which were of a political nature have engaged the attention of the Executive Council,' wrote the political correspondent of the *Irish Independent* on 12 November 1928. 'The case of the First Dáil officials who never came under the Provisional Government or the Free State received special consideration.' The correspondent specifically highlighted the civil servants who refused to take the oath and 'threw in their lot with the First Dáil', *Irish Independent*, 12 November 1928, p. 7.

[53] *Irish Examiner*, 26 March 1929, p. 8.

[54] *Irish Independent*, 7 August 1957, p. 6.

[55] *Irish Independent*, 7 August 1957, p. 6, and 9 August 1957, p. 10. O'Donoghue was sur-

vived by his wife Lucy, their son, District Justice D.L. O'Donnchadha, and their three daughters, Máire Ní Donnchadha, Mrs Eoghan O'Loinsigh and Mrs P.J. Lynch. Another son, Revd Brendan O'Donnchadha, had died.

[56] Hart (2002, 5) provided a similar time-line: 'It was not until late 1919 that any official undercover campaign was essayed in Dublin, in concert with one last attempt to rally the G with reinforcements from Belfast. This, apparently a joint effort between the Castle and Basil Thomson's Directorate of Intelligence in London, did make progress—incidentally revealing IRA vulnerabilities—but was quickly staunched by a new round of well-informed assassinations.'

[57] Kautt 2014, 43–6.

[58] Yeates 2012, Kindle location 2145.

[59] Eamon Broy, BMH WS 1280.

[60] O'Halpin 1984, 73.

[61] Ibid.

[62] Ibid., 72, referencing Bell's report to French, undated, January 1920, PRO CO 904/188/1.

[63] Hopkinson 2002, Kindle location 1367.

[64] Ibid.

[65] Four prisoners—John Savage, Michael Roche, John Newman and Thomas Russell—were paraded in front of three witnesses: a former sergeant named Donohue (probably Michael Donohue, whose bicycle had been taken), Constable Loughlin (probably Constable O'Loughlin, who was on traffic duty and wounded during the ambush) and a man called Harry Case. The four prisoners were released. At least two of them were Volunteers, but none were members of the squad or GHQ Intelligence. Michael Roche had worked in a bar with *Martin* Savage on Bachelor's Walk prior to 1916, and they had fought in the Rising, both serving under Michael McDonnell (see Joseph McCarthy, BMH WS 1497; see also Military Pensions Record: MSP34REF24799; D Coy., 2nd Batt., Dublin Brigade). John Newman also fought in 1916 in the same battalion but in a different company. Thomas Russell was possibly a 2nd lieutenant in the Borrisoleigh company in Tipperary who suffered severe ill treatment at the hands of the British military later in the conflict (see Patrick Kinnane, BMH WS 1475; see also Military Pensions Record: MA/MSPC/RO/14).

[66] Bell to French, Alan Bell, Dublin Castle Papers, NLI CO 904/188/1.

[67] Ibid.

[68] Ibid.

[69] Ibid.

[70] Ibid.

[71] Ibid.

[72] Alan Bell Notes, page marked 31, Dublin Castle Papers, NLI CO 904/188.

[73] Bell informed Lord French that constables had been monitoring activity at 42 North Great George's Street, where groups of men and women gathered at night, carrying sticks which they hid up their sleeves. One constable heard 'amid the noise of dancing a sound like the grounding of the butt of rifles'. Bell described this as 'all important as it corroborates information received by General Boyd'. He went on to say that 'I have informed him of what *my men* have seen': Bell to French, Alan Bell, Dublin Castle Papers, NLI, CO 904/188/1.

[74] There is an informant's letter in Bell's files. Full of spelling and grammatical errors, the letter implied that the shooter knew that Redmond was wearing a bulletproof

vest. The informant stated that this was known only to an inner circle within the G Division. Although difficult to decipher, he implied that some officers told Redmond prior to his shooting how leaks about raids were getting out: Alan Bell, Dublin Castle Papers, NLI CO 904/188/1.

[75] O'Halpin 1984, 73.

[76] Neligan 1999, 77.

[77] Michael Knightly, BMH WS 834.

[78] George Fitzgerald, BMH WS 684.

[79] Michael Staines, BMH WS 944.

[80] Neligan 1999, 77.

[81] Daithi O'Donoghue opened Loan accounts in Campbell's College Green office, some of which were 'very large'. This implies deposits of up to £20,000 (over $1m). Campbell had once exchanged £1,000 in notes for the equivalent in gold coin to facilitate an arms purchase before 1916 (Seán T. O'Kelly, BMH WS 1765). Christopher Tierney was the most obstructive witness. His branch on O'Connell Street cashed Sinn Féin Bank cheques and held accounts for Darrell Figgis and the Commission of Enquiry. He had worked for the bank for over 30 years. The Hibernian Bank was closely associated with the Plan of Campaign during the Land War and at one point had extended it an overdraft facility of £7,000.

[82] Michael Knightly, BMH WS 834.

[83] *Irish Times*, 19 March 1919, p. 4.

[84] See Finnegan 2012.

[85] Mackay 1996, Kindle location 2608.

[86] Béaslaí 1922, 443.

[87] David Neligan, BMH WS 380.

[88] Patrick Caldwell, BMH WS 638.

[89] Joseph Dolan, BMH WS 663.

[90] Vincent Byrne, BMH WS 423.

[91] James Slattery, BMH WS 445.

[92] 'Mick McDonnell was one of the best men in Dublin but he had one fault. He was always butting in, and on account of that he often did damage because he was too eager. He was not a member of the Squad': Major General P. Daly, BMH WS 387.

[93] *Ibid.*

Appendix

[1] 'In the issue of October 9th, 1920, "Old Ireland" published the official report of the results of the First Dáil Loan, amounting to £371,849.1.0. signed by Michael Collins': P.J. Little, BMH WS 1769.

[2] Department of Finance, Statement of Receipts and Expenditure for the half-year to 31 October 1920, with a special note bringing the figures up to 31 December 1920, NAI DE 2/7, 021.

[3] *Ibid.*: the actual figure was £17,102.

[4] O'Connor 2004, 88.

[5] 'That Loan eventually realised £400,000, and the Loan in the United States just over 5,000,000 dollars': Michael Collins, Dáil Éireann debate, 26 August 1921.

[6] Saorstat Accounts to 31 March 1927, p. 36.

7   The breakdown is based on the proceeds received up to 14 September 1920 of £370,165; Net Amounts Received at Head Office as at 14 September 1920, NAI DE 2/9, 062.

8   *Ibid.*

9   Department of Finance Report, NAI DE 2/7, 021.

10 On 5 March 1930, Blythe reported that £409,110 had been authorised for repayment. Excluding interest of 40%, this represents a principal amount of £292,221. The balance of the outstanding principal to be repaid was £86,679. According to Ernest Blythe at the time, 'We are dealing with small amounts, mostly £1 subscriptions.' If 80% of the outstanding principal of £86,679 was subscribed in £1 applications, it would represent 69,343 applications, or almost 50% of the total applications. If just 10% of the principal of £292,221 that had been authorised for repayment was subscribed in £1 applications, it would be 29,222 more applications, giving a combined 98,565 applications of £1, or 70% of the total.

11 See Evans 2012, 63; letter from Michael Collins to Terence MacSwiney, 21 July 1920 (CCCA, Lord Mayor Terence MacSwiney 1920 files, PR 4/2/25).

12 A simple average subscription amount of £2.71 can be calculated by allocating the total Loan principal repayment of £378,900 over the 140,000 total applications. Blythe reported to the Dáil on 22 June 1928 that repayment 'has, up to the present, been authorised in 70,615 cases, representing approximately £342,000, including principal *and interest*'. Deducting the interest amount of 40% leaves an authorised repayment principal of £244,286, and allocating this over the 70,615 applications gives an average subscription amount of £3.46. This higher average for the repayments authorised first probably reflects better record-keeping by those who contributed larger amounts.

13 *Irish Independent* and *Cork Examiner*, 18 August 1919.

14 See Evans 2012, 63; Dáil Éireann Secretariat files, 1919–1922, NAI DE 2/285.

15 Tadhg Kennedy, BMH WS 1413.

16 Martin Finn, BMH WS 921.

17 O'Connor 2004, 88–9.

18 Sir Ormonde Winter, *Winter's tale: an autobiography* (London, 1955), 299–300.

19 Evans 2012, 64.

20 Evans 2012, 64–5; RIC reports, September–December 1919.

21 Francis Healy, BMH WS 1694.

22 Patrick J. Little, BMH WS 1769.

23 Béaslaí 1922, 350.

24 The same act enabled the Minister for Finance to redeem the External Loan.

25 Subscribers received 28 shillings for every pound invested. The Loan Certificates were redeemable within twenty years of the international recognition of the Irish Republic at 105%.

26 Daithi O'Donoghue, BMH WS 548.

27 Dáil Éireann debate, 15 February 1928.

28 *Ibid.*

29 Dáil Éireann debate, 22 June 1928; Saorstat Accounts to 31 March 1927, p. 36.

30 Dáil Éireann debate, 5 March 1930.

31 Dáil Éireann debate, 10 June 1931.

32 Report of Finance Department, pre-20 August 1919 (date not marked), NAI DE 2/7, 158.

[33] *Freeman's Journal*, 22 August 1919.

[34] Department of Finance Report, NAI DE 2/7, 090.

[35] *Ibid.*, 089.

[36] *Ibid.*, 090.

[37] Copies of the cheque stubs for these payments are in the Collins Files in the Military Archives. Terence MacSwiney was paid £25 on 11 September 1919 (cheque stub 1704, IE_MA_CP_06_03_01).

[38] NAI DE 2/7, 171.

[39] NAI DE 2/7, 015, 177, 182.

[40] See letter from Collins to de Valera, 10 February 1920 (Béaslaí 1922, 414–16); Department of Finance report to 30 April 1920, NAI DE 2/7, 090.

[41] Béaslaí 1922, 349.

[42] *Ibid.*, 352; Daithi O'Donoghue, BMH WS 548.

[43] Béaslaí 1922, 352.

[44] *Ibid.*, 415.

[45] *Ibid.*, 352.

[46] Daithi O'Donoghue, BMH WS 548.

[47] *Ibid.*

[48] Frank Thornton, BMH WS 510.

[49] Béaslaí 1922, 351–2.

[50] Maeve MacGarry, BMH WS 826.

[51] Martin Finn, BMH WS 921.

[52] Daithi O'Donoghue, BMH WS 548.

[53] Mrs Julia A. O'Donovan, BMH WS 475.

[54] Mrs Elizabeth McGinley, BMH WS 860.

[55] George Fitzgerald, BMH WS 684.

[56] Daithi O'Donoghue, BMH WS 548.

[57] *Ibid.*

[58] O'Connor 2004, 88.

[59] Barry Keane, *Cork's revolutionary dead* (Cork, 2017), citing an unsigned and undated typescript from the Desmond Fitzgerald papers (UCDA P80/300).

[60] Daithi O'Donoghue, BMH WS 548.

Bibliography

Abbreviations

BMH	Bureau of Military History
CCCA	Cork City and County Archives
HLRO	House of Lords Record Office
IWM	Imperial War Museum
JDPF	Diaries and correspondence of John Denton Pinkstone French, kept in the Imperial War Museum
NA	National Archives of Ireland
NLI	National Library of Ireland
TNA/NAI	National Archives of Ireland
UCDA	University College Dublin Archives
WS	Witness Statement

Allen, N. 2003 *George Russell (Æ) and the New Ireland, 1905–30*. Four Courts Press, Dublin.

Andrew, C.M. and Dilks, D. (eds) 1984 *The missing dimension: governments and intelligence communities in the twentieth century*. Macmillan, London.

Barry, T. 1949 *Guerrilla days in Ireland*. Irish Press Ltd, Dublin.

Béaslaí, P. 1922 *Michael Collins and the making of a new Ireland*. The Phoenix Publishing Co. Ltd, Dublin.

Carroll, F. 2002 *Money for Ireland: finance, diplomacy, politics, and the first Dáil Éireann loans, 1919–1936*. Praeger, London.

Clare, A. 2011 *Unlikely rebels: the Gifford girls and the fight for Irish freedom*. Mercier Press, Cork.

Comerford, M. 1969 *The First Dáil, January 21st 1919*. J. Clarke, Dublin.

Coogan, T.P. 1990 *Michael Collins: a biography*. Hutchinson, London.

Coogan, T.P. 2016 *The Twelve Apostles: Michael Collins, the Squad and Ireland's fight for freedom*. Head of Zeus, London.

Costello, F.J. 1995 *Enduring the most: the life and death of Terence MacSwiney*.

Brandon, Dingle.

Costello, M. (ed.) 1997 *Michael Collins: in his own words.* Gill and Macmillan, Dublin.

Dwyer, T. Ryle 2005 *The Squad and the intelligence operations of Michael Collins.* Mercier Press, Dublin.

Evans, G. 2012 The raising of the first internal Dáil Éireann Loan and the British responses to it, 1919–1921. Unpublished MA thesis, National University of Ireland, Maynooth.

Fanning, R. 2013 *Fatal path: British government and Irish revolution 1910–1922.* Faber and Faber, London.

Ferriter, D. 2005 *The transformation of Ireland 1900–2000.* Profile Books, London.

Ferriter, D. 2015 *A nation and not a rabble: the Irish revolution 1913–23.* Profile Books, London.

Finnegan, P. 2012 *The case of the Craughwell prisoners during the Land War in Co. Galway, 1879–85.* Four Courts Press, Dublin.

Foy, M.T. 2006 *Michael Collins's intelligence war: the struggle between the British and the IRA 1919–1921.* The History Press, Stroud.

Gallant, M.M. 2005 *Money laundering and the proceeds of crime: economic crime and civil remedies.* Edward Elgar, Cheltenham.

Hart, P. (ed.) 2002 *British Intelligence in Ireland, 1920–1921: the final reports.* Cork University Press, Cork.

Hart, P. 2006 *Mick: the real Michael Collins.* Penguin, New York.

Hopkinson, M. 2002 *The Irish War of Independence.* Gill and Macmillan, Dublin.

Kautt, W.H. 2014 *Ground truths: British Army operations in the Irish War of Independence.* Irish Academic Press, Dublin.

Keyes, M. 2011 *Funding the nation: money and nationalist politics in nineteenth-century Ireland.* Gill and Macmillan, Dublin.

Lavelle, P. 2011 *James O'Mara: the story of an original Sinn Féiner.* History Publisher, Dublin.

Macardle, D. 1968 *The Irish Republic* [first published 1937]. Corgi, London.

MacDonagh, J. 1976 Unpublished memoirs. Quoted in K. Rockett, L. Gibbons and J. Hill, *Cinema and Ireland* (Routledge, London, 1987).

McGee, O. 2015 *Arthur Griffith.* Merrion Press, Dublin.

McGowan, P. 1990 *Money and banking in Ireland: origins, development and future.* Institute of Public Administration, Dublin.

Mackay, J.A. 1996 *Michael Collins: a life*. Mainstream Publishing, Edinburgh and London.

Mitchell, A. 1995 *Revolutionary government in Ireland: Dáil Éireann, 1919–22*. Gill and Macmillan, Dublin.

Neligan, D. 1999 *The Spy in the Castle*. Prendeville Publishing, London. (First published in 1968 by McGibbon and Kee, London.)

O'Connor, B. 2004 *With Michael Collins in the fight for Irish freedom*. Aubane Historical Society, Millstreet.

O'Connor, F. 1937 *The Big Fellow: Michael Collins and the Irish Revolution*. Thomas Nelson and Sons, London.

O'Halpin, E. 1984 British Intelligence in Ireland, 1914–1921. In C.M. Andrew and D. Dilks (eds), *The missing dimension: governments and intelligence communities in the twentieth century*, 55–77. Macmillan, London.

Ridley, N. 2018 *Michael Collins and the financing of violent political struggle*. Routledge, New York and Abingdon.

Ryan, E. 1995 *An Irish banking revolution*. Bank of Ireland, Dublin.

Townshend, C. 2013 *The Republic: the fight for Irish independence 1918–1923*. Penguin, London.

Valiulis, M.G. 1992 *Portrait of a revolutionary: General Richard Mulcahy and the founding of the Irish Free State*. Irish Academic Press, Dublin.

Walsh, M. 2015 *Bitter freedom: Ireland in a revolutionary world 1918–1923*. Faber and Faber, London.

Yeates, P. 2000 *Lockout: Dublin 1913*. Gill and Macmillan, Dublin.

Yeates, P. 2012 *A city in turmoil—Dublin 1919–1921: the War of Independence*. Gill and Macmillan, Dublin.

Index